08430

GR
15
C5

Clarke, Kenneth W
A folklore reader

Date Due

A Folklore Reader

A Folklore Reader

Edited by

Kenneth and Mary Clarke

New York : A. S. Barnes and Co.
London : Thomas Yoseloff Ltd.

© 1965 by A. S. Barnes and Company, Inc.

Library of Congress Catalogue Card Number: 64–21349

A. S. Barnes and Company, Inc.

8 East 36th Street

New York, N.Y. 10016

Thomas Yoseloff Ltd.

18 Charing Cross Road

London W.C.2, England

6209

Printed in the United States of America

Acknowledgments

Grateful acknowledgment is made to the following publishers and individuals for permission to reprint material which is in their copyright or of which they are the authorized publishers. These acknowledgments are in addition to those to be found on the first page of each selection.

GEORGE ALLEN & UNWIN, LTD., for British Commonwealth permission for "Presymbolic Language in Ritual" from *Language in Thought and Action* by S. I. Hayakawa.

THE BODLEY HEAD, LTD., for British Commonwealth permission for "The Two Cakes" and "The Frame Story" from *The Pentamerone of Giambattista Basile*, trans. by Bendetto Croce, ed. by N. M. Penzer.

RUPERT HART-DAVIS, LTD., for British Commonwealth permission for "Language as a Historical Product: Drift" in *Language* by Edward Sapir.

HARPER & ROW, PUBLISHERS for permission to use the brief quotation in "Silone's Use of Folk Beliefs" from *The God That Failed*, ed. Richard Crossman, Harper & Brothers.

CHARLES SCRIBNER'S SONS for the introduction of *American Ballads and Songs*, pp. xiv-xvi, by Louise Pound. (Charles Scribner's Sons, 1922).

HOUGHTON MIFFLIN COMPANY for Chapter 3 from *Laughing Boy* by Oliver LaFarge, copyright © 1929 and 1957 by Oliver LaFarge; for a portion of the introduction and texts of two ballads from *English and Scottish Popular Ballads*, ed. by Helen Child Sargent and George Lyman Kittredge, copyright © 1904 and 1932 by George Lyman Kittredge.

APPLETON-CENTURY for "The Systematization of Ideas" in *Primitive Man as Philosopher* by Paul Radin, copyright 1927 by D. Appleton & Company, renewed 1955. By permission of Appleton-Century.

CROWN PUBLISHERS, INC., for a selection from *A Treasury of American Folklore* by B. A. Botkin, copyright © 1944 by B. A. Botkin, used by permission of Crown Publishers, Inc.

THE NEW AMERICAN LIBRARY OF WORLD LITERATURE, INC., for a portion of the introduction from *American Folk Tales and Songs* by Richard Chase, copyright © 1956 by Richard Chase, published by arrangement with The New American Library of World Literature, Inc., New York.

D. C. HEATH AND COMPANY for "Literature, Music, and Dance" in *General Anthropology*, ed. by Franz Boas, copyright © 1938. By permission of D. C. Heath and Company.

HARCOURT, BRACE & WORLD, INC., for "Presymbolic Language in Ritual" from *Language in Thought and Action* by S. I. Hayakawa, copyright © 1941, 1949, by Harcourt, Brace & World, Inc. and reprinted with their permission; for "Language as a Historical Product: Drift" from *Language* by Edward Sapir, copyright © 1921 by Harcourt, Brace & World, Inc.; renewed, 1949, by Jean V. Sapir. Reprinted by permission of the publishers.

VIKING PRESS, INC., for "The Adventures of Gilgamesh" in *The Oldest Stories in the World*, edited by Theodore H. Gaster. Copyright © by Theodore H. Gaster. Reprinted by permission of the Viking Press, Inc.

THE UNIVERSITY OF CHICAGO PRESS for "The Loss of Friends" in *The Panchatantra*, translated by Arthur W. Ryder, © 1925 by the University of Chicago, by permission of the University of Chicago Press; for "Utah Mormons" reprinted from *American Folklore* by Richard Dorson, © 1959 by the University of Chicago, by permission of the University of Chicago Press; for "Epilogue" reprinted from *The Ballad Revival* by Albert B. Friedman, © 1961 by the University of Chicago, by permission of the University of Chicago Press.

E. P. DUTTON & CO., INC., for "The Two Cakes" and "The Frame Story" from *The Pentamerone of Giambattista Basile*, edited by N. M. Penzer, translated by Bendetto Croce. Reprinted by permission of the publishers, E. P. Dutton & Co., Inc.

THE WORLD PUBLISHING COMPANY for "Folk Etymology, Or Every Man a Lexicographer" from *The Miracle of Language* by Charlton Laird. Copyright 1953 by Charlton Laird. Reprinted by permission of The World Publishing Company.

THE CLARENDON PRESS, OXFORD, for "Ballads and Broadsides" from *The Ballad of Tradition*, copyright 1932. Reprinted by permission of the Clarendon Press, Oxford.

RUTGERS UNIVERSITY PRESS for "Patterns of Inclusion" from D. K. Wilgus, *Anglo-American Folksong Scholarship Since 1898*, Rutgers University Press, 1959. Copyright © 1959 by Rutgers, The State University.

OXFORD UNIVERSITY PRESS, INC., for "From Africa to the New World" from *The Story of Jazz* by Marshall Stearns, copyright 1956, 1958 by Oxford University Press, Inc. Reprinted by permission of Oxford University Press, Inc.

ATHENEUM PUBLISHERS for brief quotations in "Silone's Use of Folk Beliefs" from *Bread and Wine* by Ignazio Silone.

To Suzi

Introduction

IT IS NOT DIFFICULT TO FIND SHORT ARTICLES SUITABLE FOR an introduction to folklore studies. In fact, the volume of folklore literature is so great that the problem is to justify exclusion of selections rather than to search out those suitable for inclusion. One can find enough excellent material to fill several volumes. Merely filling a volume, however, has not been the guiding principle in this instance. The task has been to assemble materials most representative of the heritage of folklore and folklore studies as we generally know them in the middle of the twentieth century. Further, the task has been to reflect folklore scholarship in some historical depth, in several levels of relative complexity, in several areas of specialized interest, and in several definitions of the subject. This range of matter and manner developed from the recognition that many facets give the reader many opportunities to exercise discrimination and judgment. Also, to confine the selections to those which reflect only one of the various "schools" of folklore scholarship or to only one of the several "definitions" of the subject would be to distort the image of academic folklore as it actually exists.

Folklore has been an exciting field for many students precisely because it has not yet hardened into a mold of accepted doctrine. Perhaps it never will. The complex inter-relationships of folklore with other accepted areas of study appear to make the extraction of "pure folklore" an impossibility. Accordingly, we may never be confronted by a "pure folklorist," but must continue to deal with literary folklorists, historical folklorists, musical folklorists, anthropological folklorists, and (Heaven protect us!) popular fakelorists.

In recent years there has been a good deal of pushing and pulling in some quarters to get folklore to jell into an accepted body of doctrine or theory. One journal article even mentioned the "new science of folklore." Fortunately, the pushing and pulling has not been all on one side; hence the diversity of opinion continues, and there is no central authority with the power to banish its heretics. The study of folklore is not likely to become merely a science any sooner than is the study of literature or music. Language, being subject to precise observation and description, may be studied in a scientific manner, but the products of language, as infinite as the human imagination, will continue under the present scheme of designations to belong largely to the realm of the humanities.

Contents

A Folklore Reader

I

Introductory and Theoretical

LIKE ANY OTHER COMPLEX SUBJECT WHICH HAS DEVELOPED A large body of literature, folklore is treated in many ways by the specialists who approach it. As an academic discipline, folklore is sometimes baffling to the student because of its protean, interdisciplinary character. Unlike English literature or music, academic folklore will not submit to neat boundaries. Evidence of this in large universities may be seen in the composition of folklore faculties or committees. The personnel are drawn from different departments. Such a faculty may be composed of specialists in some phases of literature, language, anthropology, music, psychology, and art. What they have in common is a knowledgable interest in theories, practices, and studies pertaining to traditional expressions. Survival, transmission, and change are of interest as social processes, aesthetic manifestations, and psychological phenomena. These interests are obviously interrelated, and they extend by association to still other intellectual considerations.

The selections in this chapter have been assembled to illus-

15

trate some of the many-sided aspects of folklore, the substance and its study.

RHYS CARPENTER

Literature Without Letters*

The study of literature is an enterprise so vast that no one human mind can cope with it successfully. The multiplicity of languages, the centuries of time, are too formidable. Books and manuscripts, printed or written, recent, medieval, and ancient, make a total too great for a single lifetime's reading. And yet this terrifying array, stretching from the pyramid texts of Egypt down to the novels of our own day, derives from only a fraction of the years and a portion of the lands in which human literary activity has flourished—if we will admit the etymological contradiction that literature may exist without letters.

The craft of printing is only five hundred years old; European knowledge of paper dates back only a thousand years; the very art of writing has been known to most European peoples for less than two thousand years and nowhere, not even in China or Egypt or Mesopotamia, seems to be appreciably older than five thousand. A respectable antiquity, this last one! But how much older still are poetry and song and the craft of telling enthralling stories to attentive ears? Without benefit of writing, songs may be composed, sung, remembered, and sung again; adventures may be told, incidents, anecdotes, and marvelous happenings recounted; even poetry of great range and power and beauty may come into being and persist, nor die with the passing of its maker. Beside and beyond the known realm of written literature stretches interminably the almost unknown world of oral literature, whose merest fraction has been reduced to written or printed form.

* From *Folktale, Fiction, and Saga in Homeric Epics* by Rhys Carpenter, copyright 1946 by the Regents of the University of California.

17

Speech must be almost as old as humankind; song must be almost as old as speech; and poetry almost as old as song. Against this enormous vista, writing, on which our normal literary types depend, is almost a modernism. It is idle to ask how old is language, since no one, seemingly, yet knows securely the age of sentient loquent man; wherefore it is impossible to venture even a plausible guess at the antiquity of oral literary forms. Yet it is fairly safe to say that, with the antiquity of writing nowhere transcending five thousand years, the literature of unwritten speech must outdate its written competitor and successor by many times its measure. Attic tragedy and history, Plato and the pre-Socratics, will then be milestones set only a little distance back along the road which leads to the shadowy unwritten beginnings of literature. What seems a giant stride back into the past from Ibsen to Aeschylos is but a step that could be repeated many times before we should come to man's primal discovery of the magic of assonances and cadences, when he began to use speech for something more than the mere grunted communication of his immediate want. But these other steps behind Aeschylos are steps into darkness where it is difficult to catch even a glimmer of a lost world.

Yet we are not, like the paleontologists, seeking for things utterly extinct. Out of this immeasurable past, oral literature still survives today, both in its own right in its own true oral forms as well as in written record of itself, preserved before it died out in the past. But it has suffered and diminished greatly, and in many lands where once it flourished it is all but extinct today, because literacy, the spreading use of writing, everywhere sooner or later destroys it.

Perhaps you remember the scene in Victor Hugo's *Notre-Dame* where a cleric makes the rather cryptic remark that the printed book will ultimately destroy the carven edifice of the cathedral wherein achitecture and its attendant arts in the past had set the visual record of man's thoughts. "The book will kill the building," he insists; "this will kill that—*ceci tuera cela!*"

So it has been with the impact of writing on oral literature : *"ceci tuera cela!"* And human memory, which once perforce kept all human records, relinquished its powers to the newcomer and grew proportionately enfeebled with this cession of her strength. Most of us today can hardly credit the achievement of the *illiterati* who knew the Koran by heart or carried the entire Iliad and Odyssey in their minds. But nowadays whoever trusts his library and notebooks may no longer trust his remembrance. Only where memory cannot be displaced, as in the concert recitals of musicians or the operatic roles of singers, can we still observe its prodigious powers. But originally Mnemosyne was mother of *all* the Muses.

In the world of today, where the spread of literacy has remorselessly been destroying the oral literary forms and only the lowest cultural levels preserve their preliterate traditions, oral literature has had to take refuge with the peasant and with backward cultures. But there the strata which have escaped the schooling will continue to foster it, and in all levels the children still too young to have acquired letters will be its eager audience. But the mature, the intelligent, the gifted of mankind will despise and neglect it and let it die. For this reason it has been able to survive only in such forms as the peasant or the immature mind likes, understands, and practices. Yet it has not always been so in the past; and it is not everywhere so, even today.

World over, the gradations of oral literature seem to be three : among the fully literate nations like those of western Europe there is a prose form enshrining folk tales and *Marchen* of considerable variety; among partly literate peoples like those of eastern Europe there may also exist traditional verse forms, narrative ballads, often remembered through many generations and begetting imitative improvisations in like genre; while among wholly illiterate (but not therefore uncivilized) races there may flourish fully organized oral literature of unrestricted range and high artistic merit, such as has existed among Norse—and Celtic—and Greek-speaking peoples. It is in this latter environment that heroic epic properly belongs.

There is thus a sort of hierarchy of oral literature, with heroic epic near the highest and children's fairy tales near the lowest place; but there is a real and great difficulty in explaining how such a hierarchy is formed. If folk tale and fairy story are the last to resist the onset of literacy, shall we say that therefore these must merely be the hardest to kill, the toughest and stoutest of oral forms, able to outlive their more susceptible kindred? or shall we maintain that they more properly resemble a band of desperate survivors making their final stand in the only stronghold still uncaptured by the enemy, so that fugitives from all ranks may be found among them—from heroic epics, songs and ballads, myths and fables and adventure stories, all reduced to the lowly guise of *Marchen?* Are modern remnants of oral literature a historical residue of all that was great and good in the illiterate past? or—to change the metaphor—are they but a feeble growth of weeds in a poor man's garden from which all the statelier flowers have long since been taken?

Even if we grant that oral literature, as a genus of human artistic expression, may be a survival out of the immeasurable past before writing was invented, it does not thereby follow that its modern content, wherever it still survives, individually shares the antiquity of its kind. The date of any given piece of oral literature is the day on which it was last recited or on which it was reduced to writing. The true and proper date of those stories which the Brothers Grimm wrote down from the lips of unlettered reciters is the beginning of the nineteenth century. Most of them were uncontaminated by written literature, whose devices they ignore. In their form and pattern they often suggest great antiquity. Yet few of the stories, as they were actually told, can be oral documents handed down unaltered from a remote past, since they so often refer their surroundings to conditions recognizably recent. Manifestly, they have been retold to suit their narrator and audience. But how many times has this process of retelling already taken place? Some commentators, noting that stories of essentially the same content may be found dispersed over a huge area among races of very different speech, have concluded that such wide (even world-wide!) occurrence of comparable variants of a story is proof that once long ago, in a sort of primal Eden older than the Tower of Babel, there was told a primal story, an *Urmarchen,* from which all the modern counterparts are descended, like the animals of today which pious belief claims for descendants of the weirdly assorted zoological household afloat in Noah's ark. The theological and the folklore creed are equally naive. But it is easier to mock the dispersion theory than to find a satisfactory substitute for it. Let us grant that the range of story patterns is limited, and that more than one mind can think the same thought and construct the same story, or even that such tales, being reflections of universal wishes, hopes, and fears, must share the sameness of all human psychology. We shall still be left with a residue of inexplicable coincidences. Probably the solution is complex—almost as complex as the folklore material itself; and we shall have to be resigned to try every case on its individual merits. We shall therefore neither maintain that all the most familiar folk tales came originally from India or the

Near East or from anywhere else, nor yet hold the extreme opposite view that like begets like, that any story can spring up anywhere at any time, and that the comparative study of folk tales is merely an exploration of the behaviour of the human mind. We shall admit the possibility that there can be folk tales told today which have been told in strikingly similar form not merely centuries but thousands of years ago, since there is no good objection to such tenacity of oral memory and oral transmission. We shall admit the possibility that classical Greece was not the beginning of all Western literature, since behind its literature of reed pen and papyrus, unexplored and of vast extent, may have stretched an unwritten literature which lived by tongue and memory alone.

BENJAMIN BOTKIN

Introduction*

When I began to think of a book of American folklore, I
thought of all the good songs and stories and all the good talk
that would go into it, and of what a richly human and enter-
thought, should be as big as this country of ours—as American
as Davy Crockett and as universal as Brer Rabbit. For when
one thinks of American folklore one thinks not only of the
folklore of American life—the traditions that have sprung up
on American soil—but also of the literature of folklore—the
migratory traditions that have found a home here.

Because folklore is so elemental and folk songs and stories
are such good neighbors and pleasant companions, it is hard
to understand why American folklore is not more widely
known and appreciated. For this the word "folklore" is partly
responsible. Folklore is the scholar's word for something that is
taining book it would be. A book of American folklore, I
as simple and natural as singing songs and spinning yarns
among the folk who know the nature and the meaning but not
the name—and certainly not the scholarship—of folklore. Because the word denotes both the material and its study, and
has come to stand more for the study of the thing than for the
thing itself, folklore, in fact, seems to have become the possession of the few who study it rather than of the many who
make or use it.

The essence of folklore, however, is something that cannot
be contained in a definition but that grows upon one with folklore experience. Old songs, old stories, old sayings, old beliefs,
customs, and practices—the mindskills and handskills that
have been handed down so long that they seem to have a life

* From *A Treasury of American Folklore* edited by B. A. Botkin, copyright 1944 by B. A. Botkin, New York: Crown Publishers.

of their own, a life that cannot be destroyed by print but that constantly has to get back to the spoken word to be renewed; patterned by common experience; varied by individual repetition, inventive or forgetful; and cherished because somehow characteristic or expressive : all this, for want of a better word, is folklore.

Complementary to the "Stop me if you've heard this" aspect of folklore is the trait implied in the comeback : "That's not the way I heard it." For what makes a thing folklore is not only that you have heard it before yet want to hear it again, because it is different, but also that you want to tell it again in your own way, because it is anybody's property. On the one hand, repeated retelling establishes confidence in the rightness of what is said and how it is said. On the other hand, the beauty of a folk lyric, tune, story, or saying is that, if you don't like it, you can always change it, and, if *you* don't, someone else will.

But if folklore is old wine in new bottles, it is also new wine in old bottles. It says not only, "Back where I come from," but also, "Where do we go from here?" If this book is intended to bring the reader back to anything, it is not to the "good old days" but to an enjoyment and understanding of living American folklore for what it is and what it is worth. This is an experience in which Americans as compared with other peoples are sadly deficient. Perhaps it is because we are not one people but many peoples in one, and a young people, who have grown up too close to the machine age. The industrial folk tales and songs in this book are evidence enough that machinery does not destroy folklore. Rather, in our rapid development from a rural and agricultural to an urban and industrial folk, we have become estranged from the folklore of the past, which we cannot help feeling a little self-conscious or antiquarian about, without yet being able to recognize or appreciate the folklore of the present.

Perhaps the best way to understand the songs and stories in this book is in terms of a species of living literature which has no fixed form (in this respect differing from the classics, which it resembles in permanence and universality of appeal) and which is constantly shifting back and forth between written and unwritten tradition. Since print tends to freeze a song or a story, folklore is most alive or at home out of print, and in its purest form is associated with the "grapevine" and the bookless world. But that does not make it synonymous with illiteracy or ignorance, nor is it true that the educated do not also have their lore, or that lore ceases to be lore as soon as it is written down or published. Folk literature differs from the rest of literature only in its history: its author is the original "forgotten man."

Not only does folklore shift, but it changes as it shifts, between the top and bottom layers of culture. As it gets nearer to the world of professional poets and story-tellers, it tends to shape about itself a formal "literary" tradition of its own, as in the great collections of legends and folk tales that have come down to us from ancient and medieval times and have been pored over by scholars. But alongside of this more classic folk literature, which has acquired scholarly prestige and which gives and takes erudition, is the humbler and homelier folk literature of everyday life and the common man—today's people's literature (which the older folk literature may once have been). The difference between the two (a difference perhaps only of degree) is the difference, say, between the English and Scottish ballads and the "Dust Bowl Ballads" of Woody Guthrie.

This range of variation within the folklore field is a source of both strength and weakness. For while it enables folklore perpetually to rebuild itself from the ground up, it creates a kind of class-consciousness among folklorists. Thus the British folk-song and folk-dance expert, Cecil J. Sharp, while very much taken with the vigor and beauty of our mountain songs and dances, was unable to see in our cowboy songs anything but the fact that the "cowboy has been despoiled of his inheritance of traditional song" and has "nothing behind him" and nothing but "himself and his daily occupations to sing about, and that in a self-centered, self-conscious way, e.g., 'The Cowboy's life is a dreadful life;' 'I'm a poor lonesome cowboy;' 'I'm a lonely bull-whacker,' and so forth."

Further complicating and diversifying the picture is a third quantity, midway between "folk" and "academic"—the "popular." The latter is distinguished by its wider and more passing acceptance, the result of transmission through such "timely" media as stage, press, radio, and films. Yet the so-called lively arts—jazz, vaudeville, burlesque, comic strips, animated cartoons, pulps—often have a folk basis or give rise to new folk creations, such as Mickey Mouse and Donald Duck. Many of the innovations of popular lore are associated with new inventions: e.g., the Ford joke and the gremlins. At the same time many of our modern gags have an ancient and honorable, if somewhat wheezy, lineage. The one about the two Irishmen, the Hebrew, and the baloney ("The Three Dreams") goes back to the twelfth century, while Little Moron jokes are as old as the Turkish Nasreddin.

Also close to folk sources but to be distinguished from folk literature proper is literature about the folk. This ranges from old-timers' reminiscences . . . and homespun humor and verse to local color and regional stories and sketches, all of which throw light on the folk and folklore backgrounds, culminating in that small body of masterpieces of "folk art" mined out of the collective experience and imagination by writers, known and unknown, who have succeeded in identifying themselves with their folk tradition.

RICHARD CHASE

Introduction*

What is folklore?

Webster says: "Traditional tales, songs, dances, customs, beliefs, sayings, preserved unreflectively among a people . . . hence, the science which investigates the life and spirit of a people as revealed in such lore."

Who then are the "folk"?

Again let's consult Webster: "A group of kindred people . . . bound together by ties of race, language, religion, etc., and that great proportion of its number which determines the group character and tends to preserve its civilization."

American civilization stems from Old World sources. Our ideas of religion come from Hebraic traditions and from Christianity as it developed in the Greco-Roman world. Parts of the Bible are Jewish folklore. Much of Christianity is based on lore that preceded it in Egyptian, Hellenic, Alexandrian, and Roman civilizations. Many of our ideas of drama, poetry, architecture and sculpture come from the ancient Greeks. Greek art and literature developed from Mediterranean folklore.

Our American uses of the English language, literature, music, and folklore stem from the North of Europe. Other groups of kindred people in the United States speak French, Spanish, German, Scandinavian, and other languages—as well as English—and each tends to preserve here in our nation a great variety of Old World lore. Celtic tale-tellers *(sheen-acnies)* can be found in New York and Chicago. Basques in Montana and Washington perform their ancient ritual dances

* From *American Folk Tales and Songs* compiled by Richard Chase, copyright 1956 by Richard Chase, The New American Library of World Literature, Inc.

regularly. Folklorists have difficulty collecting Armenian songs and dances in Armenia but find them readily in Detroit!

Each "group of kindred people" coming across the Atlantic brought its own lore—things of the mind and spirit—and often "unreflectively," sometimes deliberately, have kept the identity of each individual set of folk traditions. The use of the word "American" (especially "native American") can lead to confusion in the field of folklore. The only truly American folk are the Indians, and individual tribes have to this day kept their own separate group character and civilization.

It is strange that the English-American heritage of folk tales, folk songs, and folk dances should have been so neglected by scholars and folklorists. When a certain scholar, the first to collect "The Jack Tales," approached the English Department of her university with a project for further work in the field of British folk tales in America she was told that such things did not exist.

Indian lore has been thoroughly collected. The Negro's songs and tales are widely known. Today there is an increasing interest in the folklore of many traditions, with an emphasis on Anglo-American materials, throughout the country. Our English-American folkways are still too often connected, in the minds of some, with a vulgarized idea of things "hillbilly." This is unfortunate. For there are many Americans who keep, unreflectively, these folkways : a store of traditions which they call, not "folklore," but simply the old songs, the old tales, the old ways. And those of us who know this heritage are not just mountain people, nor are we only country folk. We live in every state, and we can be found in large cities as well as out on the land.

This lore is not confined to any one geographical location— little pockets of Elizabethan culture isolated in remote mountain hollows. Such traditions are loved and remembered wherever tale-telling grandfathers and singing grandmothers are close to their children and grandchildren. For the genuine thing, carried on through generations and acquiring lively local and individual variations, always has strength, beauty, and a sort of quietness that make it convincing. Its power often resides in understatement. It does not flare into sudden "popularity" and then die out. Many of our English-American folk songs have been "popular" for seven hundred years! Our folkways are as solid, as lasting, and as adaptable as the language we use. This lore is organic, not static, and changes with each generation of singers and tale-tellers.

This book,* then, presents samples of the lore of a kindred people—those of us here in America who, whatever our origins across the Atlantic, are bound together by a common use of the English language.

One of the first to deal with British folklore as preserved here in the United States was the English scholar and musician, Cecil J. Sharp. From 1914 to 1918 he collected English folk ballads and folk songs (and one form of the English Country Dance) in the Southern Appalachians. In the years since Mr. Sharp's work was published (1932) a flood of Anglo-American folklore books has appeared, presenting such lore as found in twenty-four states and two Canadian provinces, and covering every kind of tradition, secular and sacred, from children's skip-rope rhymes to witchcraft. Folklore courses are now being taught in many colleges and schools, and The American Folklore Society, which publishes *The Journal of American Folklore,* is an active organization. The Country Dance Society of America, which developed from The English Folk Dance and Song Society in England, sponsors the social uses of all these lively traditions throughout the United States.

* *American Folk Tales and Songs.*

In this volume each song, tale, dance, or riddle will speak for itself. Notes are given telling where I learned each item. Some are well-known; some are rare. I have collated and edited the material to try to present the best and most universally usable versions, except where stated as given verbatim from the informant. Headnotes to individual songs and tales give details of my editing "for popular use."

Many of the tunes are printed in shape-notes because about twenty years ago a singer in the mountains asked me :

"You going to put these old songs in a book?"

"I hope to, some day."

"Then you be sure to get the music set down in shape-notes so we can sing it."

And I promised I would.

Shape-notes are simply an aid to sight-singing. They are in use all over the South. This device is much like the "tonic solfa" system used in England, but in our case the notes are in their usual places on the staff.

Since nearly every school child can sing the syllabus do-re-me-fa-sol-la-ti-do, once the shapes are learned, and the major scale sung by them a few times, the shape of the note head helps the singer locate the syllable and the tone. *Do* is keynote, of course, for all major tunes (Ionian mode). *Do* is movable in position but fixed in shape. In folk music there are primitive minor tunes (normal minor, pure minor, or Aeolian mode) that are sung with the keynote *la*. We might call this *"la* mode." Our folk singers never heard of the modes, however much they use them in their singing. There are six such modes, or scales : *do* to *do, sol* to *sol* (Mixolydian mode), *la* to *la, re* to *re* (Dorian mode), *mi* to *mi* (Phrygian mode), and *fa* to *fa* (Lydian mode). *Do* scale, of course, predominates. *Sol, la* and *re* scales are fairly common. *Mi* scale is infrequent, and *fa* scale rare. *Note:* In all these modes the half-steps always stand exactly where they are in the major *(do)* scale, between *mi* and *fa,* and between *ti* and *do.*

And what of the creative uses of our folk traditions?

"Great art," wrote John Jay Chapman, "does not come on call, and when it comes it is always shy." And when in the intellectual and spiritual development of a nation it does come, "it is always based on folklore, tradition, and a reverence for the past."

And Ralph Vaughan Williams says, "An art must be the reflection of the whole life of a community. Any direct and unforced expression of our common life may be the nucleus from which a great art will spring; of such expressions the folk song is the most genuine and unadulterated, besides being in itself a complete form of art."

Our nation is seeing a revival, a restoration, of various folk arts. If these traditions are kept straight and simple, and are enjoyed with the unself-conscious dignity which is their chief characteristic, then our folkways can play an important and constructive role in the work of both schools and churches. When country dancing, for example, is offered as social recreation in a community it welds any group into a highly spirited fellowship activated by an enjoyment that carries its own self-discipline, and it is self-perpetuating.

The genuine folk heritage has an immediate appeal for all ages, and as it becomes known to more and more individuals in the community it spreads naturally, toning up the whole cultural outlook. There is a living force in these old games and dances, tales and songs, that cannot be duplicated through mechanized and commercialized forms of recreation; their living social use, if thoughtfuly planned and carefully taught, often results in an awakened attitude that relates to more basic concerns of life and of art in the broadest and best sense.

A great cultural development took place in Greece just after

Athens and her allies conquered the Persian armies. The Elizabethan Age followed the defeat of the Spanish Armada. We and our allies have only recently gained a victory over forces that threatened our way of life.

There are signs that a great American art may be on its way. The outdoor dramas now being produced across the nation are full of "folklore, tradition, and a reverence for the past." Symphonic works based on Anglo-American folk music are being written. The movements of John Powell's *Symphony in A* are built around 1) country dance tunes, 2) "a love song," 3) two dramatic ballad tunes, and 4) a great triumphant march based on an ancient English ritual morris dance tune— which tune also appears in the 1835 edition of *The Southern Harmony* as "Mississippi," a Judgment Day hymn still sung in Kentucky. Stage plays based on folk ballads and tales have been attempted. Folk festivals are cropping up everywhere. And all this current interest in the word "folk" may be truly significant. Through a rediscovery of our genuine living folkways a great cultural rebirth could begin to work its leaven. It will happen slowly and quietly. Genuine culture is always shy.

A true folk singer sings "by heart" and not out of books. He never tries to impress an audience, because at his best he is a real artist. Sincerely he shares his love and knowledge of these things *with* you rather than performing *for* you. He sings "unthoughtedly," without self-consciousness. He makes his points without overdoing. He never shows his tonsils! Folk arts lose all their magic the instant they are exploited sensationally.

"It is a small demand that these things make," wrote Cecil Sharp, "—that of being known, to be loved." And wherever the work of this man[2] has become known a restoration of these traditions has flourished : in England, and, through the Mountain Folk Festival at Berea College, throughout the southern

mountains. The Berea Festival is never a "show." We meet to enjoy the old dances, to sing together, and this meeting is just another "party" to culminate the fun we have been having all winter singing and doing country dances in our own schools and communities.

In her book *The Ballad Tree*, Evelyn Wells writes: ". . . in the mountains where there was no recognition as yet (about 1918) of the value and beauty of our native songs, Cecil Sharp was able to stir a spark that has never died. Today, all over the southern mountains, a folk recreation program has developed (of which the spring festival at Berea is a part), largely because for three years a man traveled through these mountains with a divining rod which tapped the wellsprings of native music . . . nobody possesses this divining rod who does not have insight into the intrinsic fineness of human nature."

We might try to see clearly what Grundtvig did for Denmark through her folk traditions, and what Elias Lonnrot (who collected the *Kalevala* from Finnish folk singers) and Sibelius have done for Finland. Douglas Hyde, Padraic Colum, John M. Synge, and The Abbey Theatre, working with Irish tradition helped establish the New Eire. Our own cultural reawakening will follow surely, when more and more Americans discover what Cecil Sharp, Ralph Vaughan Williams, and John Powell have done for England and for us.

A full knowledge of the folk arts of our people—traditions we all share without always being conscious of it—will stir our minds and spirits as nothing else can by bringing us closer to our Old World origins—predominantly English but with delightful overlappings from other cultures and lores.

An immediate and direct awareness of our own rich heritage can most certainly inspire our makers of plays, novels, and poems toward more lasting "success," and give a fresh delight to those of us who are creative only in being alive and doing

our daily work. This experience will restore in us a cultural sincerity that can help us see the living values in all fine art in a free society like ours. Furthermore, folk arts can give coming generations a solid basis of judgment for reading good books, listening to good music, and choosing good, more really pleasurable forms of social recreation. And these traditions are not "good" because they are "old." It's the other way around! Such things last, once we have opportunities to know them, because they excite an immediate response, particularly with young people.

John Powell has said, ". . . it is for all English-speaking people . . . that this tradition has the greatest significance, for it is a vital part of that culture without which art is impossible and education can so easily become a lifeless and useless burden."

Discovery of the spontaneous "unreflective" folkways of our nation will come to many as a welcome breath of fresh air. Our ears and eyes are becoming saturated with cheap, commercialized "cultural" products consciously designed to force on us something called "amusement." And this fare is often put forth, by design, on an almost moronic level, "because that's what the public wants."

A knowledge of our folkways will open up lively and rich experiences for many who have never been moved by symphonies and other forms of art music. The inherent qualities of folk tradition do away with sham and pretense. Folk music is a sure steppingstone to a sincere understanding of the world's other music. Ralph Vaughan Williams has stated the case quite clearly : "When . . . Cecil Sharp collected and published his new discoveries in English folk songs (discoveries made on both sides of the Atlantic) he had in mind the ordinary man, the 'divine average' of Whitman. And it is the ordinary man for whose musical salvation the folk song will be responsible. For here is an ideal music . . . neither popular nor classical, highbrow nor lowbrow, but an art in which all can take part . . . a music which has for generations voiced the spiritual longings of our race."

And this current "folk movement," in England and in America, is indeed contagious. It proves, wherever it is based on actual tradition, an enlivening spiritual experience. It puts us in touch with our own individual sources, whatever they are: Anglo-American, French-American, Spanish-American, Hebrew, Negro, Indian—all. Barriers of race, language, region, fall only when one understands deeply his own individual heritage. Only then can we truly share the folkways of others, and understand that there are no "foreign" Americans. These facts give us a better understanding of the varied regions of our own nation and can play a part in creating better cultural understanding between this country and other nations of the world.

If such a movement is to become the basis for a living creative use of art in the United States, it will spread best, perhaps only, through the living word, the human touch. There can be no commercialization, no standardization, no mechanization of these things. They elude every sort of "modern sophistication." They are always "shy."

And, be it made clear: when we say "Anglo-Saxon" no kind of "superiority" is implied. (I know the beauty of Spanish folk plays of New Mexico. I know a Finn in Massachusetts whose translation into English of *The Kalevala* may prove the best ever made.) It is an awkward expression but it will have to serve. Some years ago a southern Highlander told me, "Yes, I've heard it said that here in these mountains is the best Angry-Saxon blood in the nation." And recently I heard an orator in the Appalachian region proclaim, "We are the finest Anglo-Saxon stock in the whole United States." (Much applause.) This is almost nonsensical. But the Angles, Saxons, Jutes, Danes, Vikings, Normans, all "North-men"—mixing and re-mixing with Gaels and Celts in the British Isles did develop in time certain cultural characteristics. They gave us Woden's Day and Thor's Day, and the word "Easter." They gave us the language which is spoken here between two oceans. Traditions are found amongst us today that were already ancient in the Elizabethan Age when English civilization was at a great height and our folk traditions were well known. Shakespeare wrote a play based on an old tale which you will find in this book.*

It needs to be said here, that there are no watertight compartments separating our individual American peoples. Cultural understanding transcends differences of race, and all man-made barriers, be they political or religious. Uncle Remus knew many Anglo-Celtic tales and told two versions of "Wicked John and the Devil." It is the unreflective use of such lore in our own natural environment that recreates it for each new generation.

"We in the United States," wrote the late President Franklin D. Roosevelt, "are amazingly rich in the elements from which to weave a culture. We have the best of man's past on which to draw, brought to us from all parts of the world. In binding these elements into a national fabric of strength and beauty, let us keep the original fibers so intact that the fineness of each will show in the complete handiwork."

It is the original fibers, *kept intact*, in their living uses, that are for every group of Americans the nucleus of a genuine culture. True folk traditions have the magic of all great art, whether it be a tragic ballad, a children's song, a carol, a ridiculous tall tale, a singing game, a lilting fiddle tune, a

* *American Folk Tales and Songs.*

strange-sounding "minor" hymn, or a rollicking comic tale or song.

You can tell, without being "an authority," whether it is genuine or not. You know by the feel, by a tingling of your scalp, by an indefinable something inside you when you hear the song sung, or the tale told, or the tune played. It will arouse your interest, command your respect, and finally win and hold your love.

To find your own "original fibers" you need but seek them out in your own region, your own neighborhood, or even from the older members of your own family. Here amongst my people in the Southern mountains, it is fiddlers, banjo players, the older people and the families who delight in "making music," who know these things. Often the songs and tales are buried deep in the old folks' memories and you must be patient. Sometimes the person who can tell you the most about "the old ways" will at first disclaim any knowledge of such things. But if you can tell a tale yourself, or sing some real folk song that you know, he (or she) will very likely recollect something for you sooner or later.

You might like to try it! . . . If you do try collecting folklore you may not only find something very important that has never been recorded, but you may also have opportunities to rediscover for yourself certain basic human values—traditions that lead us all to a better realization of lasting things in a changing world. For many of us are, as Gilbert Murray has put it, ". . . under the power of the enemy . . ."

This enemy is "he who always puts the letter before the spirit, cheapness and triviality before beauty. It is he who makes things only in order to sell them; who has forgotten that there is such a thing as truth and measures the world by advertisement or by profit; who daily defiles the beauty that surrounds him and makes vulgar the tragedy . . . the smart, the clever, *the counterfeiter of spiritual values*[3]—he is all about us, and worse, he has wormed his way inside so many of us . . . persecuting our peace, spoiling our insight, confusing our highest values. . . ."

Yes, our folk traditions—the hilarity and rich dry humor of our folk tales, the beauty and gaiety of our folk music, the deep sincerity of our old hymns—these are only one expression of an American culture. It is not the old songs and tales that are so important in themselves; it is a way of life, the essence of ourselves and of our kindred, and knowledge of a higher set of values in the realm of the mind and spirit, that my people here in America have taught me.

Notes

1. Such as "The Horn in the West" in Boone, North Carolina, and "Wilderness Road" at Berea, Kentucky.
2. Mr. Sharp established The English Folk Dance and Song Society in England, and the Country Dance Society in America.
3. Italics mine

STITH THOMPSON

Story-Writers and Story-Tellers*

IN THE PRESENCE OF HIS FELLOWS IN THE PURELY LITERARY fields the folklorist always feels apologetic. A large part of his time is passed in working with material which, considered as literature, is often very inferior and frequently may seem not worthy of the attention of a serious student. It is, therefore, sometimes assumed that the folklorist has no appreciation of the great literary tradition and that he romantically exaggerates the importance of the expression of common man. Yet it is no more than fair to say that the most important folklorists in this country and abroad are those who have been trained in appreciation of the great literatures. I should be particularly sorry if anyone, because my labors have largely concerned sometimes the periphery and sometimes the subsoil of written literature, should feel that I underestimate the great classics. For me, as for all of us, they are the mountain peaks of human accomplishments, and even their lesser fellows show, each in his own way, heartening achievements of the spirit of man.

But we cannot live always in contemplation of the final results of the literary process. Its whole course and extent likewise deserves our careful study. We must realize that from the point of view both of its function in society and of its chief formal manifestations, literature is not dependent on the written word. It is an activity more ancient than the pyramids and in no wise dependent on the extent of our western culture. Cheops, the great pyramid builder, 5,000 years ago had his professional story-tellers. Long before Homer and before Beowulf minstrels sang their heroic songs in the courts of kings.

* From *Philologica: The Malone Anniversary Studies,* edited by Thomas A. Kirby and Henry Bosley Woolf, copyright 1949 by The Johns Hopkins Press.

The *Iliad* and *Odyssey* themselves were oral compositions and for generations existed only in the memories of gifted men. In Africa, in the Islands of the South Seas, among primitive men everywhere are tales and songs, rituals and dramatic dances, just as there are tribal traditions and codes of conduct.

Of most interest to the student of literature are the songs and tales which thus live and have lived without benefit of writing. It is no exaggeration to guess that 95 per cent of all the stories in the world have been told for listeners rather than for readers. And a surprising number of the themes which have appeared in our literature were taken from these unrecorded tales or songs. Written literature is but a special development, under different conditions, of artistic practices current long before writing and persisting even yet among those far outside its influence.

In the field of history, students have long recognized the fact that they cannot confine themselves to written records if they would learn the story of man's activities. They utilize the results of the archaeologists' work, or themselves turn archaeologists to penetrate into the vast unrecorded stretches of prehistory, and they call on the ethnologist to help them expand their view to include all the peoples on the globe. Is it not also of importance for us who study literatures of the world to know about the behavior of story and song in times which preceded writing and among the unlettered peoples of today?

Though there was certainly never any sharp break with oral tradition in our earliest literature, and though there has always been a rather free interchange of materials, the actual behavior of the two kinds of literature shows many differences. The written word remains; the spoken vanishes. The writer goes slowly, hesitates, crosses out, revises; the speaker does none of these, though he may improve his technique for another time. The reader also may pause or reread a difficult

passage, or skip one that fails to interest him. But when he is
a listener he has only his ears to hear the speaker and he cannot slow or hurry him. What he fails to grasp he loses, and
all he can do to recover this is to hear the tale again.

This process of telling and hearing—and repeated telling
and hearing—is the principal characteristic of literature when
it is not possible by means of writing to capture and preserve
a particular form. Hence oral literature is in continual flux
with never exactly the same form manifesting itself.

This instability of form does not, however, imply that such
literature is merely kaleidoscopic in its nature. Under the
myriad surface appearances both the traditional forms and the
traditional substances show remarkable persistence. Tales and
songs known to a people cannot be changed at random in any
essential. A well-known folktale like Cinderella may appear in
all parts of the world in six or eight hundred versions, every
one different, and yet a historical and geographic study will
show that these variations are thoroughly consistent with all
the observed facts of tale-telling and transmission, combined
with the geographical situation and historical currents in
which the tale has moved.

The study of such an oral form as the folktale presents problems analogous to the investigations of written literature—
those of origin and history, of style, and of function in society
—but the approach to these problems is different. The literary
student is concerned with fixed or nearly fixed manuscripts
and books, perhaps a number of related units but always
crystallized into definite form, instead of a multitude of almost
fortuitous units representing an ever-moving, ever-changing
tradition. If his work is comparative he moves from document
to document trying to arrive at an unbroken chain in which
author A has adopted or changed or been influenced by
manuscript or book B which he has read, and if this relation

be actually established, the miles between the places of writing or the lapse of years intervening are of little, if any, importance.

The student of the purely oral tale, however, faces different problems. He finds a tale scattered over all parts of the world. If he is lucky he is able to assemble hundreds of versions—the more the better for his purpose—and from the evidence of all these he tries to tell something of the general form of the tale as it was originally invented, to hazard reasonable judgments as to about where and when it began its long career, to trace the direction of its travels and to observe the important changes the tale has undergone in different lands and times. For nearly all this he must work from internal evidence, for usually all he can tell about any versions is the place and date of its recording.

That he should have any success in spite of this handicap seems astonishing. And yet the comparative study of the folk-tale has achieved great accomplishments in the past half century. To me it seems that the most important of these has been the development of the historic-geographic method—the statement of its principles and its early application by the Finns, and its subsequent modifications and improvements by scholars of other countries. This is not the time or place to discuss this method of study. But twenty or thirty competent monographs have now demonstrated how it is possible, by a close analysis of a tale into all its parts and a consideration of minute variations in the development of these parts, to establish certainly so many local currents in a tradition that the whole movement of the tale in its complicated history becomes clearer and clearer.

The application of such a method to the investigation of an important tale is not easy. The mere language difficulty is great, for the stories will appear in a dozen tongues. The assembling of the hundreds of versions may be a matter of years, though it has been greatly facilitated by the classifications and various indexes completed in the past forty years. The arranging in geographical order, the breaking down of the tale into its significant parts, the making of tables and interpretation of these require industry and judgment. Especially does the attempt to make the final syntheses of the study present many pitfalls to the unwary scholar. But because of these very difficulties, the investigation of one of the world's great folktales furnishes a challenge to all students of comparative literature.

For often it is only a student of literary history who can be trusted with such a study. Most of our best known tales have also had literary treatment and thereby have experienced a combination of the two processes I have indicated as characteristic of written and oral material. For these the investigator must know and employ both techniques and must know where one begins and the other stops. Whether this student be primarily folklorist turned literary historian or literary historian turned folklorist makes little difference. In any case he is engaged on research that will employ all his abilities.

It is too much to expect that the student of the folktale shall have specialized training in all the fields he must cultivate. But he must at least have a very wide reading in many adjacent areas not ordinarily needed by the student of written literature. The fact that a folktale may occur in all parts of the world and may have traveled for thousands of miles, makes it imperative, for example, that the investigator have more than a casual knowledge of geography. He must continually have in mind the great water routes of the world, and must know which of the oceans and lakes have been freely navigated and which form almost impassible barriers to free communication. He must visualize clearly the mountain ranges and the deserts which have impeded and sometimes prevented transmission of tales. He must realize the importance of jungles and the attraction of fertile lands. Thus he will come to understand why it is that the tales he studies do not proceed in their distribution at an even speed in all directions, why they may remain unchanged in one place for centuries and why, in another, they may travel with the greatest mobility.

The student must also know what has actually happened in the dissemination of culture during the past centuries or milleniums. He must try to keep continually before him the accounts of all the great migrations of the past. He must know which peoples have played leading roles in the various periods and which have served only as receivers of culture. He must try to understand affinities and antipathies among various peoples and what are the conditions under which borrowing takes place freely or is retarded. For example, he must try to explain why it is that North American Indians have borrowed so freely from the French and Spanish and practically not at all from the English and Scotch. These are but a few of the historical questions which the student of the folktale must confront.

And he must also become something of an amateur psychologist. On the basis of the hundreds of versions of a particular tale, he will observe in practice the working of interesting psychological principles. That a folktale which has been told and listened to seldom, if ever, finds itself preserved completely is thoroughly understandable. The broad, general principles of forgetting details, of substituting the familiar for the unfamiliar, of changing from a third-person narrative to a first-person, or of changing a human narrative to a tale of animals —all of these may well be expected and are actually found by all investigators. But there are other, more subtle, psychological problems to be encountered. How much resistance, for example, is given to the dissemination of a tale by the crossing of a linguistic boundary? Is the tale learned in a foreign language felt to be foreign and, therefore, not properly to belong to the folklore of the receiving country? Do characteristic changes take place when tales go from country A to country B and, if so, is there any reasonable explanation for these changes? Again, what happens to a purely literary tale which is taken over by story-tellers and becomes a part of their repertory? Do they make it conform to the ordinary oral tradition, or do they keep something of the literary structure? It is well known that some of the great published collections of folktales, such as those of the Brothers Grimm and of Charles Perrault, have had great influence in spreading certain stories among those countries which have a large reading population. Do the special forms of the tale learned from Grimm or Perrault drive out the oral form, or do both exist side by side? Or is there some attempt to change the literary form so that it is more in accord with the tale as already known?

For these psychological problems, the vast collections of folktales now available furnish an excellent basis for study. It is only by approaching the problem empirically, by seeing what has actually happened to the tales in the course of their development, that the psychologist can hope to answer these questions. There is little doubt that the professional psychologist, with his special techniques, could be of great assistance to the folklorist in the study of these problems. The material for his work lies neatly arranged and only awaits his labors. Meantime, the student of the folktale must do the best he can to interpret the vast material before him, astounding as it frequently is in the variety within its unmistakable unity.

An aspect of folktale study only now in its beginning is that of oral narrative style. The successful devices of the teller of tales are greatly different from those of the story writer. Some day as a result of many men's work we may know more about this. And when we do we shall also be able to speak with more assurance about the proportion of the "popular" and the "literary" in Homer or *Beowulf*.

The growth and mutation of the *genres* of folk narrative, for example the interrelation of tales and myths, have received much attention in recent years. By the study of the myth-making process among primitive peoples in all parts of the world we may at last learn something about myths and put an end to the wild speculations of the various schools of mythologists who have only served to bring discredit on the name of serious scholarship.

The workers in our field are few, and since the war even fewer. We are frankly after able recruits. In many respects we are still pioneers. Year by year we change and seek to improve methods. Year by year new problems arise and new points of view are presented, always new challenges to originality of approach. But the way is not easy. The literature is written in at least six or eight languages and there are no translations. The material is scattered over the world, the technical work is long, the interpretation difficult. But the companionship is interesting. In this border field the scholar on successive days may be working with anthropologist, historian, sociologist, and psychologist. But, because of their close mutual relations he finds his most constant companionship with those who devote their lives to the study of literature.

MACEDWARD LEACH

Problems of Collecting Oral Literature[1]

PROBLEMS OF ORAL LITERATURE RANGE FROM THE PURELY
technical to the esthetic. A top collector must be an engineer
capable of operating and often repairing complicated recording machines; he must be a scholar and an historian, bringing
a broad knowledge of the culture he is collecting; he must be a
public relations man; he must have a sturdy stomach, capable
of digesting all manner of food, and a good head to withstand
all manner of drink; he must be physically in top shape,
capable of hiking up lonesome mountains, of rowing a boat,
even of taking a turn at cutting wood, haying, or butchering;
he must have a reassuring bedside manner, able to soothe those
who think he is planning to put their songs and stories on radio
or record and make millions for himself.

In addition to such personal problems are those involving
choice of equipment, where to collect, how to secure informants, how to conduct a recording session. There are, however, other problems which, I think, are more fundamental but
which have received less consideration. These grow out of
the general subject of *what* to collect, that is, the objectives of
the collector.

The collector has a great responsibility, for the desk scholar
can base his scholarship only on what the collector selects for
him; failure of the collector to include pertinent material,
either through ignorance or bad judgment, is as serious as a
collector's prejudging his material or collecting with only his
special interests in mind like the eighteenth century collectors

* By MacEdward Leach, *PMLA,* LXVII, No. 3 (June, 1962).
[1] This paper in somewhat different form was read before the Comparative Literature 2: Popular Literature discussion group at the MLA
convention in Philadelphia, December, 1960.

of song texts. Anthropologists have much to teach collectors of folklore and oral literature; too long have we been concerned with specifics in isolation. Certainly in a *folk* culture a song or story does not stand alone.

I believe that a collector completely fulfilling his obligations must work toward four objectives : first, he must collect and present his material as *oral* literature; second, he must collect the matrix of this material; third, he must collect the singer or tale teller; fourth, he must collect what is necessary for a presentation and a study of the folk esthetic.

Let us consider each of these objectives in detail. A collector must collect and present his material as *oral* literature. As you run through the standard collection of songs, tales, proverbs—folklore of the past—you discover that almost without exception it was collected with little reference to how it was originally presented. It is invariably collected as if it came from written sources, as if it were eye literature rather than ear literature. Since it was collected as eye literature, it is edited and judged as written literature. It is tried by the principles of sophisticated art. This same mistake has been made by students in medieval literature, much of which was also oral in origin and in presentation. Critics have conventionally found the medieval romance, for example, faulty in structure, not realizing that since it was oral it was naturally presented in oral (ear) units which when read, of course, made the work seem episodic, static, disjointed, and repetitious. Most folk tales as you meet them in collections are lifeless things and they are as static as a play read silently. As a result of our carrying over attitudes and techniques based on written literature we have failed to realize that folktale and much folk song are dramatic and that it is not the imagination of the audience that is appealed to but its sense of reality. A collection of tales like those of Grimm, even in the new translation of Magoun and Krappe,[2] can not be studied except as written literature.

The Anansi stories of the Negroes of the Caribbean, for example, as found in such collections as those of Jekyll and Beckwith,[3] are poor things when read. There is little characterization; there is a sameness of style; the action is hard to follow, and so on. It is, however, an unforgettable experience to hear an Anansi[4] tale told by a good native teller of tales to an appreciative audience. Typical is the tale of "Anansi and the Tiger" which I heard in the Blue Mountains of Jamaica a few years ago. Men, women, and children were crowded into the small room and overflowed onto the narrow porch. Some squatted on the floor; some stood around the walls; children, black eyes wide, sat at their parents' feet; the bed in the corner was loaded with women and babies. All were silent, intent on the story-teller, Arthur Wyles. Mr. Wyles was sixty-one, his hair white and kinky like sheep's wool. His eyes were unforgettable—very large, very black, and remote, expressionless. He stood throughout the story, constantly moving about. First, he would be at one side of the room taking the part of Anansi; then he would jump quickly to the other and face back as he took the role of Tiger. His voice was whining and ingratiating as Anansi; his face took on a smirk; his words were given a wheedling twist. But when he became Tiger, he drew himself up stern and dignified and majestic; his voice was deep and powerful and his walk stately. This story ends with a fight between Tiger and Death. Mr. Wyles, voice full of excitement, arms flailing, staged the fight, blow by blow, taking the parts alternately of Tiger and of Death. When the

[2] Francis P. Magoun, Jr., and Alexander H. Krappe, *The Grimms' German Folk Tales* (Carbondale,Ill., 1960).

[3] Walter Jekyll, *Jamaican Song and Story* (London, 1907); Martha W. Beckwith, *Jamaica Anansi Stories* (New York, 1924).

[4] Anansi, spider, is the hero of many West African and Caribbean tales.

climax was reached and Tiger delivered the knock-out blow conquering Death, the narrator over-reached himself and his clenched fist hit the door jamb a cruel blow that bloodied his knuckles. He seemed to feel nothing but went into the very realistic death throes of Brother Death. Though the audience had heard this story many times, they sat enthralled, eyes shining, audibly satisfied with the ending. Here, then, in the *telling* is the characterization and the drama, absent in the story when merely read, now abundantly supplied.[5]

What can a collector do with such material? Certainly he can no longer be satisfied to make a bare transcript of it. Short of making a sound movie, he can only describe what he heard and saw, can only annotate his text with elaborated stage directions, so to speak. Certainly he must collect voice—tone and inflection—gestures, facial expression, attitudes as well as words. And he must not forget the audience and their reactions. In short, he must accurately report the material as *oral* literature.

But the collector's task is not finished with simply the complete record of an oral situation. Folk culture is largely mass culture, each element of which is conditioned by its matrix, and it grows out of its matrix in a much more intimate way than an element in a sophisticated culture grows out of its matrix. There is much more of individual shaping in sophisticated culture. For this reason the collector must not be content with merely collecting the song or story; he must collect the matrix as well.

Again may I take an example from Jamaican folklore? You are collecting oral literature in Jamaica and you have

[5] For extensive discussion of this point with much concrete material, see these outstanding works: Albert B. Lord, *The Singer of Tales* (Cambridge, Mass., 1960), Part 1; Melville Jacobs, *The Content and Style of an Oral Literature* (Viking Fund Publications 26, New York, 1959); Melville Jacobs, *The People are Coming Soon* (Seattle: Univ of Washington Press, 1960).

gone to Orcabessa to collect the work songs of the stevedores
loading the banana boats. It is early evening. Already a long
line of bearers, men and women, each with a stem of bananas
on his head, is slowly moving from the lighter over the gang-
way into the steamer. Bare feet shuffle on the dry boards. The
only other sounds are the languid lapping of the water against
the side and the monotonous call of the tallyman to the
book-keeper: "Six hands, eight hands, five hands, *bunch;*
seven hands, six hands, *bunch.*" All night long it goes; the
moon climbs and descends. "Seven hands, five hands, eight
hands, *bunch.*" The line moves more slowly; hands go more
often to the weight on heads. Still comes the monotonous call
of the tallyman: "Six hands, five hands, seven hands, *bunch.*"
Then light comes in the east, at first a glow; and then, suddenly, with tropical abruptness, it is daylight and the rim of the
sun appears. At once the line quickens, backs straighten. Someone starts a slow song:

dey = there	Day oh, day oh, dey de light an' me wan' a go home;
	Day oh, day oh, dey de light an' me wan' a go home;
harse = horse	Me no ask a harse wi' bridle; me no ask house an' lan'
	Come ya, Mr. Tallyman, come tally me banana;
yah fe = here to	Me come yah fe work; me no come fe idle.
	Day oh, day oh, dey de light an' me wan' a go home;
	Day oh, day oh, dey de light an' me wan' a go home.
	Six hands, seven hands, eight hands *bunch;*
	Six hands, seven hands, eight hands *bunch*

Day oh, day oh, dey de light an me
    wan' a go home.
Six hands, seven hands, eight hands
    bunch.

On and on the song goes until the gang is dismissed for the day and they can go home to breakfast and rest. It gets them through the last hour before quitting time; it voices a protest, conscious or not, against the relentless force that drives them on, symbolized by the constant refrain, like a driver's whip, that they have been hearing all night and that now has become the driving element in the song : six hands, seven hands, eight hands, *bunch*. This is *oral* literature.

This song is highly meaningful in its cultural context; outside of that it is insignificant. The two—song and matrix—are complementary. The song seems to come spontaneously from the lips of the bearers. It is an expression of their resignation to their situation, to their fate. There is no specific protest, no social protest, no lashing out; there is only the feeling that this is the way life is. It is not the voice of the individual but of the tribe.

Harry Belafonte patterned a song after this, which he calls a folksong. His song is meaningless in relation to any *folk* culture matrix, past or present. The calypso tune in contrast to the slow-measured, functional tune of the folksong, its distortion of language through lack of understanding of the situation point up the difference. Belafonte's song is his song, reflecting his personality and his ideas, instead of the matrix creating the art form, the song. From his song we are expected to create a matrix, a culture pattern of the Negro vigorously protesting his social and economic situation—an image created by the song and the singer.

It is then the business of the collector to collect the matrix as well as the specific product, for only through knowledge of the context can one often arrive at significance. But it is important not to overstress the socio-cultural aspects of a culture and make the study of the matrix more important than the song or the story, a tendency observable among folklore anthropologists or anthropological folklorists. As I conceive it, folklorists and the students of folk literature are not cultural anthropologists or sociologists whose purpose is to study a whole culture; rather folklorists must put their emphasis on the literature—the tale, song, proverb, riddle, and the like, and collect and study the milieu only so far as it aids that study.

Not only is each oral literature nurtured by its own cultural matrix, but it may also be strongly influenced by neighboring areas—spatially and temporally. Consequently the collector must know his region intimately and its neighborhood well enough to be able to detect borrowings, influences, and regroupings. A collector of Micmac tales must know the culture and tales of the Penobscots as well, and possess general competence in all Algonquin culture.

The collector cannot collect the matrix by subjective reaction to what he sees and hears. He must get the reactions and the explanations of his informants and of the audience through such questions as: What does this story, song mean to you? Why do you sing this song? Tell this tale? Why does the character in the story act so? Moreover, each story and song should be recorded at different times from the same and different informants to study variation in text and response.

Some years ago when I was collecting tales and songs in Newfoundland I kept hearing about a fine wreck song called, "The Rose of Branch." The name was intriguing and so was the extravagant praise. I kept inquiring for it. Many knew it, had heard it, agreed that it was a wonderful song, but none could sing it. Finally, near Salmonier on St. Mary's Bay, I stayed in the home of the local midwife. She was a big mannish woman who could swing an ax like a lumberjack, who took three feet in her stride, and whose favorite cuss word was *bloody damn*. When I asked her about the "Rose of Branch" she said, "Yes, that's a wonderful song." Did she know it? "Yes," she said. Would she sing it? "No," she replied, "I can't sing it. My voice is gone." More coaxing. Well, she'd sing it the last day I was there, but with no one around. The day came; she barred the door against the neighbors. She sang. She had a big grainy voice. Halfway through she stopped. I looked up from my recording machine, thinking she had forgotten the song; great tears were coursing down her cheeks; she was sobbing audibly. "I just can't go on," she said, "It's too sad." I complimented her on her singing and on the song, told her how anxious I was to have the whole of it. Finally, her grief spent, she sang the song through to the end. "The Rose of Branch" is a ballad telling of a Newfoundland fishing vessel anchored on a dark night in St. Mary's Bay, being run down by a British Man-of-War. The pilot had not seen the boat, because she had not shown riding lights and ironically enough the man, one Jim English, whose duty it had been to set the lights, was the only person saved. The song is run-of-the-mill; the tune is without distinction; the story prosy, narrative rather than dramatic. I could not understand the informant's reaction. I asked her if a relative of hers had been lost. "Oh, no," she said. Well, had she known any of the men? No, and then she told me that it had happened over a hundred years ago, long before her father was born. When I asked her why she was so moved by the song she said only that the song always made her terribly sad. I discovered afterwards that wherever I played "The Rose of Branch" around St. Mary's Bay the song always elicited this same response. The school teacher suggested that the song evoked the ever-present dangers of the sea, a common hazard for all, and that it brought back memories of those of their relatives who had been lost; but this hardly seems an adequate explanation since other wreck songs do not bring such response. The priest explained that everyone felt sorrow for the man English who had to go through life with the terrible burden of his mates' death on his heart. Whatever the explanation this general response seems rather silly, certainly unmotivated. That such a routine story lacking any kind of literary distinction should stimulate such a response one hundred years after the event it chronicles is astonishing to us and difficult to understand. The important thing, however, is that it did, and that is more important than the song itself, and consequently it should be carefully explored and noted in detail by the collector.

The collector not only must collect folk literature as oral literature and in its cultural context, but he must go beyond that and collect the singer of the songs and the teller of the tales. In some folk communities dozens of people sing and dozens tell tales; all are capable of giving some information about their culture. But most informants do not sing well or tell a story well; nonetheless, all can express in varying degrees of worth their common mass folk culture. Information from such informants is worth collecting because it does often throw light on the meaning and history of stories, songs, and beliefs.

In every community, however, there are individuals who have more songs or more stories than the others and usually they sing better or tell a tale better. Although all in a folk community know the stock cures, the granny woman is the expert. Likewise, in any community you will find the best songs in the keeping of one or two individuals. Often the position is hereditary. Mrs. Brown of Falkland[6] is typical, not accidental. In the summer of 1960 I collected in eight little outports of Labrador. In each outport there was an outstanding singer or storyteller : Peter Letto in Launce au Clair; Andrew Roberts in Forteau; George Trim in Englishtown; Ned Odell in Pinware. So I have found it in Jamaica, in Cape Breton, in Virginia. We need a detailed study of this matter—the continuing tradition of the scop, the filid, the makar, the poet, and we need fuller information from present-day collectors about these superior informants. We need answers to questions like these : Where did they get their songs? Why do they cling to them? Is there a family tradition? Do they ever deliberately change a song, or tune, or story? I, for one, am quite convinced that new songs and stories, new groupings of material, variations, selective changes—all the processes by which folk literature improves—are due directly or indirectly to these few individuals in each culture. It is these who make an oral literature more complex, who extend it by borrowing from their fellows across the borders. Every field worker in anthropology who has the slightest understanding of literature knows that literary artists exist in every pre-literate community, that they are recognized as such by the community, and that, moreover, fictional and semi-historical narratives are told for the sheer delight of telling them. That presupposes, of course, an audience willing to listen and able to evaluate and appreciate.

In this connection I think of Angus The Ridge MacDonald —named The Ridge to distinguish from the other five Angus MacDonalds in his Cape Breton neighborhood. For seventy-five years he had lived on the north shore of Lake Katrine— singing, fiddling, piping, telling stories, making songs. "It's in my blood," he says, "back to the MacDonalds of the glens."

[6] See Francis J. Child, *English and Scottish Popular Ballads* (Boston, 1892–98), v, 397.

Across the lake lives his friend Robert MacIsaac. "Robert is a hard worker," Angus says, "I looks out and I see Robbie across there sawing wood, digging, working like a beast. I always thought that the good Lord never intended man to work like a beast and I feels sorry for Robbie and I puts on me kilts and I takes me pipes and I walks up and down and I plays me sweet music for him and its braw comin' over the water, and it eases his heart while he's workin'." There you have it. Go to Angus for the good song well sung and the good story well told. And it is he who will make up the new song about the white sleigh was seen near Benacadie Pond and the little green man running alongside.

Our collectors must tell more of these persons—their inheritance, the processes of the creativity, their evaluation of their stock of songs and stories, for a study of these specialists would throw much light on all folk culture, its origins, development, interrelations, and meanings.

And this leads us to the collectors' concern with the folk esthetic. I am aware that the idea of a folk esthetic as distinct from the esthetic of sophisticated art is controversial or perhaps is a matter of definition. But whatever name you give it I am convinced that there is a kind of *folk* art that is not just casual, untutored, naive, accidental. Moreover, I am quite convinced that the folk esthetic cuts across language and geographical barriers and, more importantly, also cuts across genres. A common thread runs through folk song, story, dance, ritual, painting, sculpture. In this connection, Paul Radin's *African Folktales and Sculpture*[7] is highly instructive because of its wide selection of African folktales presented along with reproductions of African sculpture, and likewise the similar book, LeRoy H. Appleton's *Indian Art of the Americas*,[8]

[7] New York, 1952.
[8] New York, 1950.

which contains a representative selection of Indian tales and songs, liberal reproductions of Indian sculpture, paintings, and pottery. Both of these books point up the kinship among all of these folk types. Limiting enumeration of details largely to the verbal arts, I suggest that the folk esthetic is worked through combinations of the following : highly concrete and specific diction and detail, sense of drama, formulae, cliché, archaism of style and culture, personification to the point of animism, understatement, naturalness, simple repetition, repetition with increment, montage rather than expository connective, pathos, mystery, translation of time and of space into action, compression rather than diffusion.

The folk esthetic is, I think, the most important aspect of folklore and for this reason the collector must keep constantly in mind the elements which demonstrate it and which furnish the basis for the study of it by the desk scholars. Failure to recognize and understand the folk esthetic accounts for the urge to do something to folklore, to rewrite it, to piece different versions of songs together, to censor it, to re-arrange it, to try to make it more like sophisticated art. And so we get Child ballads arranged for the piano and for group singing around camp fires, texts of ballads obscured by guitar or banjo, folk tales "cutiefied" up for children, folklore vulgarized by articles like the recent series in *Life* magazine.

The collector must have experienced enough of folk life and folk literature to have become aware of the folk esthetic and of the techniques behind the folk esthetic. His task in this respect is twofold. First, from his informants, especially the most gifted, he must elicit answers to such questions as : Do you think this is a fine story or song? Why? Why have you continued to sing it or tell it? He will get the stock responses : It is a good story because it is true; it really happened. I like it because my mother used to sing it and it reminds me of her.

I like it because it teaches a good lesson. It shows what happens to murderers or drunkards. But the collector must go beyond these stock responses, valuable as they are, to try to determine a set of artistic values among the people.

And, secondly and more importantly, the collector will present all the data from texts and from the general culture of the folk that will serve as a basis for a study of the folk esthetic.

For example, one of the characters in a well-known Anansi story is Sister Hen. The term is immediately identifying and highly characterizing. A good collector will determine the source of its use and will discover that it is not casual but deliberate. Sister is used to denote a very responsible woman of middle age, a leader, one who is looked up to, one who would lay out the dead, who would be at the head of the table in a Pocomanian meeting. So the term makes this hen as distinctive and special as Chaucer's Dame Partlet. The story says: "Sister hen him a (she was) thirsty and him stop a pond and him drink and each time him drink and lif' up him head, him say thank you, thank you." This is not only vivid picturization, as anyone who has ever observed a chicken will agree, it is more. The "lif' up him head and say thank you, thank you" is an additional humanizing and characterizing touch. And there is just a neat, subtle suggestion of satire of humankind, who so often take the good gifts without lifting up their heads to say thank you. This is proved by the well-known Jamaican proverb: When fowl drink him say thank you.

Collection then should be on as wide a base as possible. When one is collecting tales, he must also collect or be aware of the songs, riddles, proverbs, and language arts, for all are related and through them all the folk esthetic is created. Especially must the collector give attention to the language of the culture being recorded and the language habits. Folk languages and folktales make constant use of repetition—repe-

tition of words, phrases, ideas, and details. Repetition is used to
secure emphasis, but also to indicate progression of action and
duration of time. "We started walkin', and we walked an'
walked and walked, and by and by we looked back and my it
was a long way back." In this way the folk esthetic builds on
basic language habits, but it goes beyond the simple repetition
by the addition of increment, pace, variation, and balance.
Consider the Caribbean version of the old ballad "The Maid
Freed from the Gallows" (Child 95):

> Mourn, Saylen, mourn oh! Mourn, Saylen Mourn
> Mourn, Saylen, mourn oh! Mourn, Saylen Mourn.
> I came to town to see you hang,
> Hang you mus be hang.

Note the artfulness of the repetitions here in connection with
the pace of the lines, and note the effectiveness of the caesural
stop and the resumption of the refrain on a lower note.

But a collector who collects folk literature as oral literature,
who collects the matrix of that literature, who collects the folk
artist, story teller, or singer, and who collects the material for
a study and appreciation of the folk esthetic will not come
back from the field with hundreds of songs and stories. It's a
big task, best done perhaps by a group of collectors working
together. Boas spoke against the dragnet method of collecting
as early as 1904, suggesting that twelve to eighteen tales
properly collected is a good summer's work.

THELMA JAMES

Problems of Archives*

Problems of archiving texts collected in American folklore are complicated by a number of factors. Chief among these is a lack of central registry for the many kinds of collecting activity and archiving programs currently being carried on. The American Folklore Society has taken an important first step in listing the state and regional societies, but communication between them on the above problems is limited to rather casual knowledge of work being done by individuals.

The Committee on Archiving was established to determine the number and kind of archives and their systems of classification. Also, it was hoped that there might be developed some principles of archiving that would be of national usefulness. Two years ago letters asking for specific information were sent to all the collectors and institutions known to be engaged in archiving their materials. The replies showed an almost complete absence of agreement on principles and practices. Subsequently, we developed a decimal division system at Wayne State University and sent copies of it to our former correspondents. Reactions ranged from reserved admiration to horror. The extreme detail was designed to serve a purpose of rather clear identification in areas where specific numbering is lacking. For the folktale, the Thompson Tale and Motif numbers are always standard. But what standards can be as widely accepted for proverb, riddle, superstition, charm, folk medicine, children's games, weather lore—to name but a few of the areas? When Professor Wayland Hand's projected *Dictionary of American Popular Beliefs and Superstitions* is completed, there will be a definitive identification system

* From *The Folklore and Folk Music Archivist,* Vol. I. No. 2 (June, 1958). Bloomington: Indiana University.

established. Meantime, his edition of the *Frank C. Brown Collection of North Carolina Folklore*, Volume V, *Superstitions*, has to serve. Ray B. Browne's *Popular Beliefs and Practices from Alabama* (University of California Press, 1958) is a valuable extension of the Frank C. Brown items.

Although Archer Taylor's *Proverbial Comparisons and Similes from California* (University of California Press, 1954) is proving, by virtue of its early publication, to be extremely helpful, we may have to await the publication of Professor Margaret Bryant's nation-wide study of the proverb under the sponsorship of the American Dialect Society.

The riddle, in English, is superbly classified by use of Archer Taylor's *English Riddles from Oral Tradition* (University of California Press, 1951). The riddles of other peoples are well collected as is indicated in the Preface to Hull and Taylor's *A Collection of Irish Riddles* (University of California Press, 1955).

For the English ballad, the Child numbers and additions thereto will suffice. A recent valuable help is G. Malcolm Laws' *American Balladry from British Broadsides* (American Folklore Society, 1957). For the ballad tunes, as for all folk music, we have a great need of more specific indentification systems. For folk dance acceptable choreographic notation seems to be developing, and Gertrude Prokosch Kurath's excellent article "Dance: Folk and Primitive" (*Standard Dictionary of Folklore*, I, pp. 276–296) will continue to be a basis for structural and functional classification.

In short, we may have been fortunate in being late in developing a series of national archive classifications in the United States. It seems increasingly correct that the archive systems should evolve from the recognized standard studies in each field, rather than to have archival problems determine the trend of the practices. This brief discussion points up the necessity for authoritative study in all of the folklore fields recognized in this country, and ultimately to a need for a far clearer definition of folklore itself. If we are to continue to move in the direction of broader interpretations of the term to include much of folk culture and craft, we may need to copy the practices of the Swedish and Irish Archives which, up to now, cannot be adopted without almost destructive adaptations. Furthermore, if we are to be concerned with aspects of description of function, of analysis of the informant's role, of regional and family environmental and historical factors, we face problems hitherto unmentioned in American archiving.

Ultimately, the function of the archiving process is to make clear the contents of any archive so that the holder, knowing his own resources, may develop them, exchange items with collectors and scholars, and thus fill in the details of the national holdings. Thus, there emerges the necessity for establishment and acceptance of a nation-wide system, known and used by archives, large and small, and into which new materials will fit easily, and in the use of which students may be trained.

Experimentally, the various systems sent in response to inquiry are being tested in the Archives of Wayne State University.

FRANZ BOAS

Literature, Music, and Dance*

Among some of the most primitive tribes very few objects of artistic value are found. This is easily understood, for the roaming life of the hunter and the necessity of constant application for obtaining the bare necessities of life do not leave much time for manual work beyond that required for the pursuit of game and the collection of other kinds of food. Furthermore, the whole amount of property that can be carried along is very small. The family cannot burden itself with many unnecessary or unfinished products, and the completion of artistic work requires time. The Eskimo who returns to his semipermanent house every day and whose hunting gear is in good condition may amuse himself with the ivory-carving, which he may take up in long evenings or during snowstorms that make hunting impossible, but the total amount of such work and its size are necessarily restricted. Still more unfavorable are conditions for the Bushman who has to travel on foot and who has still less leisure to follow artistic inclinations. Leisure is indispensable for artistic handiwork, and a certain amount of stability or transportation by means of animals seems indispensable for its development. Stone work, stone architecture, and heavy wood work presuppose stability of residence.

Such restrictions are not present in the arts of literature, music, and dance, for the hunter watching for game or leisurely attending to his traps may give free rein to his imagination without interfering with his watchful waiting. Out of the daydreams of the hunter and of the woman attending to her housework, stories and songs may be spun.

* "Literature, Music, and Dance," by Franz Boas, in *General Anthropology*, ed. by Franz Boas, D. C. Heath and Co., New York, 1938.

The world-wide distribution of tales and songs shows that these considerations are valid. The Bushman and the eastern Eskimo, although poor in the production of art, are rich in tales and songs, of which they possess a well-nigh inexhaustible treasure. The poor hunters of the Malay peninsula and the Australians have their literature no less than economically more advanced people. Songs and tales are found all over the world. These are the fundamental forms of literature among primitive people.

The essential traits of song are rhythm and melody. Rhythm belongs not only to song but also to prose. Repetition, particularly rhythmic repetition, is a fundamental trait of both. All prose narrative consists in part of free elements the form of which is dependent upon the taste and ability of the narrator. Inserted among these passages we find others of fixed form which give to the narrative its formal attractiveness. Often these passages consist of conversation between the actors, in which deviations from the fixed formula are not permitted. In other cases they are of rhythmic form and must be considered poetry or chants rather than prose.

It is very difficult to gain a correct understanding of the form of primitive prose, because most of the available material has been recorded in European languages only, and it is impossible to determine the accuracy of the rendering. In most of the records there is an obvious attempt to adopt European literary styles. Even when the material is available in the original text we may assume that, at least in the majority of cases, it does not reach the standard of excellence of the native narrative. The difficulty of phonetic rendering of foreign languages requires such slowness of dictation that the artistic style necessarily suffers. The number of collectors who have complete mastery of the native language is altogether too small. The best approximation to the art of narrative of primitive people is probably found in those cases in which educated natives write down the texts, or in the records taken down by missionaries who, in long years of personal, intimate contact with the people, have acquired complete control of their language, and who are willing to give us just what they hear. In some cases natives have been trained to write with such ease that their writings may be considered as good representation of style. Early examples of this kind are tales published by Eskimos. Recently some attempts have been made to take down texts on the phonograph and to have them redictated sentence by sentence.

In almost all reliable collections the fixed formal parts are of considerable importance. It is not easy to form a correct opinion regarding the rhythmic character of the formal prose, partly because the rhythmic sense of primitive people is much more highly developed than our own. The simplification of the rhythm of modern folk song, and of poetry intended to appeal to popular taste, has dulled our feeling for rhythmic form. It requires careful study to understand the structure of primitive rhythm, more so in prose than in song, because in this case the help of the melodic pattern is lacking.

I believe the liking for the frequent repetition of single motives is in part due to the pleasure given by rhythmic repetition. For example, the tales of the Chinook Indians are always so constructed that five brothers, one after another, have the same adventure. The four eldest perish while the youngest one comes out successful. The tale is repeated verbatim for all the brothers, and its length, which to our ear and taste is intolerable, probably gives pleasure by the repeated form. Conditions are quite similar in European fairy tales relating the fates of three brothers, two of whom perish or fail in their tasks while the youngest one succeeds.

Repetitions leading to a climax are also found. Thus in

Tsimshian tales[1] an eagle is said to screech every morning. The hero comes out of the house following the call and finds every day a larger animal on the beach in front of his house. A similar device occurs in the German tales of the fisherman whose wife sends him day after day to ask a wonderful fish to give him ever greater gifts. Every time he uses the same verse when calling the fish.

In the tales of the Pueblo Indians[2] the same incident is repeated four times, happening to four sisters : the yellow, red, blue, and white girl. In a Papua tale from New Guinea[3] the birds come one after another and try to peck open the stomach of a drowned person so as to let the water he has swallowed run out. In a New Ireland tale[4] the birds try to throw the cassowary off the branch of a tree on which it is perched. One after another alights next to him on the same branch but nearer the trunk. Then he is compelled to move out farther and farther until finally he drops down. Similar repetitions are found in the German tale of Red Ridinghood, in the widely spread European story of the rooster who goes to bury his mate, and in the story of the Three Bears. In Oriental tales the incidents of the tale are sometimes repeated verbatim, being retold by one of the heroes.

Much more striking are rhythmic repetitions in the formal parts of tales or in those cases in which connecting discussion is omitted. An example is the following Eskimo tale[5] of a woman and the spirit of the singing-house :

"Where is its owner? Where is its master?
Has the singing-house an owner? Has the singing-house a master?
It has no owner."—"Here he is, there he is !"
"Where are his feet? Where are the calves of his legs? Where are his knees? Where are his thighs?"—"Here they are, there they are !"

"Where is his stomach?"—"Here it is, there it is!"
"Where is his chest? Where is his arm? Where is his neck?
Where is his head?"—"Here it is, there it is!"
He had no hair.*

Sometimes these parts of tales are in an archaic form or in a foreign language, so that they may be quite unintelligible. Their impressiveness rests on their form and the general emotional trend of the passages in which they occur.[6]

In oratory, rhythmic repetitions are used for purposes of emphasis and impressiveness. An Indian who welcomes his guests in his house and who wishes to recall the greatness of his ancestors addresses his hearers as follows:[7]

"This is the house of my great-great-grandfather Mahwa who invited you here.
This is the house of my great-grandfather Mahwa who invited you at Sandy Beach.
This is the house of my grandfather Mahwa who invited you at Crooked Beach.
This is the feasting house of my father who invited you at Tide Beach.
Now I have taken the place of my father. I invited you, tribes, that you should come and see my house here."

Similar are the Polynesian chants in which the ancestors are enumerated:

Hulihonua the husband,
Keakahulilani the wife;
Laka the husband, Kapapaiakele the wife;
Kamooalewa the husband,
Nanawahine the wife;

and so on through twenty-seven pairs.[8]

* This means that the woman felt for the supernatural owner of the singing-house. He is supposed to have bandy legs, no hair, and no occipital bone. To touch his soft head is immediate death.

In oratory rhythm is also applied to give fixed form to free discourse. This is sometimes obtained by a delivery in which the phrases are given somewhat equal length with accent on the last, sometimes an added, syllable. Thus the Kwakiutl will address his guests : "Welcome-ai, brothers-ai, at my feast-ai," always connecting the -*ai* firmly with the preceding word; or by introducing every phrase with *ha*. Similar devices are used in the recital of myths, as when the Fox Indians repeat after every phrase of their Culture Hero myth the syllables *nootchee nootchee*.[9] Sometimes the phrasing is made by a pause in which the listeners supply the rhythmic break. Thus, in Africa, the narrator may tell, "The Turtle killed the Leopard," and the audience will repeat, clapping their hands, "The Leopard, the Leopard."

More definite and clearer rhythmic structure appears in poetry. Primitive rhythmic poetry that is not sung is, as far as I am aware, unknown. It is therefore more correct to speak of song rather than of poetry. All song is accompanied by body movements that are often associated with noise, such as hand-clapping or stamping the ground; also by swaying the body. Therefore poetry, music, and dance form an inextricable unit. Only gradually is poetry dissociated from music and dance, and music from dance, while dance seems to be almost indissolubly connected with music.

Since song is so often accompanied by movement, there is commonly a coordination of two kinds of rhythms : that of song and that of movement. On the whole the regularity of emphasis on every second, third, or fourth time-interval which is characteristic of modern folk music, forming our regular two, three, and four part measures, is not the rule in primitive music. Longer units are found, such as five or seven part rhythms as well as long units that cannot be divided into regular measures, but which are regularly repeated.

The coordination of song and movement is also often different from ours. We are accustomed to move in accord with the accented measures, but very commonly the coordination follows different patterns leading to various types of syncope, to the combination of one rhythm in song with another movement. When the movement is accompanied by sound, as in hand-clapping or stamping, we have a new acoustic rhythm developing through the combination of the two. In Africa this multiplicity of interweaving rhythms is augmented by the independence of rhythmic movements of different parts of the body, particularly of the two hands and the two feet, which create new complexities.

The great variety of forms in which rhythm appears, as rhythm of time in music and dance, rhythm of space in decorative art, shows that the theory of Bucher,[10] who derives rhythm from the regularity of movements in communal work, or the parallel theory of Wundt,[11] who derives it from dance, cannot be maintained. The pleasure given by regular repetition of embroidery designs, paintings, or the complex arrangement of strings in rhythmically repeated order cannot be explained by conditions imposed by the technique, and there is no indication that this rhythm is later than the one determined by motor habits.

In primitive music we find numerous songs in which the melody is carried solely by vocables, like our la-la-la in songs the words of which are not familiar to us, or in the frequent refrains. The musical elements of such songs are solely tune and rhythm. Sometimes the vocable itself may have a significance indicating a certain emotion or situation. Such are the vocables of wails or those suggesting the cries of animals or of definite spirits. In other cases the song may be interspersed with a single word here and there, like an outcry adjusted to the regular course of the tune, while the rest is carried on by vocables. In many cases the words, even when forming continuous sentences, are distorted by lengthening or abbreviation —an extended use of the method we employ in using the apostrophe, wrong accents, or extraordinary lengthening in order to fit words to a tune. This, however, is not always the case. In recitations and chants the words are often controlling, and musical phrases are added or omitted when the words require it. In the music of the Dakota Indian we find both tendencies, the words adapted to the tunes and the tunes adapted to the words.[12]

The contents of poetry are as varied as the cultural interests of the people. It is difficult for us to appreciate the poetic value they may have for the composer or singer, since the contents may have no emotional appeal to us. When the Eskimo women sing, "Our husbands are coming down there, I am going to eat!" it may sound utterly prosaic to us who do not know the privations of Eskimo life, and it may well be that the combined joy of seeing the safe return of the men from the dangers of the chase and the prospect of a jolly evening when all the people are assembled over the meal and are joking and conversing finds exuberant relief in these insignificant lines. The effect of poetry does not depend upon the power of description that releases clear and beautiful images, but upon its ability to arouse strong emotion.

As we may underestimate the poetic value of such trifling songs, we may easily overestimate the acual poetic value of stereotyped symbolic poetry that appeals to us on account of its strange imagery, but that may have to the native no other than the emotional appeal of the ritual.

When the occasions of singing are varied we find commonly distinctive types of song for every one of these. Thus the Kwakiutl Indians of Vancouver Island have children's songs which father or mother sings, letting the child dance on the arms; love songs, generally sung in chorus by the young men walking up and down the street; feast songs praising the greatness of the host; war songs; and various types of ritual songs sung in their religious ceremonials. The types are clearly distinct and easily recognizable. They are built on a common principle, but each has its own style.

While the style of songs may be defined by a study of their rhythm and melody, it is much more difficult to define the style of prose—even setting aside the paucity of reliable material. The style depends to a great extent upon linguistic form. What may be appealing in one language may be repellent in one of different form. Thus the structure of many American languages compels the narrator to express himself explicitly in regard to the location where an event happens while other languages remain vague in regard to this point. To one accustomed to strict localization the latter style is lacking in color.

The inclination to diffuse detail characterizes the style of some tales while others may strive for such pregnant conciseness that the most intimate knowledge of the culture is required to make the contents intelligible. Devices for securing emphasis are probably present everywhere. There are pathos and fun. A generalized treatment of prose style seems hardly possible.

Certain devices may be discussed. One of these is characterization of individuals by peculiar ways of behaving or talking. The mere introduction of a trickster in a tale arouses the expectation of some exhilarating exploit. Often he and other actors in the tale are characterized by peculiar mannerisms of speech that set them off from other personalities. The character of various animals or persons is liable to be stereotyped, and their mere introduction may call forth the expectation of events that conform to their supposed nature.

Similes are found more often in songs and oratory than in

narrative prose. Still, they are not lacking in prose. The Polynesians seem to appreciate their poetic value. Thus we read in the Fornander collection of Hawaiian tales : "His skin was like a ripe banana. His eyeballs were like the young buds of a banana. His body was straight and without blemish and he was without an equal." In the Hawaiian story of Laiei-kawai[13] it is said : "I am not the mistress of this shore. I came from inland, from the top of the mountain which is clothed in a white garment."

In Indian oratory there is ample use of similes. I will confine my remarks to their use among the Kwakiutl,[14] with whose speech forms I am familiar. Similes are used particularly when describing the greatness of a chief or of a warrior. The chief is compared with a mountain; a precipice (from which rolls down wealth overwhelming the tribe); a rock that cannot be climbed; the post of heaven (that supports the world); the only great tree (that raises its crown over the lower trees of the woods or that rises in lonely height on an island); a loaded canoe at anchor; the one who makes the whole world smoky (from the smoke of the fire in the house in which he gives feasts); the thick tree; the thick root (of the tribe). Through his great acts he burns up the tribes (relating to warlike exploits). The people follow him as the young sawbill ducks follow the mother bird. He makes the people suffer with his shortlife maker; he shoves away the tribes. The greatness of the chief is called the weight of his name. When he marries a princess he lifts her weight from the floor; his wealth of blankets (which are piled up before being distributed) is a mountain that rises through our heavens; in the feast, surrounded by his tribe, he stands on his fortress. Wealth is the salmon caught by him.

Examples of similar kind may be found in the oratory and poetry of many peoples. They occur also commonly in sayings.

The Tsimshian of British Columbia say, "A deer, though toothless, may accomplish something."

Allusions are also a device used particularly in oratory. The Tsimshian, to whom I referred before, have a saying, "Is this war, father?" which refers to a story in which a boy who has been told by his father that there will be a great war, endures many hardships and asks every time this question. The Dakota Indians say, "Did you not see his palate?" referring to the striped palate of the trickster of their mythology and implying that the person referred to is unreliable and tricky. Such allusions are intelligible only to those who know the tribal lore. Therefore, they are not often found in published material. Allusions of this kind are common in African proverbs. A Lamba saying is, "The slave was redeemed through his castor-oil," referring to the story of a slave who paid for his freedom by presenting his master with oil from plants he had sowed.[15] Another is: "It is an evil omen of the Nsenga. We shall question it on our return."[16] This means that one will not be discouraged easily. It refers to the tale of a trading expedition to the Nsenga country on which many evil omens were encountered. The leader refused to be discouraged and on his return journey received satisfactory explanation of every one of them. A Djagga proverb says, "Do not cheat me like Kitiko who cheated Ivere."[17] This refers to two men who bet that they could fast for ten days. Kitiko was fed by his wife, although he was being watched, and thus won the bet.

There are great differences in the manner of composition. Some people have a preference for long, complex stories; among others, brief anecdotic tales prevail. On the whole the incidents of which complex stories are built up are brief, disconnected anecdotes which are woven into a whole by various devices. Often this is accomplished by concentrating all the anecdotes around one personage. When this person is given a definite character a somewhat greater unity is secured. Thus the Raven tale of Alaska consists entirely of unrelated episodes.[18] The only connecting link, besides the identity of the hero, is the voracity of the Raven. Similar in structure are the Spider tales of Africa,[19] the Dwarf Antelope tales of Malaysia,[20] and the Fox tales of Europe.[21]

Notes

1. Boas, F., *Tsimshian Mythology,* Annual Report of the Bureau of American Ethnology, vol. 31 (1916), pp. 225 ff.
2. Boas, F., *Keresan Texts,* Publications of the American Ethnological Society, vol. 8, Part 1 (1928), pp. 82 ff.; Benedict, R., *Tales of the Cochiti Indians,* Bulletin of the Bureau of American Ethnology, vol. 98 (1931), pp. 49 ff.
3. Ker, A., *Papuan Fairy Tales* (London, 1910), p. 106.
4. Meier, P. J., *Mythen and Erzählungen der Küstenbewohner der Gazelle-Halbinsel* (Munster, 1909), p. 106.
5. Boas, F., "Eskimo Tales and Songs," *Journal of American Folk-Lore,* vol. 7 (1894), p. 45.
6. See for instance, Boas, F., *Keresan Texts, op. cit.,* Part II (1925), pp. 342, 343.
7. Boas, F., *The Social Organization and the Secret Societies of the Kwakiutl Indians,* Report of the United National Museum for 1895 (1897).
8. *Fornander Collection of Hawaiian Antiquities and Folk-lore,* Memoirs of the Bernice P. Bishop Museum, vol. 4, Part II (Honolulu, 1917), p. 371.
9. Jones, W., *Fox Texts,* Publication of the American Ethnological Society, vol. 1 (Leyden, 1907), p. 337.
10. Bucher, K., *Arbeit und Rhythmus* (Leipzig, 1909).
11. Wundt, W. *Völkerpsychologie,* vol. 3 (Leipzig, 1919), p. 507.
12. Densmore, F., *Teton Sioux Music,* Bulletin of the Bureau of American Ethnology, vol. 61 (1918), p. 162.
13. Beckwith, M. W., *The Hawaiian Romance of Laieikawai,* Annual Report of the Bureau of American Ethnology, vol. 33 (1919), p. 403.
14. Boas, F., *The Social Organization and the Secret Societies of the Kwakiutl Indians,* p. 346.
15. Doke, C. M., *Lamba Folk-Lore,* Memoirs of the American Folk-Lore Society, vol. 20 (1927), p. 357.
16. *Ibid.,* p. 403.
17. Gutmann, B., *Volksbuch der Wadschagga* (Leipzig, 1914), p. 244.
18. Boas, F., *Tsimshian Mythology,* pp. 567 ff.
19. Cronise, F., and Ward, H., *Cunnie Rabbit, Mr. Spider and Other Beef* (1903); Tremearne, A. J. N., *Hausa Superstitions and Customs* (London, 1913).
20. Skeat, W., *Fables and Folk Tales from an Eastern Forest* (Cambridge, 1904).
21. Dähnhardt, O., *Natursagen,* vol. 4 (Leipzig, 1912), pp. 217 ff.

J. A. HADFIELD

Dreams as Archetypal*

The Archetypes

The *forms* in which these primordial images manifest themselves in conscious life Jung calls 'Archetypal Images' and the potentialities themselves the 'Archetypes.' Archetypes may be described, therefore, as the forms taken by the archaic potentialities in the collective unconscious.

Jung's idea of the archetype differs considerably from the idea of the instincts as described for instance by MacDougall.[1] Both are universally transmitted potentialities, but the instincts are inherited patterns of behaviour like fear and sex, whereas Jung's archetypes consist rather of images, or 'thought-feelings' as he puts it elsewhere, patterns of thought such as we find in myths and in dreams. It is one thing to have an inherited instinct to run away from danger, quite another to have an inherited image of a monster, or at least a potentiality toward such an image. It is true that he says that it is not the ideas or images themselves which are transmitted but their potentialities, but these potentialities are nevertheless of specific ideas and images.

Instances of the archetypes, constantly appearing in myths and in dreams, are the Hero (the Deliverer, the Saviour, the Messiah, the Man of the Moment, the 'Strong Man' that the nations of Europe in their distress are looking for), the Terrible Mother (portrayed as the witch, the avenging goddess, the cruel stepmother, the ogre), and others. These ideas or images, constantly recurring in dreams and in myths, represent deep-seated racial experiences in man.

* From Chapter 3 of *Dreams and Nightmares* by J. A. Hadfield, a Pelican Book, copyright 1954 by Penguin Books, Ltd. Excerpts are from pages 42–43, 44, 46–48.

[1] *Social Psychology.*

78

The idea of sacrifice is archetypal, the need for sacrifice being a basic factor in life throughout nature, the sloughing off the old for the new, the sacrifice of a good for a greater good. In mythology the idea is embodied in the Phoenix, whose body is burned to give rise to a new being. Sacrifice also appears in most religions as a propitiation for guilt, showing how deep-rooted is this idea of guilt in human nature, as well as the need to propitiate. . . .

Animus and *anima* are figures which constantly appear in mythology. They 'are natural archetypes, primordial figures of the unconscious, and have given rise to the mythological gods and goddesses.' 'They live in a world quite different from our own.'[2] 'It is therefore rather a futile undertaking to disinfect Olympus with rational enlightenment'—for men and women will continue to believe in gods in spite of all scepticism and rationalism because they stand for something real in themselves!

In ancient mythology the *anima* is represented by such figures as Helen of Troy and Venus;[3] in medieval times by Mother Church or the Queen of Heaven. In modern times it has been vividly represented in Rider Haggard's 'She,' in Faust's 'Gretchen,' as representing the fallen woman, and in the Virgin Mary representing the immaculate woman. The *anima* is also represented in Tennyson's 'Lady of the Lake,' who 'knows a subtler magic'; dwells down in a deep; calm whatever storms shall shake the world—'a mist of incense curl'd about her, and her face well-nigh was hidden.' All these figures obviously have reference beyond the personal and individual, for they stand for the eternal feminine, the ideal woman, the 'woman of my dreams.' . . .

[2] Jung, *The Integration of the Personality,* pp. 23 and 25.
[3] *Ibid.,* p. 78.

These archetypes, relating as they do to deep-seated ideas and feelings in the collective unconscious, cannot adequately be expressed in the language of reason and therefore take form in fairy stories, in myths of the race, and in dreams, and also find expression in music and the primitive as well as in modern art.

There would be no function for the artist and musician to perform if all that we experience could be expressed in words, for art and music can give expression to feelings which cannot be otherwise expressed, nor otherwise appreciated. So these archetypal images can sometimes be best expressed in symbolic art forms, which are pictorial representations of what is going on in the personality and especially in the unconscious. This is particularly obvious in the automatic drawings of the insane, from which a study of the archetypes may be made, for in them have appeared strange ideas and imaginings which never were on land or sea; also in the automatic drawings of children through which we may interpret the child's difficulties and problems. Such drawings are constantly used by the physician, for by them he can diagnose the nature of the patient's disorder.

Many archaic modes of thought are to be found in religious practice, which can be expressed only in symbol and justify the use of ritual in religious worship. The idea of baptism represents new birth, and the sacred meal which in primitive life takes the form of eating the totem animal of the tribe, and thus 'eating the God,'[4] persists in the Christian Sacrament, which some still take to mean the eating of the actual body of Christ, or God; whereas others, taking it more symbolically as representing partaking of the life of God, the source of all life and goodness, or the acceptance of Christ's sacrifice. It is impossible to express these experiences adequately in words,

[4] See Robertson Smith's *Religion of the Semites.*

because they are mystical and matters of feeling rather than of thought, and they must therefore be expressed symbolically. To attempt to tie them down to ordinary and logical thinking would be to destroy their meaning. In any case, in many people the symbol or ritual is capable of arousing deeper emotions and feelings than the expression of the corresponding idea in words, for by the expression of such ideas we gain in clarity but lose in depth of feeling and emotion.

Archetypal ideas emerge also in fairy stories: they depict men fighting against giants, like Jack the Giant Killer, St. George and the Dragon, Beowulf, and others, all of which represent man's struggle against the primitive force in his unconscious. There are stories such as Joseph in the Old Testament, despised of his brothers, reaching to great fame; and the story of the Princess shut up in the Tower who has all she needs except that which she needs most of all, namely love, but she is ultimately rescued by the hero; and the story of Cinderella, which originated in China and has travelled all over the world, depicting the theme of the ignored and neglected person coming at last into her own. All these stories relate to common feelings, problems, experiences, and cravings of the human soul. Therefore human beings love to hear these stories over and over again, just as children love to hear the stories such as Little Black Sambo over and over again until they can repeat them word for word, because they relate to some experience or problem in themselves which they but dimly appreciate. Dreams also, as we shall see, repeat the same experience, or the same theme, over and over again because they represent and help to clarify some deap-seated problem in us.

These archetypes also appear in myths, which are the attempts to give expression to collective experience, attempts to solve racial problems, and these also are repeated over and over again, and from generation to generation. A well-known illustration is that of Pygmalion and Galatea, which gives expression to latent potentialities in ourselves and of petrified feelings which come to life and warmth within us. The myth of Prometheus likewise is expressive, among other things, of the rebellion of youth against authority and of its consequences, as is the story of Lucifer's rebellion against God.

What myths are to the race, dreams are to the individual, for in dreams, as in myths, there also appear those primitive emotions and feelings in the form of giants, heroes, dragons, serpents, and blood-sucking vampires; representations of guilt, retribution, and fate; of lust and of power, of monsters of the deep (the unconscious) and of unknown but overwhelming beings which fill our nights with nightmarish dream and make us fear to sleep, but which, rightly used, can be fruitfully integrated into our personality.

So close is this parallel between myths and dreams that Jung often has resort to myths to help in the interpretation of dreams. This is a method complementary to that of free association, for it may be maintained that even free association cannot plumb the depths of the unconscious mind. When, therefore, the symbolism of a dream is in doubt, corresponding myths may suggest a true interpretation. Indeed Jung maintains that the symbols used so readily in Eastern religions originally came from dreams and visions, and were not the invention of some church Father.[5] The symbolism of the cave, referred to later, often appears in mythology and also in dreams as representing the unconscious with its dark secret recesses. Similarly, to dream of a return to the womb may represent a need to get back to a condition of safety and security; but it may mean a return to the womb of the unconscious out of which springs all life. There is also the symbolism

[5] *The Integration of the Personality,* p. 127.

of the snake, which is often depicted as coming out of the cave, and which Freud would interpret as a phallic symbol, the cave as representing the uterus. But in mythology the snake is often the symbol of healing. The serpent which was lifted by Moses in the wilderness so that whoever looked upon it should be cured of their diseases was a symbol of healing and was adopted by Aesculapius in the Temple of Healing. It now appears in the badge of the Royal Army Medical Corps. The snake is also the symbol of rebirth, because of the sloughing of its skin. In mythology it is the symbol of wisdom.

S. I. HAYAKAWA

Presymbolic Language in Ritual*

Sermons, political caucuses, conventions, "pep rallies," and other ceremonial gatherings illustrate the fact that all groups —religious, political, patriotic, scientific, and occupational —like to gather together at intervals for the purpose of sharing certain accustomed activities, wearing special costumes (vestments in religious organizations, regalia in lodges, uniforms in patriotic societies, and so on), eating together (banquets), displaying the flags, ribbons, or emblems of their group, and marching in processions. Among these ritual activities is always included a number of speeches, either traditionally worded or specially composed for the occasion, whose principal function is *not* to give the audience information it did not have before, *not* to create new ways of feeling, but something else altogether. . . .

Let us look at what happens at a "pep rally" such as precedes college football games. The members of "our team" are "introduced" to a crowd that already knows them. Called upon to make speeches, the players mutter a few incoherent and often ungrammatical remarks, which are received with wild applause. The leaders of the rally make fantastic promises about the mayhem to be performed on the opposing team the next day. The crowd utters "cheers," which normally consist of animalistic noises arranged in extremely primitive rhythms. *No one comes out any wiser or better informed than he was before he went in.*

To some extent religious ceremonies are equally puzzling at first glance. The priest or clergyman in charge utters set

* From *Language in Thought and Action* by S. I. Hayakawa. Copyright 1939–1940 by S. I. Hayakawa. Copyright 1941, 1949 by Harcourt, Brace and Company, Inc.

speeches, *often in a language incomprehensible to the congregation* (Hebrew in orthodox Jewish synagogues, Latin in the Roman Catholic Church, Sanskrit in Chinese and Japanese temples), with the result that, as often as not, no information is communicated to those present.

If we approach these linguistic events from a detached point of view, and if also we examine our own reactions when we enter into the spirit of such occasions, we cannot help observing that, whatever the words used in ritual utterance may signify, we often do not think very much about their signification during the course of the ritual. Most of us, for example, have often repeated the Lord's Prayer or sung "The Star-Spangled Banner" without thinking about the words at all. As children we are taught to repeat such sets of words before we can understand them, and many of us continue to say them for the rest of our lives without bothering about their signification. Only the superficial, however, will dismiss these facts as "simply showing what fools human beings are." We cannot regard such utterances as "meaningless," because they have a genuine effect upon us. We may come out of church, for example, with no clear memory of what the sermon was about, with a sense nevertheless that the service has somehow "done us good."

What is the "good" that is done us in ritual utterances? It is the *reaffirmation of social cohesion:* the Christian feels closer to his fellow-Christians, the Elk feels more united with his brother Elks, the American feels more American and the Frenchman more French, as the result of these rituals. Societies are held together by such bonds of common reactions to sets of linguistic stimuli.

Ritualistic utterances, therefore, whether made up of words that have symbolic significance at other times, of words in foreign or obsolete tongues, or of meaningless syllables, may be regarded as consisting in large part of presymbolic uses of language : that is, *accustomed sets of noises* which convey no information, but to which feelings (often group feelings) are attached. Such utterances rarely make sense to anyone not a member of the group. The abracadabra of a lodge meeting is absurd to anyone not a member of the lodge. When language becomes ritual, that is to say, its effect becomes to a considerable extent independent of whatever significations the words once possessed.

Advice to the Literal-minded

Presymbolic uses of language have this characteristic in common : their functions can be performed, if necessary, without the use of grammatically and syntactically articulated symbolic words. They can even be performed without recognizable speech at all. Group feelings may be established, for example, among animals by collective barking or howling, and among human beings by college cheers, community singing, and such collective noise-making activities. Indications of friendliness such as we give when we say "Good morning" or "Nice day, isn't it?" can be given by smiles, gestures, or, as among animals, by nuzzling or sniffing. Frowning, laughing, smiling, jumping up and down, can satisfy a large number of needs for expression, without the use of verbal symbols. But the use of verbal symbols is more customary among human beings, so that instead of expressing our feelings by knocking a man down, we often verbally blast him to perdition; instead of forming social groups by huddling together like puppies, we write constitutions and bylaws and invent rituals for the vocal expression of our cohesion.

To understand the presymbolic elements that enter into our everyday language is extremely important. We cannot restrict our speech to the giving and asking of factual information; we cannot confine ourselves strictly to statements that are literally true, or we should often be unable to say even "Pleased to meet you" when the occasion demanded. The intellectually persnickety often tell us that we ought to "say what we mean" and "mean what we say," and "talk only when we have something to talk about." These are, of course, impossible prescriptions.

Ignorance of the existence of these presymbolic uses of language is not so common among uneducated people (who often perceive such things intuitively) as it is among the educated. The educated often listen to the chatter at teas and receptions and conclude from the triviality of the conversation that all the guests (except themselves) are fools. They may discover that people often come away from church services without any clear memory of the sermon and conclude that churchgoers are either fools or hypocrites. They may hear political oratory and wonder "how anybody can believe such rot," and sometimes conclude therefrom that people in general are so unintelligent that it would be impossible for democracy to be made to work. Almost all such gloomy conclusions about the stupidity or hypocrisy of our friends and neighbors are unjustifiable on such evidence, because they usually come from applying the standards of symbolic language to linguistic events that are either partly or wholly presymbolic in character.

One further illustration may make this clearer. Let us suppose that we are on the roadside struggling with a flat tire. A not-very-bright-looking but friendly youth comes up and asks, "Got a flat tire?" If we insist upon interpreting his words literally, we will regard this as an extremely silly question and our answer may be, "Can't you see I have, you dumb ox?" If we pay no attention to what the words say, however, and understand his meaning, we will return his gesture of friendly interest by showing equal friendliness, and in a short while he may be helping us to change the tire.[1] In a similar way, many situations in life as well as in literature demand that we pay no attention to what the words say, since the meaning may often be a great deal more intelligent and intelligible than the surface *sense* of the words themselves. It is probable that a great deal of our pessimism about the words, about humanity, and about democracy may be due in part to the fact that unconsciously we apply the standards of symbolic language to presymbolic utterances.

Notes

1. Dr. Karl Menninger, in *Love Against Hate* (Harcourt, Brace, 1942), comments on this passage and offers the following translation of "Got a flat tire?" in terms of its psychological meaning: "Hello—I see you are in trouble. I'm a stranger to you but I might be your friend now that I have a chance to be if I had any assurance that my friendship would be welcomed. Are you approachable? Are you a decent fellow? Would you appreciate it if I helped you? I would like to do so but I don't want to be rebuffed. This is what my voice sounds like. What does your voice sound like?" Why does not the youth simply say directly, "I would be glad to help you"? Dr. Menninger explains: "But people are too timid and mutually distrustful to be so direct. They want to hear one another's voices. People need assurance that others are just like themselves."

DAVID BIDNEY

The Concept of Myth*

3. The Psychocultural Approach to Myth

From the perspective of the psychocultural approach advanced here, Boas' objection that the same tale could not be classed at one time as a myth and at another time as a folk tale is not insurmountable. Since the object of myth, as Tylor noted, varies with the social standard of possibility, it follows that a given tale may at one time be classed as myth and at another as a folk tale, depending upon the degree of credence attached to it by a given society. Lowie, in particular, has noted[18] that folk tales are sometimes utilized for purposes of etiological rationalization of rites and that priestly adaptation may convert fiction into sacred myth. Conversely, in the process of time myths can become great literature having lasting symbolic value for subsequent generations, for example, Goethe's *Faust*, Cervantes' *Don Quixote*, and Melville's *Moby Dick*.

Boas himself has noted that folk tales are taken lightly by their originators, while myths are taken seriously, but he interpreted this psychological observation in a static, fixed sense rather than from a changing, relativistic psychocultural perspective. By natives tales are taken seriously not because they are myths; they are evaluated by us as myths because they are, or were, taken seriously by those who recounted them. It is not only the nature of the metaphysical concepts involved or the distance of the prehistoric space-time in which the

* From Chapter 10 of *Theoretical Anthropology* by David Bidney, copyright 1953 by the Columbia University Press. Excerpts are from pages 293–297, 300–301, 322–326.
[18] Lowie, *Primitive Religion*.

events narrated occurred which determines whether or not a given tale is to be regarded as a myth; it is rather the psycho-cultural attitude or degree of belief of those who recount them. Thus, the accepted belief or subjective truth of one epoch may become myth for the next. In all instances, it is the psycho-cultural context, rather than the subject matter, which determines how a given narrative is to be classified.

According to my thesis, the term "belief" is an epistemically neutral term in the sense of being beyond truth and falsity. To say that one believes a given statement tells us nothing of its scientific or objective validity, that is, whether the given statement is in accordance with empirically established facts. But myth is not a scientifically neutral term; on the contrary, it is a value-charged term and implies a negative evaluation concerning the validity of a given narrative. In other words, myth is correlative to belief and implies a priori that the narrative or explanation described as mythological is not true or credible. It is important to note, furthermore, that a myth is evaluated as such only from the perspective of those who do not share the ideas and beliefs under consideration. From the perspective of those who accept the ideas and beliefs as true or valid, the latter are not myths at all. What we may regard as "myths" are, psychologically, charters of belief for those who accept them and live by them. Belief is essential to the acceptance of "myth" and accounts for its effectiveness in a given cultural context, but the very fact of belief implies that subjectively, that is, for the believer, the object of belief is not mythological. Hence, nonbelief in a given narrative, tradition, or explanation is essential for its acceptance as an effective element of culture. In this way, the distinction between belief, myth, and truth is retained, while the relativity of myth to belief and an accepted cultural standard of credibility is recognized.

We must distinguish, furthermore, between myth and superstition. Myth involves a belief of a special kind, namely, an incredible belief or the idea of a credible impossibility. A superstition, on the other hand, is a mode of fear based on some irrational or mythological belief and usually involves some taboo in practice. Myths may give rise to superstitions, and the later may stimulate the invention of myths. Superstitions may, however, arise from any irrational association of ideas, whether speculative or empirical, such as the idea of a black cat as an omen of bad luck, and hence do not necessarily arise from mythical narratives or notions of the supernatural. Furthermore, since a superstition is essentially an irrational fear, it is to be distinguished from precritical folk beliefs in general, some of which may comprise elements of empirical knowledge. Some recent collections of "superstitions" apparently do not make this distinction.[19]

Since belief may be objectively either true or false, it follows that what a given individual regards as myth may reflect his own unbelief rather than objective truth, just as his subjective "truth" may be objective myth. In this sense myth is a function of cultural belief and unbelief. Since Nietzsche and Kierkegaard, many modern philosophers, theologians, and social scientists have tended to evaluate "truth" subjectively or "existentially" and to deny the validity of any objective metaphysical truth. In particular, moral values have been explained as functions and mythological rationalizations of a "will to power" on the part of social classes. Thus, the "transvaluation of all values" by Nietzsche has led many modern thinkers to regard traditional metaphysical and moral truths as a "mythology of dangerous ancient ideas." The term "myth" has become a term of abuse whereby to discredit the liberal, democratic tradition, with its rational "ascetic ideals" and belief in

[19] De Lys, *A Treasury of American Superstitions.*

a common humanity. Instead, we have the "truth" of the new "supermen" which posits a new morality in the interests of political power. Contemporary political propaganda and the "cold war" between the East and the West provide many instances of this relativistic interpretation of myth.

The relativity of myth to belief in general renders intelligible the continuous change in the evaluation of a particular myth, or mythological system, to be found at different periods of culture history. The firm faith of one generation becomes the myth of the next. Thus, the Greek folk deities and religious traditions have become the myths of classical scholars. Where belief is not guided by critical, self-correcting, scientific intelligence, the fortunes of a given myth vary from time to time and culture to culture, depending upon the changing psycho-cultural orientation of the society concerned. Thus, it may happen that what one society regards as mere fable or legend unworthy of credence may become the accepted faith, or dogma, of another. In the process of historical acculturation, it may be shown, many primitive religious traditions have become folktales, while the folktales of one culture have often been used to rationalize or validate the ritual and customs of another.

Objectively and normatively, however, myth is relative to established knowledge, and to this extent myth may be described as belief, usually expressed in narrative form, that is incompatible with scientific and rational knowledge. Insofar as knowledge is demonstrable and potentially universal, the category of myth may be said to refer by comparison, to propositions and narratives which, though once accepted and believed, are no longer worthy of rational credence. For example, theories of disease which explain disease as due to evil spirits are mythological because they are incompatible with scientific medicine, not merely because they are no longer believed by civilized societies.

This explains why so many scientists and philosophers belittle and regret myth-making, although they recognize its great influence in sociocultural life. Insofar as it is acknowledged that there is a normative body of well-authenticated truth and that human reason is capable of distinguishing truth from falsity and fiction, responsible and mature minds will prefer objective truth and well-founded faith to fictions and myths, regardless of the latter's so-called pragmatic value. To regard myth as a neutral term beyond truth and falsity and to interpret the culture of scientific rationalism as if it also were based on myth, is to undermine the very basis of rational and scientific thought. From this perspective, the greatest myth of the twentieth-century is the identification of all cultural ideology with myth in the name of social science.

. . . .

As against this thesis,* I maintain that in the term "belief" we already have a neutral term indifferent to truth and falsity. Myth, on the other hand, by common usage is a value-centered term and implies a negative evaluation of the truth of a given belief. MacIver admits that myths are "value-impregnated beliefs" and yet holds that they are neutral, or beyond truth and falsity. My point is that it is not possible to separate the social and cultural values of myths from their truth-value. The force of a "myth" in a given culture is due to its uncritical acceptance by its adherents as true or valid for themselves; the moment this belief is questioned it becomes a myth and ceases to be effective as a guide to conduct. MacIver's use of the term "myth" blurs the distinction between philosophy, religion, and superstition.

. . . .

* Bidney quotes from R. M. MacIver's *The Web of Government*, pp. 4–5.

I should distinguish, then, three categories of belief. First, there is scientific belief which may be verified. Secondly, there is myth which refers relatively to any belief which we discredit, although acceptable to others in the past or the present. Objectively and normatively, myth refers to belief incompatible with scientific fact. Thirdly, there is a sphere of belief which lies between science and myth. Religious beliefs, such as the belief in God, are neither scientific nor mythological. The concept of God is not a scientific concept, because it does not refer to an object which may be empirically verified. Neither does the concept of God refer to a mythological entity, since there is nothing in scientific knowledge to disprove the existence of such a being.

That is why religion is essentially the sphere of faith—faith which may be in accord with scientific knowledge, but may not be reduced to scientific truth or disproved by scientific knowledge. Some aspects of religious belief may be found to be incompatible with scientific knowledge, such as belief in a multitude of anthropomorphic gods constantly intervening in natural processes, and hence there is bound to be a close relation between historical religions and mythology. There may, in other words, be said to be a continuous growth in religious experience in general. I see no valid ground, however, for setting up a narrow dichotomy, as the positivists are inclined to do, of science, on the one hand, and myth, superstition, and fiction, on the other. There is, I should say, a realm of rational belief which may be in accord with scientific knowledge and which goes beyond strict empirical verification. There are postulates of experience which we introduce to render experience intelligible and significant, and these are metascientific presuppositions which we can never verify empirically. Philosophy and religion belong in this general sphere.

.   .   .   .

9. Symbolism, Art, and Science

Our survey of the history of mythological theory has demonstrated that there have been two basic approaches to the interpretation of myth, the literal and the symbolic. On the whole, ethnologists, whether evolutionists or functionalists, have been inclined to interpret myth literally. Evolutionary ethnologists, such as Tylor, and classical scholars, such as C. O. Müller, sought to evaluate myth as an expression of primitive thought and as a mode of thinking destined to be superseded by scientific thought. The functionalists, such as Malinowski, evaluate myth as a universal human phenomenon having a pragmatic function in resolving critical problems not amenable to empirical investigation and scientific procedures. Myth deals with the sphere of the supernatural and supersensuous, as does religion; both have a vital meaning for their adherents and serve to validate their cultural institutions. On the other hand, philosophers, historians, theologians, and psychologists from ancient to modern times have been inclined to evaluate myths as expressing some absolute metaphysical, historical, or psychological truth which underlies the apparently irrational and absurd tales. Philosophers have been inclined to see their own philosophical systems reflected in the myths, and contemporary analytical psychological processes and types which they have conceived quite independently. Those who have adopted a symbolical interpretation have been wont to select some one single kind or reality as the referent of myth and the object of its truth. On the whole, it may be said that the latter have tended to reduce myth to a kind of allegory, since they were concerned to reduce the mythical narrative to some form of timeless truth and to minimize the literal significance of the narrative itself.

Thus, the phrase "a science of mythology" turns out to be

ambiguous. For the ethnologist it usually means a scientific study of the origin and function of myth in the history of human culture. Here scientific, empirical method is applied to the study of myth, but no attempt is made to reduce myth itself to science. On the other hand, for those who interpret myth symbolically, the term "science of myth" has been interpreted to mean the scientific knowledge to be found in the analysis of myth. For the latter, therefore, a science of myth involves the application of scientific method for the purpose of ascertaining the cross-cultural, scientific validity, or significance, of myth regardless of the variety of cultural contexts. In this way myth is reduced to science and the dividing line between science and myth is eliminated. This may be compared with the implicit, converse attempt to reduce science itself to myth by evaluating scientific concepts and cultural ideologies as fictions of the imagination serving a pragmatic function.

My own thesis is that a scientific study of myth should refer to the study of myth from an ethnological point of view. Myths are elements of culture and are to be investigated with the same empirical and critical methods employed in the study of culture in general. Such a scientific approach does not preclude a symbolical interpretation of myth provided it is clearly understood that in doing so one is engaging in literary art. The great myths suggest to each critical reader some moral or psychological truth which may not even have occurred to their original adherents. Thus, a later generation may find degrees of truth in mythological narratives beyond the perspective of their originators, who accepted them literally. What one finds in myth depends upon the content of the mind one brings to it.

Thus, myth may have an artistic, allegorical, and philosophical value for critical thought which it did not have for its poetic originators, and in this sense myth may have timeless value as a work of art, even though it may no longer be believed literally. As noted, the myth of Adam and Eve still exercises a potent charm over the imagination of thoughtful men, who discern in it, each according to his own insight, some imaginative psychological, moral, or philosophical truth. Myth, like great fictional and dramatic literature in general, may have profound symbolic or allegorical value for us of a later generation, not because myth necessarily contains such latent wisdom, but because the plot or theme suggests universal patterns of action where comparable problems arise. That is, the original and literal value of a myth for us and the actual historical significance of the myth for its poetic originators are identical. The nature and degree of truth found in a given myth will vary with the cultural context and the special intuitive insight of its interpreters.

My point is that myths are not "higher" forms of latent, unconscious truth which the conscious mind, through labored analysis, may abstract and delineate in part. Myths are the first approximations to truth in a primitive culture which, because they are reflections upon elemental problems, continue to retain a measure of artistic value as marking the dawn of human intelligence. Myths have an objective ethnological truth-value and a subjective, artistic symbolic value in spite of the fact that we evaluate them as myths.

From the perspective of culture theory the concept of natural, universal, biologically conditioned mythological symbols which emerge into consciousness from the collective unconscious is not tenable. If culture is not biologically inherited, then the concept of innate cultural symbols is self-contradictory and involves the naturalistic fallacy of attempting to deduce culture from nature. Mythological symbols are historically and ontogenetically acquired, as are cultural symbols in general, and their significance, therefore, will vary with their cultural contexts. Through the processes of suggestion and cultural diffusion some culturally acquired symbols may, in time, become generally accepted and may affect the artistic achievements and psychological experiences of individuals of other cultures also. In this sense, as Roheim has suggested, cultural symbols are potentially universal, but never actually so. The fact that cultural symbols are products of the creative intelligence of man leads me to deny the validity of all attempts at a monistic reductionistic interpretation of mythological symbols. As C.O. Müller noted long ago, "we have no ground whatever for excluding beforehand any class of thoughts and ideas from the mythic representation, if it can be at all supposed that they lay within the sphere of intellectual activity in those primitive ages."[95] Besides, as Müller has also shown, there is no exact correspondence between symbolic objects and particular ideas in classical mythology. The connotation of symbols varies with cultural modes of intuition.

10. Myth and the Psychocultural Evolution of Thought

If it be granted that myth is a universal cultural phenomenon originating in a plurality of motives and involving all mental faculties which may contribute to social illusion and delusion, then it seems reasonable to accept the thesis of the continuity of precritical, critical, and scientific thought. A comparative, psychocultural and ethnohistorical study of human thought reveals the essential similarity of the processes at work in the formation of myth, while allowing for differences in the types of myth which prevail at different times and cultures. From the perspective of modern critical thought, animistic thought is "mythopoeic" because it represents a

[95] Müller, *Introduction to a Scientific System of Mythology,* p. 19.

mode of thinking which is no longer characteristic of our age. In reality, all that has changed is the mode of expression. In precritical cultures animistic tales of culture heroes and of magic and epic cosmogonic and theogonic myths tend to prevail. In critical, prescientific cultures myths of the miraculous and supernatural gain currency. In scientific thought, there is a tendency to discount narratives of the miraculous and supernatural, but to accept secular myths instead. In our so-called scientific culture we have the secular beliefs of pseudo-science, such as the myths of racial superiority and the stereotypes of racial and national character. That is why the struggle of man against myth[96] demands such ceaseless vigilance and self-conscious analysis. Myth is most potent when it is assumed complacently that one is free from it.

The sociopolitical myths of our time are the products of the divorce of scientific thought from the social values which underlie our effective social beliefs and institutions. In fact, modern social scientists and philosophers have encouraged this trend by putting a new positive value upon myth. In order to safeguard the "autonomy" of moral and religious values they have made the validity of the latter independent of scientific truth-values. In this way rational thought has proved itself capable of undermining its own foundations by espousing myth as a "higher" form of truth in the interests of personal "peace of mind" and of national "solidarity." The "myth of modernity," with its glorifications of the present age, has replaced the "myth of progress," which envisaged a better world in the future.[97] The modern "myth of the proletariat" has served to sanction revolutionary activity with a view to realizing in our time the eschatological myth of a stateless and classless society.[98] Normative, critical, and scientific thought

[96] Dunham, *Man against Myth.*
[97] Baudouin, *The Myth of Modernity,* ch. 1.
[98] Berdyaev, *The Russian Idea,* p. 249.

provides the only tested, self-correcting means of combatting the growth of myth, but it may do so only on condition that it retain its own integrity and does not mistake reason for rationalization. Otherwise, in order to preserve life we may cast away the reasons for living.[99]

[99] Baudouin, *The Myth of Modernity,* p. 19.

2

Folklore in Literature, Ancient, Medieval, and Modern

IN MOST DEFINITIONS, FOLK NARRATIVE IS UNDERSTOOD TO BE the folktales and other narrative material maintained in *oral* tradition. The fact that narratives have been passed from one person to another, from one comunity to another, and from one century to another strictly by word of mouth without intervention of writing is well established. Even when such narratives are abstracted from the stream of oral literature and fixed in print by collectors or literary artists, the oral tradition continues. Though the term seems self-contradictory, *oral literature* is the one commonly used to refer to the literature of non-literate peoples, and, of course, to the countless generations of people who maintained a literature prior to the invention of writing.

Such evidence as is available suggests rather strongly that early written literature drew directly from the oral literature of the time and place in which the written records were established. From inscribed clay tablets and similar early records, scholars have established that the sources of much written literature have been the ever-renewing springs of folklore.

Once the written record and the oral traditions become concurrent, however, a new force is at work: literary convention, which reshapes the narratives and, in some cases, feeds new elements back into the stream of oral literature.

Students who begin their explorations of literature are sometimes surprised to learn that a tale from Chaucer's *The Canterbury Tales* or some similarly venerable literary monument had circulated widely as an oral anecdote prior to the time the artist picked it up for literary treatment. To learn that "literature" may have been told briefly as a joke or lengthened to make a tale is to learn a new dimension of studies in literature. Some who fail to make this discovery may continue even to advanced stages of scholarship maintaining a literary blind spot—an illusion that studies in literature can be confined to consideration of only that which has been written.

Though it is true that the modern scholar may never personally encounter an orally transmitted version of the motif he is examining, the possibility of such a version should not escape his attention. Twentieth-century authors are fully as capable of incorporating or alluding to elements from their aural environment as were Chaucer, Shakespeare, and Homer. If an obscure allusion in one of Ezra Pound's sonnets has eluded the most rigorous library search, the searcher may find it in the barber shop next door, on the nearest playground, or in a fraternity bull session. Since the researcher can hardly be expected to extend his search to these primary sources, he must turn to some of the many available bibliographic tools of folklore.

Unlike some medieval writers who expended their creative

talents on the reshaping of old stories possibly already well known to their readers, modern writers weave folklore into their creations in two ways : *consciously*, with an awareness of the appeal of what they are using; and *unconsciously*, as a reflection of the folk processes which are a part of the lives of all people and which emerge spontaneously in their expressions.

The unconscious use of folklore is less easy to illustrate with certainty, for to do so one would have to see into the mental processes of the writer. But the use of proverbial expressions, allusions to customs, amusements, and beliefs, and even the local idiom may be the unconscious reflection of the writer's necessary involvement in the lore of his culture.

The conscious use of folklore by a writer who knows and appreciates the traditions of his subjects is illustrated in Hardy's description of the peasant's use of black magic. His intimate knowledge of the beliefs and practices of Wessex country folk enabled him to add an extra dimension to his novels. He exploited this insight regularly, as do many modern writers who are aware of the appeal of folk materials in literature.

The selections in this chapter have been assembled to illustrate the process of literary adaptation and readaptation of folklore.

THEODORE GASTER

The Adventures of Gilgamesh*

Once upon a time there lived in the city of Erech a great and terrible being whose name was Gilgamesh. Two-thirds of him were god, and only one-third was human. He was the mightiest warrior in the whole of the East; none could match him in combat, nor could anyone's spear prevail against him. Because of his power and strength all the people of Erech were brought beneath his sway, and he ruled them with an iron hand, seizing youths for his service and taking to himself any maiden he wished.

At length they could endure it no longer, and prayed to heaven for relief. The lord of heaven heard their prayer and summoned the goddess Aruru—that same goddess who, in olden times, had fashioned man out of clay.

"Go," said he, "and mold out of clay a being who will prove the equal of this tyrant, and let him fight with him and beat him, that the people may have relief."

Thereupon the goddess wetted her hands, and taking clay from the ground, kneaded it into a monstrous creature, whom she named Enkidu. Fierce he was, like the god of battle, and his whole body was covered with hair. His tresses hung long like a woman's, and he was clothed in skins. All day long he roamed with the beasts of the field, and like them he fed on grass and herbs and drank from the brooks.

But no one in Erech yet knew that he existed.

One day a huntsman who had gone out trapping noticed the strange creature refreshing himself beside the herds at the fountain. The mere sight was sufficient to turn the huntsman pale. His face drawn and haggard, his heart pounding and

* From *The Oldest Stories in the World* by Theodore H. Gaster, copyright 1952 by Theodore H. Gaster. Published as a Beacon Paperback (Boston: Beacon Press) 1958.

thumping, he rushed home in terror, screaming with dismay.

The next day he went out into the fields to continue his trapping, only to find that all the pits he had dug had been filled in and all the snares he had lain torn up, and there was Enkidu himself releasing the captured beasts from the toils!

On the third day, when the same thing happened once more, the huntsman went and consulted his father. The latter advised him to go to Erech and report the matter to Gilgamesh.

When Gilgamesh heard what had happened, and learned of the wild creature who was interfering with the labors of his subjects, he instructed the huntsman to choose a girl from the streets and take her with him to the place where the cattle drank. When Enkidu came thither for water she was to strip off her clothing and entice him with her charms. Once he embraced her the animals would recognize that he was not of their kind, and they would immediately forsake him. Thus he would be drawn into the world of men and be forced to give up his savage ways.

The huntsman did as he was ordered and, after three days' journey, arrived with the girl at the place where the cattle drank. For two days they sat and waited. On the third day, sure enough, the strange and savage creature came down with the herd for water. As soon as she caught sight of him the girl stripped off her clothing and revealed her charms. The monster was enraptured and clasped her wildly to his breast and embraced her.

For a whole week he dallied with her, until at least, sated with her charms, he rose to rejoin the herd. But the hinds and gazelles knew him no more for one of their own, and when he approached them they shied away and scampered off. Enkidu tried to run after them, but even as he ran he felt his legs begin to drag and his limbs grow taut, and all of a sudden he became aware that he was no longer a beast but had become a man.

Faint and out of breath, he turned back to the girl. But now it was a changed being who sat at her feet, gazing up into her eyes and hanging intently upon her lips.

Presently she turned toward him. "Enkidu," she said softly, "you have grown handsome as a god. Why should you go on roving with the beasts? Come, let me take you to Erech, the broad city of men. Let me take you to the gleaming temple where the god and goddess sit enthroned. It is there, by the way, that Gilgamesh is rampaging like a bull, holding the people at his mercy."

At these words Enkidu was overjoyed; for, now that he was no longer a beast, he longed for the converse and companionship of men.

"Lead on," said he, "to the city of Erech, to the gleaming temple of the god and goddess. As for Gilgamesh and his rampaging, I will soon alter that. I will fling a challenge in his face and dare him, and show him, once for all, that country lads are no weaklings!" . . .

Gilgamesh strode forward to meet his opponent, and in a few moments they were locked in battle, raging and butting like bulls. At last Gilgamesh sank to the ground and knew that he had indeed met his match.

But Enkidu was chivalrous as well as strong, and saw at once that his opponent was not simply a blustering tyrant, as he had been led to believe, but a brave and stout-hearted warrior, who had courageously accepted his challenge and not flinched from the fight.

"Gilgamesh," said he, "you have proved full well that you are the child of a goddess and that heaven itself has set you on your throne. I shall no longer oppose you. Let us be friends."

And, raising him to his feet, he embraced him.

Now Gilgamesh loved adventure and could never resist a hazard. One day he proposed to Enkidu that they go together into the mountains and, as an act of daring, cut down one of the cedars in the sacred forest of the gods.

"That is not easy," replied his friend, "for the forest is guarded by a fierce and terrible monster called Humbaba. Often, when I lived with the beasts, I beheld his works. His voice is a whirlwind, and he snorts fire, and his breath is the plague."

"For shame!" retorted Gilgamesh. "Should a brave warrior like you be frightened of battle? Only the gods can escape death; and how will you face your children when they ask you what you did in the day when Gilgamesh fell?". . .

Eagerly and impetuously the two stalwarts set out on their journey, covering in three days the distance of six weeks' march. At length they came to a dense forest, and at the entrance of the forest there was a huge door. Enkidu pushed it open a trifle and peered within.

"Hurry," he whispered, beckoning to his companion, "and we can take him by surprise. Whenever he wanders abroad Humbaba always bundles himself up in seven layers of garments. Now he is sitting wearing only his vest. We can get him before he goes out!"

But even as he spoke the huge door swung upon its hinges and slammed shut, crushing his hand.

For twelve days Enkidu lay writhing in anguish, and all the while kept imploring his comrade to give up the wild adventure. But Gilgamesh refused to pay heed to his words.

"Are we such puny weaklings," he cried, "as to be put out by the first mishap? We have traveled a long way. Shall we now turn back defeated? For shame! Your wounds will soon be healed; and if we cannot engage the monster in his house, let us wait for him in the thicket!"

So on they went to the forest and at last they reached the Mountain of Cedars itself—that high and towering mountain on the summit of which the gods held session. Fatigued by the long journey, they lay down beneath the shade of the trees and were soon asleep.

But in the middle of the night Gilgamesh suddenly awoke with a start. "Did you wake me?" he called to his companion. "If not, it must have been the force of my dream. For I dreamed that a mountain was toppling upon me, when all of a sudden there appeared before me the most handsome man in all the world, and he dragged me out from under the weight and raised me to my feet."

"Friend," replied Enkidu, "your dream is an omen, for the mountain which you saw is yon monstrous Humbaba. Now it is clear that even if he falls upon us we shall escape and win!"

Then they turned upon their sides, and sleep fell on them once more. But this time it was Enkidu who woke suddenly with a start.

"Did you wake me?" he called to his companion. "If not it must have been the force of my dream. For I dreamed that the sky rumbled and the earth shook, and the day grew black and darkness fell, and lightning flashed and a fire blazed, and death poured down. And then, all of a sudden, the glare faded and the fire went out and the sparks which had fallen turned to ashes."

Gilgamesh knew full well that the dream portended ill for his friend. Nevertheless he encouraged him not to give up; and presently they had risen and were deep in the forest.

Then Gilgamesh grasped his ax and felled one of the sacred cedars. The tree fell to earth with a loud crash, and out rushed Humbaba from his house, growling and roaring.

Now the monster had a strange and terrible face, with one eye in the middle, which could turn to stone any upon whom it gazed. As he came storming through the thicket, nearer and nearer, and as the tearing and cracking of branches announced his approach, Gilgamesh for the first time grew truly frightened.

But the sun-god remembered his promise and called to Gilgamesh out of the heavens, bidding him go forth unafraid to the combat. And even as the leaves of the thicket parted and the terrible face bore down upon the heroes, the sun-god sent mighty, searing winds from every quarter of the heavens, and they beat against the eye of the monster until they blinded his vision and he could move neither backward nor forward.

Then as he stood there, thrashing with his arms, Gilgamesh and Enkidu closed in upon him, until at last he begged for grace. But the heroes would grant him none. They drew their swords and severed the horrible head from his giant frame. . . .

But the gods are not mocked; whatsoever a man sows, that shall he also reap.

One night Enkidu had a strange dream. He dreamed that the gods were sitting in council, trying to decide whether he or Gilgamesh was the more to blame for the slaying of Humbaba and the heavenly bull.* The more guilty, they had ruled, was to be put to death.

For a long while the debate raged back and forth, but when at length they had still not made up their minds, Anu, the father of the gods, proposed a way out.

"In my opinion," he declared, "Gilgamesh is the greater culprit, for not only did he slay the monster but he also cut down the sacred cedar."

---

* Gilgamesh and Enkidu had offended the gods by killing a sacred bull. A similar offense committed by Odysseus's crew on the Island of the Sun is another familiar reminder of the importance of cattle in religious cults. See *The Odyssey*, E. V. Rieu, tr., Penguin Classics, pp. 198–199.

No sooner, however, had he uttered these words than pandemonium broke loose, and soon the gods were at sixes and sevens, each roundly abusing the other.

"Gilgamesh?" screamed the god of the winds. "It is Enkidu who is the real villain, for it was he that led the way!"

"Indeed!" roared the sun-god, wheeling sharply upon him. "What right have *you* to talk? It was *you* who hurled the winds into Humbaba's face!"

"And what about *you*? retorted the other, shaking with anger. "What about *you*? If it hadn't been for you, neither of them would have done these things! It was *you* that encouraged them and kept coming to their aid!"

Fiercely they argued and fiercely they wrangled, their tempers growing hotter and hotter by the minute and their voices louder and louder. But before they could come to a decision—Enkidu woke up.

He was now firmly convinced that he was doomed to die. But when he told the dream to his companion it seemed to Gilgamesh that the real punishment was destined, after all, for himself. . . .

For nine days Enkidu languished upon his bed, growing weaker and weaker, while Gilgamesh watched beside him, torn with grief. . . .

And even as he cried he saw that his companion no longer stirred nor opened his eyes; and when he felt Enkidu's heart it was beating no more.

Then Gilgamesh took a cloth and veiled the face of Enkidu, even as men veil a bride on the day of her espousal. And he paced to and fro and cried aloud, and his voice was the voice of a lioness robbed of her whelps. And he stripped off his garments and tore his hair and gave himself up to mourning.

All night long he gazed upon the prostrate form of his companion and saw him grow stiff and wizened, and all the beauty was departed from him. "Now," said Gilgamesh, "I have seen the face of death and am sore afraid. One day I too shall be like Enkidu."

When morning came he had made a bold resolve.

On an island at the far ends of the earth, so rumor had it, lived the only mortal in the world who had ever escaped death—an old, old man, whose name was Utnapishtim. Gilgamesh decided to seek him out and to learn from him the secret of eternal life.

As soon as the sun was up he set out on his journey, and at last, after traveling long and far, he came to the end of the world and saw before him a huge mountain whose twin peaks touched the sky and whose roots reached down to nethermost hell. In front of the mountain there was a massive gate, and the gate was guarded by fearsome and terrible creatures, half man and half scorpion.

Gilgamesh flinched for a moment and screened his eyes from their hideous gaze. Then he recovered himself and strode boldly to meet them.

When the monsters saw that he was unafraid, and when they looked on the beauty of his body, they knew at once that no ordinary mortal was before them. Nevertheless they challenged his passage and asked the purpose of his coming.

Gilgamesh told them that he was on his way to Utnapishtim, to learn the secret of eternal life.

"That," replied their captain, "is a thing which none has ever learned, nor was there ever a mortal who succeeded in reaching that ageless sage. For the path which we guard is the path of the sun, a gloomy tunnel leagues long, a road where the foot of man may not tread."

"Be it never so long," rejoined the hero, "and never so dark, be the pains and the perils never so great, be the heat never so searing and the cold never so sharp, I am resolved to tread it!"

At the sound of these words the sentinels knew for certain that one who was more than a mortal was standing before them, and at once they threw open the gate. . . .

"Young man," said the sage,"that which you seek you will never find. For there is nothing eternal on earth. When men draw up a contract they set a term. What they acquire today, tomorrow they must leave to others. Age-long feuds in time die out. Rivers which rise and swell, in the end subside. When the butterfly leaves the cocoon it lives but a day. Time and seasons are appointed for all."

"True" replied the hero. "But you yourself are a mortal, no whit different from me; yet you live forever. Tell me how you found the secret of life, to make yourself like the gods."

A faraway look came into the eyes of the old man. It seemed as though all the days of all the years were passing in procession before him. Then, after a long pause, he lifted his head and smiled.

"Gilgamesh," he said slowly, "I will tell you the secret—a secret high and holy, which no one knows save the gods and myself." And he told him the story of the great flood which the gods had sent upon the earth in the days of old, and how Ea, the kindly lord of wisdom, had sent him warning of it in the whistle of the wind which soughed through the wattles of his hut. At Ea's command he had built an ark, and sealed it with pitch and asphalt, and loaded his kin and his cattle within it, and sailed for seven days and seven nights while the waters rose and the storms raged and the lightnings flashed. And on the seventh day the ark had grounded on a mountain at the end of the world, and he had opened a window in the ark and sent out a dove, to see if the waters had subsided. But the dove had returned, for want of place to rest. Then he had sent out a swallow, and the swallow too had come back. And at last he had sent out a raven, and the raven had not returned. Then he led forth his kinsmen and his cattle and offered thanksgiving to the gods. But suddenly the god of the winds had come down from heaven and led him back into the ark, along with his wife, and set it afloat upon the waters once more, until it came to the island on the far horizon, and there the gods had set him to dwell forever.

When Gilgamesh heard the tale he knew at once that his quest had been vain, for now it was clear that the old man had no secret formula to give him. He had become immortal, as he now revealed, by a special grace of the gods and not, as Gilgamesh had imagined, by possession of some hidden knowledge. The sun-god had been right, and the scorpion-men had been right, and the alewife had been right: that which he had sought he would never find—at least on this side of the grave. . . .

Thereupon Utnapishtim ordered him to wash and cleanse himself and make ready for the journey home. But even as the hero stepped into his boat to depart Utnapishtim's wife drew near.

"Utnapishtim," said she, "you cannot send him away empty-handed. He has journeyed hither with great effort and pain, and you must give him a parting gift."

The old man raised his eyes and gazed earnestly at the hero. "Gilgamesh," he said, "I will tell you a secret. In the depths of the sea lies a plant. It looks like a buckthorn and pricks like a rose. If any man come into possession of it, he can, by tasting it, regain his youth!"

When Gilgamesh heard these words he tied heavy stones to his feet and let himself down into the depths of the sea; and there, on the bed of the ocean, he espied the plant. Caring little that it pricked him, he grasped it between his fingers, cut the stones from his feet, and waited for the tide to wash him ashore.

Then he showed the plant to Urshanabi the boatman. "Look," he cried, "it's the famous plant called Graybeard-grow-young! Whoever tastes it, gets a new lease on life! I will carry it back to Erech and give it to the people to eat. So will I at least have some reward for my pains!"

After they had crossed the perilous waters and reached land, Gilgamesh and his companion began the long journey on foot to the city of Erech. When they had traveled fifty leagues the sun was already beginning to set, and they looked for a place to pass the night. Suddenly they came upon a cool spring.

"Here let us rest," said the hero, "and I will go bathe."

So he stripped off his clothes and placed the plant on the ground and went to bathe in the cool spring. But as soon as his back was turned a serpent came out of the waters and, sniffing the fragrance of the plant, carried it away. And no sooner had it tasted of it than at once it sloughed off its skin and regained its youth.

When Gilgamesh saw that the precious plant had now passed from his hands forever he sat down and wept. But soon he stood up and, resigned at last to the fate of all mankind, he returned to the city of Erech, back to the land whence he had come.

THE PANCHATANTRA

Book I

The Loss of Friends*

Here then begins Book I, called "The Loss of Friends." The first verse runs:

> The forest lion and the bull
> Were linked in friendship, growing, full:
> A jackal then estranged the friends
> For greedy and malicious ends.

And this is how it happened.

In the southern country was a city called Maiden's Delight. It rivaled the city of heaven's King, so abounding in every urban excellence as to form the central jewel of Earth's diadem. Its contour was like that of Kailasa Peak. Its gates and palaces were stocked with machines, missile weapons, and chariots in great variety. Its central portal, massive as Indrakila Mountain, was fitted with bolt and bar, panel and arch, all formidable, impressive, solid. Its numerous temples listed their firm bulk near spacious squares and crossings. It wore a moat-girdled zone of walls that recalled the high-uplifted Himalayas.

In this city lived a merchant named Increase. He possessed a heap of numerous virtues, and a heap of money, a result of the accumulation of merit in earlier lives.

As he once pondered in the dead of night, his conclusions took this form: "Even an abundant store of wealth, if pecked at, sinks together like a pile of soot. A very little, if added to, grows like an ant-hill. Hence, even though money be abundant, it should be increased. Riches unearned should be

* From *The Panchatantra,* translated by Arthur W. Ryder, copyright 1925 by the University of Chicago Press.

115

earned. What is earned, should be guarded. What is guarded, should be enlarged and heedfully invested. Money, even if hoarded in commonplace fashion, is likely to go in a flash, the hindrances being many. Money unemployed when opportunities arise, is the same as money unpossessed. Therefore, money once acquired should be guarded, increased, employed. As the proverb says:

> Release the money you have earned;
>   So keep it safely still :
> The surplus water of a tank
>   Must find a way to spill.
>
> Wild elephants are caught by tame;
> With capital it is the same :
> In business, beggars have no scope
> Whose stock-in-trade is empty hope.
>
> If any fail to use his fate
> For joy in this or future state,
> His riches serve as foolish fetters;
> He simply keeps them for his betters.

Having thus set his mind in order, he collected merchandise bound for the city of Mathura, assembled his servants, and after saying farewell to his parents when asterism and lunar station were auspicious, set forth from the city, with his people following and with blare of conchshell and beat of drum preceding. At the first water he bade his friends turn back, while he proceeded.

To bear the yoke he had two bulls of good omen. Their names were Joyful and Lively; they looked like white clouds, and their chests were girded with golden bells.

Presently he reached a forest lovely with grisleas, acacias, dhaks, and sals, densely planted with other trees of charming aspect; fearsome with elephants, wild oxen, buffaloes, deer, grunting-cows, boars, tigers, leopards, and bears; abounding in water that issued from the flanks of mountains; rich in caves and thickets.

Here the bull Lively was overcome, partly by the excessive weight of the wagon, partly because one foot sank helpless where far-flung water from cascades made a muddy spot. At this spot the bull somehow snapped the yoke and sank in a heap. When the driver saw that he was down, he jumped excitedly from the wagon, ran to the merchant not far away, and humbly bowing, said : "Oh, my lord ! Lively was wearied by the trip, and sank in the mud."

On hearing this, merchant Increase was deeply dejected. He halted for five nights, but when the poor bull did not return to health, he left caretakers with a supply of fodder, and said : "You must join me later, bringing Lively, if he lives; if he dies, after performing the last sad rites." Having given these directions, he started for his destination.

On the next day, the men, fearing the many drawbacks of the forest, started also and made a false report to their master. "Poor Lively died," they said, "and we performed the last sad rites with fire and everything else." And the merchant, feeling grieved for a mere moment, out of gratitude performed a ceremony that included rites for the departed, then journeyed without hindrance to Mathura.

In the meantime, Lively, since his fate willed it and further life was predestined, hobbled step by step to the bank of the Jumna, his body invigorated by a mist of spray from the cascades. There he browsed on the emerald tips of grass-blades, and in a few days grew plump as Shiva's bull, high-humped, and full of energy. Every day he tore the tops of ant-hills with goring horns, and frisked like an elephant.

But one day a lion named Rusty, with a retinue of all kinds of animals, came down to the bank of the Jumna for water.

There he heard Lively's prodigious bellow. The sound troubled his heart exceedingly, but he concealed his inner feelings while beneath a spreading banyan tree he drew up his company in what is called the Circle of Four.

Now the divisions of the Circle of Four are given as : (1) the lion, (2) the lion's guard, (3) the understrappers, (4) the menials. In all cities, capitals, towns, hamlets, market-centers, settlements, border-posts, land-grants, monasteries, and communities there is just one occupant of the lion's post. Relatively few are active in the lion's guard. The understrappers are the indiscriminate throng. The menials are posted on the outskirts. The three classes are each divided into members high, middle, and low.

Now Rusty, with counselors and intimates, enjoyed a kingship of the following order. His royal office, though lacking the pomp of umbrella, flyflap, fan, vehicle, and amorous display, was held erect by sheer pride in the sentiment of unaffected pluck. It showed unbroken haughtiness and abounding self-esteem. It manifested a native zeal for unchecked power that brooked no rival. It was ignorant of cringing speech, which it delegated to those who like that sort of thing. It functioned by means of impatience, wrath, haste, and hauteur. Its manly goal was fearlessness, disdaining fawning, strange to obsequiousness, unalarmed. It made use of no wheedling artifices, but glittered in its reliance on enterprise, valor, dignity. It was independent, unattached, free from selfish worry. It advertised the reward of manliness by its pleasure in benefiting others. It was unconquered, free from constraint and meanness, while it had no thought of elaborating defensive works. It kept no account of revenue and expenditure. It knew no deviousness nor time-serving, but was prickly with the energy earned by loftiness of spirit. It wasted no deliberation on the conventional six expedients, nor did it hoard weapons or jewelry. It had an uncommon appetite for power, never adopted subterfuges, was never an object of suspicion. It paid no heed to wives or ambush-layers, to their torrents of tears or their squeals. It was without reproach. It had no artificial training in the use of weapons, but it did not disappoint expectations. It found satisfactory food and shelter without dependence on servants. It had no timidity about any foreign forest, and no alarms. Its head was high. As the proverb says :

> The lion needs, in forest station,
> No trappings and no education,
>   But lonely power and pride;
> And all the song his subjects sing,
> Is in the words : "O King! O King!"
>   No epithet beside.

And again :

> The lion needs, for his appointing,
> No ceremony, no annointing;
> His deeds of heroism bring
> Him fortune. Nature crowns him king.

> The elephant is the lion's meat,
> With drops of trickling ichor sweet;
> Though lack thereof should come to pass,
> The lion does not nibble grass.

Now Rusty had in his train two jackals, sons of counselors, but out of a job. Their names were Cheek and Victor. These two conferred secretly, and Victor said : "My dear Cheek, just look at our master Rusty. He came this way for water. For what reason does he crouch here so disconsolate?" "Why meddle, my dear fellow?" said Cheek. "There is a saying :

> Death pursues the meddling flunkey :
> Note the wedge-extracting monkey."

"How was that?" asked Victor. And Cheek told the story of

The Wedge-pulling Monkey

There was a city in a certain region. In a grove near by, a merchant was having a temple built. Each day at the noon hour the foreman and workers would go to the city for lunch.

Now one day a troop of monkeys came upon the half-built temple. There lay a tremendous anjana log, which a mechanic had begun to split, a wedge of acacia-wood being thrust in at the top.

There the monkeys began their playful frolics upon tree-top, lofty roof, and woodpile. Then one of them, whose doom was near, thoughtlessly bestrode the log, thinking: "Who stuck a wedge in this queer place?" So he seized it with both hands and started to work it loose. Now what happened when the wedge gave at the spot where his private parts entered the cleft, that, sir, you know without being told.

"And that is why I say that meddling should be avoided by the intelligent. And you know," he continued, "that we two pick up a fair living just from his leavings."

"But," said Victor, "how can you give first-rate service merely from a desire for food with no desire for distinction? There is wisdom in the saying:

> In hurting foes and helping friends
> The wise perceive the proper ends
> Of serving kings. The belly's call
> To answer, is no job at all.

And again:

> When many lives on one depend,
>   Then life is life indeed:
> A crow, with beak equipped, can fill
>   His belly's selfish need.

If loving kindness be not shown
   To friends and souls in pain,
To teachers, servants, and one's self,
   What use in life, what gain?
A crow will live for many years
   And eat the offered grain.

A dog is quite contened if
   He gets a meatless bone,
A dirty thing with gristle-strings
   And marrow-fat lone—
And not enough of it at that
   To still his belly's moan.

The lion scorns the jackal, though
   Between his paws, to smite
The elephant. For everyone,
   However sad his plight,
Demands the recompense that he
   Esteems his native right.

Dogs wag their tails and fawn and roll,
   Bare mouth and belly, at your feet :
Bull-elephants show self-esteem,
   Demand much coaxing ere they eat.

A tiny rill
Is quick to fill,
   And quick a mouse's paws;
So seedy men
Are grateful, when
   There is but little cause.

For if there be no mind
   Debating good and ill,
And if religion send
   No challenge to the will,
If only greed be there
   For some material feast,
How draw a line between
   The man-beast and the beast?

Or more accurately yet:

> Since cattle draw the plow
>   Through rough and level soil,
> And bend their patient necks
>   To heavy wagons' toil,
> Are kind, of sinless birth,
>   And find in grass a feast,
> How can they be compared
>   With any human beast?"

"But at present," said Cheek, "we two hold no job at court. So why meddle?" "My dear fellow," said Victor, "after a little the jobless man does hold a job. As the saying goes:

> The jobless man is hired
>   For careful serving;
> The holder may be fired,
>   If undeserving.

> No character moves up or down
> At others' smile or others' frown;
> But honor or contempt on earth
> Will follow conduct's inner worth.

And once more:

> It costs an effort still
> To carry stones uphill;
> They tumble in a trice:
> So virtue, and so vice."

"Well," said Cheek, "what do you wish to imply?" And Victor answered: "You see, our master is frightened, his servants are frightened, and he does not know what to do." "How can you be sure of that?" asked Cheek, and Victor said: "Isn't it plain?

An ox can understand, of course,
The spoken word; a driven horse
Or elephant, exerts his force;

But men of wisdom can infer
Unuttered thought from features' stir—
For wit rewards its worshiper.

And again :

From feature, gesture, gait,
From twitch, or word,
From change in eye or face
Is thought inferred.

So by virtue of native intelligence I intend to get him into my power this very day."

"Why," said Cheek, "you do not know how to make yourself useful to a superior. So tell me. How can you establish power over him?"

"And why, my good fellow, do I not know how to make myself useful?" said Victor. "The saintly poet Vyasa has sung the entry of the Pandu princes into Virata's court. From his poem I learned the whole duty of a functionary. You have heard the proverb :

No burden enervates the strong;
To enterprise no road is long;
The well-informed all countries range;
To flatterers no man is strange."

But Cheek objected : "He might perhaps despise you for forcing yourself into a position that does not belong to you." "Yes," said Victor, "there is point in that. However, I am also a judge of occasions. And there are rules, as follows :

> The Lord of Learning, speaking to
>   A false occasion,
> Will meet with hatred, and of course
> Lack all persuasion.

And again :

> The favorite's business comes to be
> A sudden source of king's *ennui,*
> When he is thoughtful, trying scents,
> Retiring, or in conference.

And once again :

> On hours of talk or squabbling rude,
> Of physic, barber, flirting, food,
> A gentleman does not intrude.

> Let everyone be cautious
>   In palaces of kings;
> And let not students rummage
>   In their professor's things :
> For naughty meddlers suffer
>   Destruction swift and sure.
> Like evening candles, lighted
>   In houses of the poor.

Or put it this way :

> On entering a palace,
>   Adjust a modest dress;
> Go slowly, bowing lowly
>   In timely humbleness;
> And sound the kingly temper,
>   And kingly whims no less.

Or this way :

> Though ignorant and common,
>   Unworth the honoring,
> Men win to royal favor
>   By standing near the king :

For kings and vines and maidens
To nearest neighbors cling.

And once again :

The servant in his master's face
Discerns the signs of wrath and grace,
And though the master jerk and tack,
The servant slowly mounts his back.

And finally :

The brave, the learned, he who wins
To bureaucratic power—
These three, alone of all mankind,
Can pluck earth's golden flower.

"Now let me inform you how power is gained by dancing attendance on a master.

Win the friendly counselors,
To the monarch dear,
Win persuasive speakers; so
Gain the royal ear.

On the undiscerning mob
'Tis not wise to toil :
No man reaps a harvest by
Plowing barren soil.

Serve a king of merit, though
Friendless, destitute;
After some delay, you pluck
Long-enduring fruit.

Hate your master, and you fill
Servant's meanest state :
Not discerning whom to serve,
'Tis yourself you hate.

Treat the dowager, the queen,
And the king-to-be,
Chaplain, porter, counselor,
Most obsequiously.

One who seeks the van in fights,
    In the palace clings,
In the city walks behind,
    Is beloved of kings.

One who flatters when addressed,
    Does the proper things,
Acts without expressing doubts,
    Is beloved of kings.

One, the royal gifts of cash
    Prudently who flings,
Wearing gifts of garments, he
    Is beloved of kings.

One who never makes reply
    That his master stings,
Never boisterously laughs,
    Is beloved of kings.

One who never hearkens to
    Queenly whisperings,
In the women's quarters dumb,
    Is beloved of kings.

One who, even in distress,
    Never boasts and sings
Of his master's favor, he
    Is beloved of kings.

One who hates his master's foe,
    Loves his friend, and brings
Pain or joy to either one,
    Is beloved of kings.

One who never disagrees,
    Blames, or pulls the strings
Of intrigue with enemies,
    Is beloved of kings.

One who finds in battle, peace
    Free from questionings,

> Thinks of exile as of home,
>> Is beloved of kings.

> One who thinks of dice as death,
>> Wine as poison-stings,
> Others' wives as statues, he
>> Is beloved of kings."

"Well," said Cheek, "when you come into his presence, what do you intend to say first? Please tell me that." And Victor replied:

> "Answers, after speech begins,
>> Further answers breed,
> As a seed, with timely rain,
>> Ripens other seed.

And besides:

> A clever servant shows his master
> The gleam of triumph or disaster
> From good or evil courses springing,
> And shows him wit, decision-bringing.

> The man possessing such a wit
> Should magnify and foster it;
> Thereby he earns a livelihood
> And public honor from the good.

And there is a saying:

> Let anyone who does not seek
> His master's fall, unbidden speak;
> So act at least the excellent:
> The other kind are different."

"But," said Cheek, "kings are hard to conciliate. There is a saying:

> In sensuous coil
> And heartless toil,
> In sinuous course

And armored force,
In savage harms
That yield to charms—
In all these things
Are snakes like kings.

Uneven, rough,
And high enough—
Yet low folk roam
Their flanks as home,
And wild things haunt
Them, hungry, gaunt—
In all these things
Are hills like kings.

The things that claw, and the things that gore
 Are unreliable things;
And so is a man with a sword in his hand,
 And rivers, and women, and kings."

"Quite true," said Victor. "However:

The clever man soon penetrates
The subject's mind, and captivates.

Cringe, and flatter him when angry;
 Love his friend and hate his foe;
Duly advertise his presents—
 Trust no magic—win him so.

And yet:

If a man excel in action,
 Learning, fluent word,

Make yourself his humble servant
 While his power is stirred,
Quick to leave him at the moment
 When he grows absurd.

Plant your words where profit lies:
Whiter cloth takes faster dyes.

> Till you know his power and manhood,
> Effort has no scope :
> Moonlight's glitter vainly rivals
> Himalaya's slope."

And Cheek replied : "If you have made up your mind, then seek the feet of the king. Blest be your journeys. May your purpose be accomplished.

> Be heedful in the presence of the king;
> We also to your health and fortune cling."

Then Victor bowed to his friend, and went to meet Rusty.

Now when Rusty saw Victor approaching, he said to the doorkeeper : "Away with your reed of office! This is an old acquaintance, the counselor's son Victor. He has free entrance. Let him come in. He belongs to the second circle." So Victor entered, bowed to Rusty, and sat down on the seat indicated to him.

Then Rusty extended a right paw adorned with claws as formidable as thunderbolts, and said respectfully : "Do you enjoy health? Why has so long a time passed since you were last visible?" And Victor replied : "Even though my royal master has no present need of me, still I ought to report at the proper time. For there is nothing that may not render service to a king. As the saying goes :

> To clean a tooth or scratch an ear
> A straw may serve a king :
> A man, with speech and action, is
> A higher kind of thing.

"Besides, we who are ancestral servants of our royal master, follow him even in disasters. For us there is no other course. Now the proverb says :

> Set in firm position each
> Gem or serving man;

No tiaras on the toes,
Just because you can.

Servants leave the kings who their
Qualities ignore,
Even kings of lofty line,
Wealthy, served of yore.

Lacking honor from their equals,
Jobless, *déclassé*,
Servants give their master notice
That they will not stay.

And again :

If set in tin, a gem that would
Adorn a golden frame,
Will never scream nor fail to gleam,
Yet tells its wearer's shame.

The king who reads a servant's mind—
Dull, faithless, faithful, wise—
May servants find of every kind
For every enterprise.

"And as for my master's remark : 'It is long since you were
last visible,' pray hear the reason of that :

Where just distinction is not drawn
Between the left and right,
The self-respecting, if they can,
Will quickly take to flight.

If masters no distinction make
Among their servants, then
They lose the zealous offices
Of energetic men.

And in a market where it seems
That no distinctions hold
Between red-eye and ruby, how
Can precious gems be sold?

There must be bonds of union
In all their dealings, since
No prince can lack his servants
Nor servants lack a prince.

"Yet the nature of the servant also depends on the master's quality. As the saying goes :

In case of horse or book or sword,
Of woman, man or lute or word,
The use of uselessness depends
On qualities the user lends.

"And another point. You do wrong to despise me because I am a jackal. For

Silk comes from worms, and gold from stone;
From cow's hair sacred grass is grown;
The water-lily springs from mud;
From cow-dung sprouts the lotus-bud;
The moon its rise from ocean takes;
And gems proceed from hoods of snakes;
From cows' bile yellow dyestuffs come;
And fire in wood is quite at home :
The worthy, by display of worth,
Attain distinction, not by birth.

And again :

Kill, although domestic born,
Any hurtful mouse :
Bribe an alien cat who will
Help to clean the house.

And once again :

How use the faithful, lacking power?
Or strong, who evil do?
But me, O King, you should not scorn,
For I am strong and true.

Scorn not the wise who penetrate
Truth's universal law;
They are not men to be restrained
By money's petty straw :
When beauty glistens on their cheeks
By trickling ichor lent,
Bull-elephants feel lotus-chains
As no impediment."

"Oh," said Rusty, "you must not say such things. You are our counselor's son, an old retainer." "O King," said Victor, "there is something that should be said." And the king replied : "My good fellow, reveal what is in your heart."

Then Victor began : "My master set out to take water. Why did he turn back and camp here?" And Rusty, concealing his inner feelings, said : "Victor, it just happened so." "O King," said the jackal, "if it is not a thing to disclose, then let it be.

Some things a man should tell his wife,
Some things to friend and some to son;
All these are trusted. He should not
Tell everything to everyone."

Hereupon Rusty reflected : "He seems trustworthy. I will tell him what I have in mind. For the proverb says :

You find repose, in sore disaster,
By telling things to powerful master,
To honest servant, faithful friend,
Or wife who loves you till the end.

Friend Victor, did you hear a great voice in the distance?" "Yes, master, I did," said Victor. "What of it?"

And Rusty continued : "My good fellow, I intend to leave this forest." "Why?" said Victor. "Because," said Rusty, "there has come into our forest some prodigious creature,

from whom we hear this great voice. His nature must correspond to his voice, and his power to his nature."

"What!" said Victor. "Is our master frightened by a mere
voice? You know the proverb:

> Water undermines the dikes;
> Love dissolves when malice strikes;
> Secrets melt when babblings start;
> Simple words melt dastard hearts.

So it would be improper if our master abruptly left the forest
which was won by his ancestors and has been so long in the
family. For they say:

> Wisely move one foot; the other
> Should its vantage hold;
> Till assured of some new dwelling,
> Do not leave the old.

"Besides, many kinds of sounds are heard here. Yet they
are nothing but noises, not a warning of danger. For example,
we hear the sounds made by thunder, wind among the reeds,
lutes, drums, tambourines, conch-shells, bells, wagons, bang-
ing doors, machines, and other things. They are nothing to
be afraid of. As the verse says:

> If a king be brave, however
> Fierce the foe and grim,
> Sorrows of humiliation
> Do not wait for him.

And again:

> Bravest bosoms do not falter,
> Fearing heaven's threat;
> Summer dries the pools; the Indus
> Rises, greater yet.

And once again:

> Mothers bear on rare occasions
> To the world a chief,
> Glad in luck and brave in battle,
> Undepressed in grief.

And yet again :

> Do not act as does the grass-blade.
> Lacking honest pride,
> Drooping low in feeble meanness,
> Lightly brushed aside.

My master must take this point of view and reinforce his resolution, not fear a mere sound. As the saying goes :

> I thought at first that it was full
> Of fat; I crept within
> And there I did not find a thing
> Except some wood and skin."

"How was that?" asked Rusty. And Victor told the story of

The Jackal and the War-Drum

In a certain region was a jackal whose throat was pinched by hunger. While wandering in search of food, he came upon a king's battle ground in the midst of a forest. And as he lingered a moment there he heard a great sound.

This sound troubled his heart exceedingly, so that he fell into deep dejection and said : "Ah me ! Disaster is upon me. I am as good as dead already. Who made that sound? What kind of a creature?"

But on peering about, he spied a war-drum that loomed like a mountain-peak, and he thought : "Was that sound its natural voice, or was it induced from without?" Now when the drum was struck by the tips of grasses swaying in the wind, it made the sound, but was dumb at other times.

So he recognized its helplessness, and crept quite near. Indeed his curiosity led him to strike it himself on both heads, and he became gleeful at the thought: "Aha! After long waiting food comes even to me. For this is sure to be stuffed with meat and fat."

Having come to this conclusion, he picked a spot, gnawed a hole, and crept in. And though the leather covering was tough, still he had the luck not to break his teeth. But he was disappointed to find it pure wood and skin, and recited a stanza:

> Its voice was fierce; I thought it stuffed
> With fat, so crept within;
> And there I did not find a thing
> Except some wood and skin.

So he backed out, laughing to himself, and said:

> I thought at first that it was full
> Of fat, . . .

and the rest of it.

AESOP

The Introduction*

Aesop

By the latter part of the fifth century, Aesop (Aisōpos) had become a familiar name in Greece, and he was commonly spoken of not merely as *an* author, but as *the* author, of fables. We possess very little certain information about him, and it has even been held that no such person ever lived, and that the name represents nothing more than an imaginary inventor of the fable—for the Greeks liked to ascribe each kind of composition to a real or fictitious 'finder out.' There is, however, early and reliable authority for the actual existence of Aesop in the *Histories* of Herodotus,[1] who, writing in the second half of the fifth century, (1) states that Aesop the maker of stories lived in the time of the Egyptian pharoah Amasis (i.e. the middle of the sixth century) and was connected with the island of Samos; (2) gives reason for thinking that he was a slave belonging to a Samian citizen called Iadmon; (3) implies that Aesop met his death at the hands of the people of Delphi. Herodotus speaks of him as a well-known person and assumes that the place and manner of his death are common knowledge; and there is no reason for doubting the truth of what he says. As to Aesop's being a slave, the position is not quite clear. Herodotus gives good cause for believing that, if he was a slave, he was a slave of the Samian Iadmon; but he does not tell us how he knows that Aesop was a slave at all, and the evidence which he adduces would be equally consistent with his being not a

[1] II 134.

* From *Fables of Aesop,* translated by S. A. Handford, The Penguin Classics, 1954.

slave but a relative of Iadmon. However, his servile condition was universally accepted in antiquity, and it may well have been an established fact, too well known to need any proof.

The statements of later writers about Aesop must be accepted with caution, because we generally have no means of knowing whether they rest on good authority. They tell us that he was by birth a Thracian, or a Phrygian, and they give more or less circumstantial accounts of his death. Aristophanes[2] says the Delphians accused him of stealing a cup from their temple. Plutarch[3] says that he gave offence to the Delphians, who in revenge trumped up a charge of sacrilege against him and put him to death by hurling him from a rock. A commentator on Aristophanes adds a further detail: they 'planted' a gold cup belonging to the temple in Aesop's baggage—a story suspiciously like other stories, such as that of Joseph and Benjamin in Genesis. Eventually his name became the centre of fantastic legends. He was alleged to have been a preternaturally ugly, misshapen little man, whose hideous appearance contrasted strikingly with his brilliant sallies of wisdom. He made everyone laugh not only by the cleverness of his story-telling but by his grotesque manner and his stammering speech. Finally, after he died he came back to life and fought at the battle of Thermopylae!

From the fifth century onwards the Aesopian fable and the tradition of Aesop the story-teller became very popular, especially at Athens, as is shown by many references to him or to fables attributed to him—in Aristophanes, Xenophon, Plato, Aristotle, and other writers. We do not know whether Aesop's own versions of any fables were written down by him or by any of his contemporaries; and even supposing that some of them were written, it is very unlikely that they are preserved

[2] *Wasps*, 1446–7.
[3] *De sera numinis vindicta,* 12.

in the versions that we possess. It is clear that Aesop's name was so closely associated with this kind of story that *any* fable came to be spoken of as a fable of Aesop. Aristophanes' attributes to Aesop the fable of the eagle and the vixen which was known to Archilochus a century and a half before Aesop's time, and it appears later in collections of 'Fables of Aesop.'

Later History of the Fable

After Aesop's lifetime, newly invented fables were nearly always attributed to him. Most of them, old and new, would certainly be current in different forms, expanded or abridged, and would be continually varied in the detail. There is evidence that, before the beginning of the Christian era, the adaptation or invention of fables became a regular part of a rhetorical training.

The earliest recorded collection was made at Athens about 300 B.C., but nothing is known about it beyond the fact that it was compiled by Demetrius, a famous citizen of the Attic deme of Phalerum. A few fables occur in Greek and Latin literature of the second and first centuries. Horace alludes to several and narrates or summarizes three. . . . The earliest extant collection was made in Latin verse by Phaedrus, a slave born in Macedonia who lived most of his life at Rome and became a freedman of the emperor Augustus. It includes many fables of which we have also Greek versions; others which, though not elsewhere known, are doubtless of Greek origin; and some—clearly Phaedrus' own invention—which refer to contemporary social and political conditions. Most of these stories are simply and concisely told in language made attractive by its liveliness and charm.

⁴ *Birds,* 651–3.

A Communist Dictator

A wolf which had been made leader of the other wolves established a law that each of them should put into a pool everything he caught in the chase and share it equally with all the rest, so that they should not be driven by hunger to eat one another. But an ass came forward and, shaking his mane, said : 'Out of the mind of the wolf has come forth a noble thought. But how is it, wolf, that you yourself laid up in your den the quarry you took yesterday? Put it in the common store and share it.' This exposure shamed the wolf into annulling his laws.

*The very men who pretend to legislate justly do not themselves abide by the laws which they enact and administer.

Delusion

Wandering in a lonely place as the sun went down, a wolf noticed the long shadow cast by his body. 'Fancy a big fellow like me being afraid of a lion!' he said. 'Why, I must be thirty yards long! I'll make myself king and rule all the animals, every single one of them.' But for all his boasting, a strong lion caught him and sat down to devour him. Too late, he regretted his mistake. 'Conceit,' he wailed, 'has helped to bring about my ruin.'

Making the Punishment Fit the Crime

A land rat, in an evil hour, struck up a friendship with a frog, who played a mean trick on him. He tied the rat's foot to his own. They started out on dry land to get themselves a dinner. But when they came to the edge of a pond, the frog dived in. *He* revelled in the water and kept on uttering his familiar croak, while the unlucky rat, who was dragged down with him, swallowed a bellyful and was drowned. But his dead body floated, still made fast to the frog's foot. A kite that spotted it snatched it up in its claws, and the frog, unable to free himself, was hoisted up with it. So the kite ate him too.

*Even when you are dead you can get even with an enemy. For nothing escapes the eye of divine Justice; it weighs crimes in the balance and allots the appropriate punishment.

Killed by Kindness

It is said that apes produce twins, on one of which they lavish affection, feeding it with great care, while they turn against the other and neglect it. But by a curious dispensation of providence, the one that the mother delights to care for and strains tightly to her breast is smothered to death, while the rejected one reaches maturity.

*No forethought can prevail against destiny.

Tit for Tat

Do not do an ill turn to anyone. But if someone injures you, he deserves, according to the fable which I am going to relate, to be paid back in his own coin.

The story is that a stork which had arrived from foreign parts received an invitation to dinner from a fox, who served her with clear soup on a smooth slab of marble, so that the hungry bird could not taste a drop of it. Returning the invitation, the stork produced a flagon filled with pap, into which she stuck her bill and had a good meal, while her guest was tormented with hunger. 'You set the example,' she said, 'and you must not complain at my following it.'

OVID

The Story of Orpheus and Eurydice*

So Hymen left there, clad in saffron robe,
Through the great reach of air, and took his way
To the Ciconian country, where the voice
Of Orpheus called him, all in vain. He came there,
True, but brought with him no auspicious words,
No joyful faces, lucky omens. The torch
Sputtered and filled the eyes with smoke; when swung,
It would not blaze : bad as the omens were,
The end was worse, for as the bride went walking
Across the lawn, attended by her naiads,
A serpent bit her ankle, and she was gone.
Orpheus mourned her to the upper world,
And then, lest he should leave the shades untried,
Dared to descend to Styx, passing the portal
Men call Taenarian. Through the phantom dwellers,
The buried ghosts, he passed, came to the king
Of that sad realm, and to Persephone,
His consort, and he swept the strings, and chanted :
"Gods of the world below the world, to whom
All of us mortals come, if I may speak
Without deceit, the simple truth is this :
I came here, not to see dark Tartarus,
Nor yet to bind the triple-throated monster
Medusa's offspring, rough with snakes. I came
For my wife's sake, whose growing years were taken
By a snake's venom. I wanted to be able
To bear this; I have tried to. Love has conquered.
This god is famous in the world above,
But here, I do not know. I think he may be
Or is it all a lie, that ancient story
Of an old ravishment, and how he brought
The two of you together? By these places
All full of fear, by this immense confusion,

* From Ovid's *Metamorphoses*, tr. by Rolfe Humphries, copyright 1955
by Indiana University Press.

141

By this vast kingdom's silences, I beg you,
Weave over Eurydice's life, run through too soon.
To you we all, people and things, belong,
Sooner or later, to this single dwelling
All of us come, to our last home; you hold
Longest dominion over humankind.
She will come back again, to be your subject,
After the ripeness of her years; I am asking
A loan and not a gift. If fate denies us
This privilege for my wife, one thing is certain :
I do not want to go back either; triumph
In the death of two."
                    And with his words, the music
Made the pale phantoms weep : Ixion's wheel
Was still, Tityos' vultures left the liver,
Tantalus tried no more to reach for the water,
And Belus' daughters rested from their urns,
And Sisyphus climbed on his rock to listen.
That was the first time ever in all the world
The Furies wept. Neither the king nor consort
Had harshness to refuse him, and they called her,
Eurydice. She was there, limping a little
From her late wound, with the new shades of Hell.
And Orpheus received her, but one term
Was set : he must not, till he passed Avernus,
Turn back his gaze, or the gift would be in vain.

They climbed the upward path, through absolute silence,
Up the steep murk, clouded in pitchy darkness,
They were near the margin, near the upper land,
When he, afraid that she might falter, eager to see her,
Looked back in love, and she was gone, in a moment.
Was it he, or she, reaching out arms and trying
To hold or to be held, and clasping nothing
But empty air? Dying the second time,
She had no reproach to bring against her husband,
What was there to complain of? One thing, only :
He loved her. He could hardly hear her calling
Farewell! when she was gone.

The double death
Stunned Orpheus, like the man who turned to stone
At sight of Cerberus, or the couple of rock,
Olenos and Lethaea, hearts so joined
One shared the other's guilt, and Ida's mountain,
Where the rivers run, still holds them, both together.
In vain the prayers of Orpheus and his longing
To cross the river once more; the boatman Charon
Drove him away. For seven days he sat there
Beside the bank, in filthy garments, and tasting
No food whatever. Trouble, grief, and tears
Were all his sustenance. At last, complaining
The gods of Hell were cruel, he wandered on
To Rhodope and Haemus, swept by the north winds,
Where, for three years, he lived without a woman
Either because marriage had meant misfortune
Or he had made a promise. But many women
Wanted this poet for their own, and many
Grieved over their rejection. His love was given
To young boys only, and he told the Thracians
That was the better way : *enjoy the springtime,*
Take those first flowers!
                              There was a hill, and on it
A wide-extending plain, all green, but lacking
The darker green of shade, and when the singer
Came there and ran his fingers over the strings,
The shade came there to listen. The oak-tree came,
And many poplars, and the gentle lindens,
The beech, the virgin laurel, and the hazel
Easily broken, the ash men use for spears,
The shining silver-fir, the ilex bending
Under its acorns, the friend sycamore,
The changing-colored maple, and the willows
That love the river-waters, and the lotus
Favoring pools, and the green boxwood came,
Slim tamarisks, and myrtle, and viburnum
With dark-blue berries, and the pliant ivy,
The tendrilled grape, the elms, all dressed with vines,
The rowan-trees, the pitch-pines, and the arbute

With the red fruit, the palm, the victor's triumph,
The bare-trunked pine with spreading leafy crest,
Dear to the mother of the gods since Attis
Put off his human form, took on that likeness,
And the cone-shaped cypress joined them, now a tree,
But once a boy, loved by the god Apollo
Master of lyre and bow-string, both together.

The Story of Cyparissus

There was a deer, whom the Carthean nymphs
Held sacred, a great stag, whose spreading antlers
Were his own shade-tree. Golden shone those horns,
And round his glossy neck a string of jewels
Fell to his shoulders, and a silver bubble,
Fastened with little straps, gleamed on his forehead,
With earrings, made of bronze, at either temple.
He had no fear at all, would enter houses,
Let even unfamiliar people pet him,
But most of all he was fond of Cyparissus,
The handsomest youth in Cea. Cyparissus
Would lead the animal to the green pastures,
Beside the running brooks, wreathe garlands for him
Of many-colored flowers, or ride him, bareback,
Guiding him gently with the crimson bridle.
One summer noon-day, when the heat of the sun
Held hot around the seashore, the deer was lying,
Tired, with his body on the grassy ground,
Under a tree's cool shadow, and Cyparissus
Shot him, by some ill luck, with pointed arrow,
And as he saw him dying from the wound,
Wanted to die himself. Apollo offered
Such consolation as he could, advised him
To keep his grief within some proper limit,
But he kept grieving still, and prayed the gods,
As a last boon, to let him grieve forever.
And his blood grew thin from that incessant weeping,
His limbs were green in color, and the hair

Over his snowy forehead, bristled, roughened
Like any bush, rose, tapering, toward Heaven.
Apollo spoke in sorrow : "I shall mourn you,
As you shall mourn for other, an attendant
On all who mourn for their dead." And still the cypress
Remains a tree of mourning.
                                        Such was the grove
Orpheus had drawn to hear him, and the beasts
And birds made a circle around him.
He tried the chords with his thumb, and found the tones
Different but harmonious, and began :
"From Jove, O Muse, my mother, for all things come
From Jove, inspire my song! I have often sung
His power before, his wars against the giants,
His thunderbolts, but now the occasion seeks
A gentler lyre, for I would sing of boys
Loved by the gods, and girls inflamed by love
To things forbidden, and earned punishment."

THE ARABIAN NIGHTS' ENTERTAINMENTS

*King Shahryar and his Brother**

"O my daughter," asked he, "and how shall that profit thee
when thou shalt have thrown away thy life?" and she answered, "O my father it must be, come of it what will!" The
Wazir was again moved to fury and blamed and reproached
her, ending with, "In very deed I fear lest the same befal thee
which befel the Bull and the Ass with the Husbandman."
"And what," asked she, "befel them, O my father?" Whereupon the Wazir began

The Tale of the Bull and the Ass

Know, O my daughter, that there was once a merchant
who owned much money and many men, and who was rich in
cattle and camels; he had also a wife and family and he dwelt
in the country, being experienced in husbandry and devoted to
agriculture. Now Allah Most High had endowed him with
understanding the tongues of beasts and birds of every kind,
but under pain of death if he divulged the gift to any. So he
kept it secret for very fear. He had in his cow-house a Bull
and an Ass each tethered in his own stall one hard by the other.
As the merchant was sitting near hand one day with his servants and his children were playing about him, he heard the
Bull say to the Ass, "Hail and health to thee O Father of
Waking!¹ for that thou enjoyest rest and good ministering;
all under thee is cleanswept and fresh-sprinkled; men wait
upon thee and feed thee, and thy provaunt is sifted barley
and thy drink pure spring-water, while I (unhappy creature!)

* From *The Arabian Nights' Entertainments* or *The Book of a Thous-
and Nights and a Night*, translated by Richard F. Burton, selected by
Bennett A. Cerf for the Modern Library Edition, copyright 1932 by
Bennett A. Cerf. New York: Random House, 1932.

am led forth in the middle of the night, when they set on my neck the plough and a something called Yoke; and I tire at cleaving the earth from dawn of day till set of sun. I am forced to do more than I can and to bear all manner of ill-treatment from night to night; after which they take me back with my sides torn, my neck flayed, my legs aching and mine eyelids sored with tears. Then they shut me up in the byre and throw me beans and crushed-straw, mixed with dirt and chaff; and I lie in dung and filth and foul stinks through the livelong night. But thou art ever in a place swept and sprinkled and cleansed, and thou art always lying at ease, save when it happens, when he mounts thee and rides thee to town and returns with thee forthright. So it happens that I am toiling and distrest while thou takest thine ease and thy rest; thou sleepest while I am sleepless; I hunger still while thou eatest thy fill, and I win contempt while thou winnest good will." When the Bull ceased speaking, the Ass turned towards him and said, "O Broad-o'-Brow, O thou lost one! he lied not who dubbed thee Bull-head, for thou, O father of a Bull, hast neither forethought nor contrivance; thou art the simplest of simpletons, and thou knowest naught of good advisers. Hast thou not heard the saying of the wise :—

> For others these hardships and labours I bear
> And theirs is the pleasure and mine is the care;
> As the bleacher who blacketh his brow in the sun
> To whiten the raiment which other men wear.

But thou, O fool, art full of zeal and thou toilest and moilest before the master; and thou tearest and wearest and slayest thyself for the comfort of another. Hast thou never heard the saw that saith, None to guide and from the way go wide? Thou wendest forth at the call to dawn-prayer and thou returnest not till sundown; and through the livelong day thou endurest all manner hardships; to wit, beating and belabouring and bad language. Now hearken to me, Sir Bull! when they tie thee to thy stinking manger, thou pawest the ground with thy forehand and lashes out with thy hind hoofs and pushest with thy horns and bellowest aloud, so they deem thee contented. And when they throw thee thy fodder thou fallest on it with greed and hastenest to line thy fair fat paunch. But if thou accept my advice it will be better for thee and thou wilt lead an easier life even than mine. When thou goest a-field and they lay the thing called Yoke on thy neck, lie down and rise not again though haply they swinge thee; and, if thou rise, lie down a second time; and when they bring thee home and offer thee thy beans, fall backwards and only sniff at thy meat and withdraw thee and taste it not, and be satisfied with thy crushed straw and chaff; and on this wise feign thou art sick, and cease not doing thus for a day or two days or even three days, so shalt thou have rest from toil and moil." When the Bull heard these words he knew the Ass to be his friend and thanked him, saying, "Right is thy rede;" and prayed that all blessings might requite him, and cried, "O Father Wakener! thou hast made up for my failings." (Now the merchant, O my daughter, understood all that passed between them.) Next day the driver took the Bull, and settling his plough on his neck, made him work as wont; but the Bull began to shirk his ploughing, according to the advice of the Ass, and the ploughman drubbed him till he broke the yoke and made off; but the man caught him and leathered him till he despaired of his life. Not the less, however, would he do nothing but stand still and drop down till the evening. Then the herd led him home and stabled him in his stall; but he drew back from his manger and neither stamped nor ramped nor butted nor bellowed as he was wont to do; whereat the man wondered. He brought him the beans and husks, but he sniffed at them and left them and lay down as far from them as he could and passed the whole night fasting. The peasant came next morning; and, seeing the manger full of beans, the crushed-straw untasted and the ox lying on his back in sorriest plight, with legs outstretched and swollen belly, he was concerned for him, and said, to himself, "By Allah, he hath assuredly sickened, and this is the cause why he would not plough yesterday." Then he went to the merchant and reported, "O my master, the Bull is ailing; he refused his fodder last night; nay more, he hath not tasted a scrap of it this morning." Now the merchant-farmer understood what all this meant, because he had overheard the talk between the Bull and the Ass, so quoth he, "Take that rascal donkey, and set the yoke on his neck, and bind him to the plough and make him do Bull's work." Thereupon the ploughman took the Ass, and worked him through the livelong day at the Bull's task; and, when he failed for weakness, he made him eat stick till his ribs were sore and his sides were sunken and his neck was flayed by the yoke; and when he came home in the evening he could hardly drag his limbs along, either fore-hand or hindlegs. But as for the Bull, he had passed the day lying at full length and had eaten his fodder with an excellent appetite, and he ceased not calling down blessings on the Ass for his good advice, unknowing what had come to him on his account. So when night set in and the Ass returned to the byre the Bull rose up before him in honour, and said, "May good tidings gladden thy heart, O Father Wakener! through thee I have rested all this day and I have eaten my meat in peace and quiet." But the Ass returned no reply, for wrath and heart-burning and fatigue and the beating he had gotten; and he repented with the most grievous of repentance; and quoth he to himself: "This cometh of my folly in giving good counsel; as the saw saith, I was in joy and gladness, nought save my officiousness brought me this sadness. And now I must take thought and put a trick upon him and return him to his place, else I die." Then he went aweary to his manger, while the Bull thanked him and blessed him. And even so, O my daughter, said the Wazir, thou wilt die for lack of wits; therefore sit thee still and say naught and expose not thy life to such stress; for, by Allah, I offer thee the best advice, which cometh of my affection and kindly solicitude for thee. "O my father," she answered, "needs must I go up to this King and be married to him." Quoth he, "Do not this deed;" and quoth she, "Of a truth I will:" whereat he rejoined, "If thou be not silent and bide still, I will do with thee even what the merchant did with his wife." "And what did he?" asked she. Know then, answered the Wazir, that after the return of the Ass the merchant came out on the terrace-roof with his wife and family, for it was a moonlit night and the moon at its full. Now the terrace overlooked the cowhouse and presently, as he sat there with his children playing about him, the trader heard the Ass say to the Bull, "Tell me, O father Broad-o'-Brow, what thou purposest to do to-morrow?" The Bull answered, "What but continue to follow thy counsel, O Aliboron? Indeed it was as good as good could be and it hath given me rest and repose; nor will I now depart from it one tittle: so, when they bring me my meat, I will refuse it and blow out my belly and counterfeit crank." The Ass shook his head and said, "Beware of so doing, O Father of a Bull!" The Bull asked, "Why," and the Ass answered, "Know that I am about to give thee the best of counsel, for verily I heard our owner say to the herd, If the Bull rise not from his place to do his work this morning and if he retire from his fodder this day, make him over to the butcher that he may slaughter him and give his flesh to the poor, and fashion a bit of leather from his hide. Now I fear for thee on account of this. So take my advice ere a calamity befal thee; and when they bring thee thy fodder eat it and rise up and bellow and paw the ground, or our master will assuredly slay thee : and peace be with thee!" Thereupon the Bull arose and lowed aloud and thanked the Ass, and said, "To-morrow I will readily go forth with them;" and he at once ate up all his meat and even licked the manger. (All this took place and the owner was listening to their talk.) Next morning the trader and his wife went to the Bull's crib and sat down, and the driver came and led forth the Bull who, seeing his owner, whisked his tail and brake wind, and frisked about so lustily that the merchant laughed a loud laugh and kept laughing till he fell on his back. His wife asked him, "Whereat laughest thou with such loud laughter as this?"; and he answered her, "I laughed at a secret something which I have heard and seen but cannot say lest I die my death." She returned, "Perforce thou must discover it to me, and disclose the cause of thy laughing even if thou come by thy death!" But he rejoined, "I cannot reveal what beasts and birds say in their lingo for fear I die." Then quoth she. "By Allah, thou liest! this is a mere pretext : thou laughest at none save me, and now thou wouldest hide somewhat from me. But by the Lord of the Heaven! If thou disclose not the cause I will no longer co-habit with thee : I will leave thee at once." And she sat down and cried. Whereupon quoth the merchant, "Woe betide thee! what means thy weeping? Fear Allah and leave these words and query me no more questions." "Needs must thou tell me the cause of that laugh," said she, and he replied, "Thou wottest that when I prayed Allah to vouchsafe me understanding of the tongues of beasts and birds, I made a vow never to disclose the secret to any under pain of dying on the spot." "No matter," cried she, "tell me what secret passed between the Bull and the Ass and die this very hour an thou be so minded;" and she ceased not to importune him till he was worn out and clean distraught. So at last he said,

"Summon thy father and thy mother and our kith and kin and sundry of our neighbours," which she did; and he sent for the Kazi and his assessors, intending to make his will and reveal to her his secret and die the death; for he loved her with love exceeding because she was his cousin, the daughter of his father's brother, and the mother of his children, and he had lived with her a life of an hundred and twenty years. Then, having assembled all the family and the folk of his neighbourhood, he said to them, "By me there hangeth a strange story, and 'tis such that if I discover the secret to any, I am a dead man." Therefore quoth every one of those present to the woman, "Allah upon thee, leave this sinful obstinacy and recognise the right of this matter, lest haply thy husband and the father of thy children die." But she rejoined, "I will not turn from it till he tell me, even though he come by his death." So they ceased to urge her; and the trader rose from amongst them and repaired to an outhouse to perform the Wuzu-ablution, and he purposed thereafter to return and to tell them his secret and to die. Now, daughter Shahrazad, that merchant had in his outhouses some fifty hens under one cock, and whilst making ready to farewell his folk he heard one of his many farm-dogs thus address in his own tongue the Cock, who was flapping his wings and crowing lustily and jumping from one hen's back to another and treading all in turn, saying "O Chanticleer! how mean is thy wit and how shameless is thy conduct! Be he disappointed who brought thee up? Art thou not ashamed of thy doings on such a day as this?" "And what," asked the Rooster, "hath occurred this day?", when the Dog answered, "Dost thou not know that our master is this day making ready for his death? His wife is resolved that he shall discolse the secret taught to him by Allah, and the moment he so doeth he shall surely die. We dogs are all a-mourning; but thou clapest thy wings and clarionest

thy loudest and treadest hen after hen. Is this an hour for
pastime and pleasuring? Art thou not ashamed of thyself?"
"Then by Allah," quoth the Cock, "is our master a
lack-wit and a man scanty of sense: if he cannot manage
matters with a single wife, his life is not worth pro-
longing. Now I have some fifty Dame Partlets; and I please
this and provoke that and starve one and stuff another; and
through my good governance they are all well under my control. This our master pretendeth to wit and wisdom, and he
hath but one wife, and yet knoweth not how to manage her."
Asked the Dog, "What then, O Cock, should the master do to
win clear of his strait?" "He should arise forthright," answered the Cock, "and take some twigs from yon mulberry-
tree and give her a regular back-basting and rib-roasting till
she cry:—I repent, O my lord! I will never ask thee a question as long as I live! Then let him beat her once more and
soundly, and when he shall have done this he shall sleep free
from care and enjoy life. But this master of ours owns neither
sense nor judgment." "Now, daughter Shahrazad," continued
the Wazir, "I will do to thee as did that husband to that wife."
Said Shahrazad, "And what did he do?" He replied, "When
the merchant heard the wise words spoken by his Cock to his
Dog, he arose in haste and sought his wife's chamber, after
cutting for her some mulberry-twigs and hiding them there;
and then he called to her, "Come into the closet that I may
tell thee the secret while no one seeth me and then die." She
entered with him and he locked the door and came down upon
her with so sound a beating of back and shoulders, ribs, arms
and legs, saying the while, "Wilt thou ever be asking questions,
about what concerneth thee not?" that she was well nigh
senseless. Presently she cried out, "I am of the repentant!
By Allah, I will ask thee no more questions, and indeed
I repent sincerely and wholesomely." Then she kissed his

hand and feet and he led her out of the room submissive
as a wife should be. Her parents and all the company
rejoiced and sadness and mourning were changed into joy
and gladness. Thus the merchant learnt family discipline from
his Cock and he and his wife lived together the happiest of
lives until death. And thou also, O my daughter! continued
the Wazir, "Unless thou turn from this matter I will do by
thee what that trader did to his wife." But she answered him
with much decision, "I will never desist, O my father, nor
shall this tale change my purpose. Leave such talk and tattle.
I will not listen to thy words and, if thou deny me, I will
marry myself to him despite the nose of thee. And first I will
go up to the King myself and alone and I will say to him : —
I prayed my father to wive me with thee, but he refused, being
resolved to disappoint his lord, grudging the like of me to the
like of thee." Her father asked, "Must this needs be?" and she
answered, "Even so." Hereupon the Wazir being weary of
lamenting and contending, persuading and dissuading her, all
to no purpose, went up to King Shahryar and, after blessing
him and kissing the ground before him, told him all about his
dispute with his daughter from first to last and how he designed to bring her to him that night. The King wondered
with exceeding wonder; for he had made an especial exception
of the Wazir's daughter, and said to him, "O most faithful of
Counsellors, how is this? Thou wottest that I have sworn by
the Raiser of the Heavens that after I have gone into her this
night I shall say to thee on the morrow's morning :—Take
her and slay her! and, if thou slay her not, I will slay thee
in her stead without fail." "Allah guide thee to glory and
lengthen thy life, O King of the age," answered the Wazir,
"it is she that hath so determined : all this I have told her
and more; but she will not hearken to me and she persisteth
in passing this coming night with the King's Majesty." So

Shahryar rejoiced greatly and said, " 'Tis well; go get her ready and this night bring her to me." The Wazir returned to his daughter and reported to her the command saying, "Allah make not thy father desolate by thy loss!" But Shahrazad rejoiced with exceeding joy and gat ready all she required and said to her younger sister, Dunyazad, "Note well what directions I entrust to thee! When I have gone into the King I will send for thee and when thou comest to me and seest that he hath had his carnal will of me, do thou say to me :—O my sister, an thou be not sleepy, relate to me some new story, delectable and delightsome, the better to speed our waking hours; and I will tell thee a tale which shall be our deliverance, if so Allah please, and which shall turn the King from his blood-thirsty custom." Dunyazad answered "With love and gladness." So when it was night their father the Wazir carried Shahrazad to the King who was gladdened at the sight and asked, "Hast thou brought me my need?" and he answered, "I have." But when the King took her to his bed and fell to toying with her and wished to go in to her she wept; which made him ask, "What aileth thee?" She replied, "O King of the age, I have a younger sister and lief would I take leave of her this night before I see the dawn." So he sent at once for Dunyazad and she came and kissed the ground between his hands, when he permitted her to take her seat near the foot of the couch. Then the King arose and did away with his bride's maidenhead and the three fell asleep. But when it was midnight Shahrazad awoke and signalled to her sister Dunyazad who sat up and said, "Allah upon thee, O my sister, recite to us some new story, delightsome and delectable, wherewith to while away the waking hours of our latter night." "With joy and goodly gree," answered Shahrazad, "if this pious and auspicious King permit me." "Tell on," quoth the King who chanced to be sleepless and restless and therefore was pleased with the prospect of hearing her story. So Shahrazad rejoiced; and thus, on the first night of the Thousand Nights and a Night, she began her recitations.

Notes

1.   Arab. "Abu Yakzan" = the Wakener; because the ass brays at dawn—Burton's note.

GIAMBATTISTA BASILE

Seventh Diversion

of the Fourth Day

*The Two Cakes**[1]

Marziella, having shown kindness to an old woman, is given a charm; but her aunt, envious of her good fortune, throws her into the sea, where she is kept imprisoned for a long time by a siren. After some time she is set free by her brother, she becomes a Queen, and the aunt receives due punishment for her crime.

The Prince and Princess would certainly have said that this story of Antonella's surpassed[2] all those previously narrated, had they not feared to discourage Ciulla, who, having rested the lance of her tongue, now hit[3] the mark of Thaddeus' and his wife's taste in the following manner :

I have always heard it said that to give pleasure is to receive pleasure : the bell of Manfredonia says, "Give me, and I will give to you."[4] He who does not bait the hook of affection with kindness and courtesy will not catch the fish of favour. If you wish to hear the proof of this, listen to this story, and then say if the miser does not lose more than the generous man.

Once upon a time there were two sisters, Lucida and Troccola, who each had a daughter, one called Marziella and the other Puccia. Marziella was as fair to behold as she was good at heart. But the heart and face of Puccia, in following the same rule, had formed, on the contrary, a crabbed face and

* From *The Pentamerone of Giambattista Basile*, translated from the Italian of Bendetto Croce, ed. by N. M. Penzer, 2 vols., London : E. P. Dutton and Company, 1932.

157

pestilential heart; and in this she was like her parents, for Troccola was a harpy within and without.

It happened one day that Lucida, who wanted to boil a few parsnips to fry them up afterwards with some green sauce, said to her daughter: "Marziella, my darling, go to the fountain and fetch me a pitcherful of water." "Willingly, my mother," replied the daughter, "but if you love me give me a cake, for I should like to eat one with that fresh water." "Certainly," said her mother, and took out of a basket hanging on a nail a nice cake (for they had had the oven on for baking the day before), which she gave to Marziella. Then Marziella, putting the pitcher on her head on a little pad, went to the fountain, which, like a charlatan on a marble bench, to the sound of falling water, was selling the secrets which drive away thirst.

Whilst she was filling the pitcher, there came an old woman acting the tragedy of Time on the stage of her great hunchback. Seeing the nice cake Marzialla held in her hand and was just about to bite, the old woman said: "My pretty one, give me a bit of that cake, and may Heaven send you good fortune." Marziella, with the manners of a Queen, replied: "Here, you shall have it all, my good old woman; I am only sorry it is not made of sugar and almonds, for I would still give it to you with all my heart."

The old woman, having thus tasted of Marziella's kindness, said to her: "Go, and may Heaven always prosper you for the goodness you have shown me. I pray all the stars that you may be contented and happy; that as you breathe, roses and jessamines may come out of your mouth; that when you comb your hair, pearls and garnets may fall from your head; that when you put your feet to the ground, violets and lilies may spring up."

The young girl thanked her and went home, where, when

her mother had done the cooking, they satisfied nature's debt to the body. The next morning, when the Sun had set out in the market-place of the celestial fields his merchandise of light, brought from the Orient, Marziella in putting up her hair again, saw pearls and garnets raining down into her lap. Joyfully she called her mother and together they picked up the jewels and put them in a basket and went to a jeweller, a friend of Lucida's, to sell him some.

In the meantime, Troccola came to visit her sister, and finding Marziella bustling about over the pearls, she asked her how and when they had come into her possession. And the young girl, who never stirred up mud in a clear stream, and perhaps did not know that proverb which says: "Do not use all your strength, do not eat as much as you would like, do not spend all you have, do not tell all you know," let out the whole story to her aunt.

She had not finished her story when the aunt, without waiting for her sister, ran back to her own house, gave a cake to her daughter, and sent her off to the fountain. Puccia found the same old woman there; but when she was asked for a piece of cake she replied: "As if I should think of giving the cake to you! Do you take me for an ass, asking me for my own things? Look you, our teeth are nearer than our relatives." So saying, she gobbled up the cake in four mouthfuls, making the old woman's mouth water. When she saw the last piece, and with it all hope, disappear, the old woman, in a perfect frenzy of rage, said: "Begone! and whenever you breathe may you foam at the mouth like the doctor's mule;⁵ when you comb your hair may lice in swarms fall from your head; wherever you set foot may bracken and thistles spring up."

When Troccola saw her daughter returning with the water she was all impatience to begin combing her hair. She spread out a fine large towel on her lap, and bent her head over it, but as soon as she began to use the comb on her daughter's head there fell from it a shower of those little alchemistic animals which can even stop quicksilver.⁶ Words cannot describe the state of the mother; flames and smoke came from her nostrils and mouth as she added the fire of her wrath to the snow of envy.

Now it happened shortly after this that Ciommo, the brother of Marziella, was at the court of the King of Chiunzo,⁷ and that they were discussing the charms of various ladies, when he, without being asked, joined in the conversation, saying that if his sister were to appear, all the other ladies might as well go and throw bones over the bridge;⁸ for besides the beauty of her person, which was the counterpoint to the *canto fermo* of her beautiful nature, she possessed in her hair, in her mouth, and in her feet a charm given to her by a fairy. When the King heard this boast he bade Ciommo bring his sister before him, saying that if he found her such as she had been described he would take her for his wife.

Ciommo thought that this was not an opportunity to lose, and sent a special messenger to his mother to tell her what had happened and to beg her to come at once with her daughter and not to let slip this good fortune. Lucida was not very well, and, without realising that she was delivering the sheep to the wolf, asked her sister to accompany Marziella to the court of Chiunzo for this particular business, and Troccola, seeing that things were going just as she wished, promised to conduct the young girl safely to her brother.

She embarked on a ship, taking with her both Marziella and Puccia; but in the middle of the sea, choosing a moment when the sailors were asleep, she pushed Marziella into the water. The unfortunate girl was on the point of drowning, when a beautiful siren caught her in her arms and carried her off.

When Troccola arrived at Chiunzo, Ciommo, who, owing to his long separation from his sister, had forgotten her appearance, received Puccia as if she had been Marziella, and at once took her before the King. He ordered that her hair should be combed, and saw falling out of it those little animals,' the enemies of truth which always annoy witnesses; he looked into her face and saw that, breathing heavily from the fatigue of her journey, she had foamed so much at the mouth that it looked like a soapy wash-tub; he glanced on the ground, and his stomach was turned by the sight of the fetid plants at her feet. In a fury he drove Puccia and her mother away without further ado, and, to punish Ciommo, sent him to look after the geese belonging to the court. In despair over what had happened, and not knowing how to account for it, Ciommo took the geese into the fields and, letting them wander as they liked along the shore, went into a little straw-covered hut, where he wept and bemoaned his sad fate till it was time to stretch himself out and go to sleep. But whilst the geese were running about on the shore, Marziella came up out of the water and fed them with sweet pastry and gave them rose-water to drink, so that they all became as big as sheep, and so fat that they could hardly open their eyes. In the evening they would push their way into a little garden just under one of the King's windows and then they would begin to sing :

> Pire, pire, pire !
> Fair is the sun and fair is the moon,
> But the maid who feeds us is fairer still.

The King, hearing this goosy music every evening, sent for Ciommo, and wanted to know what he fed the geese on, to which Ciommo replied : "I give them nothing to eat but the fresh grass of the fields." But the King was not convinced by this answer, and secretly sent a trusty servant to follow Ciommo and see where he took the geese. The servant, following Ciommo's footsteps, saw him go into the little hut, leaving the geese to stray off alone to the sea-shore. When they came to the water's edge Marziella came up out of the sea, and I think that the mother[10] of that blind boy, who, as the poet said, asks no other alms but tears, was not more beautiful as she rose from the waves. The King's servant, quite enchanted and full of wonder, ran back to his master and described to him the beautiful scene he had witnessed on the stage of the shore. The King's curiosity was excited, and he was moved to go to see the spectacle for himself. So the next morning, when the cock, the leader[11] of the birds, had roused them to arm every living soul against Night, the King followed Ciommo when he went off with the geese to the usual place, and never once lost sight of him. Ciommo stopped in the little straw hut, and the geese went on towards the shore, where the King saw Marziella come out of the water and give the geese a basketful of sweet-meats and a bowl of rose-water. Then she seated herself on a rock and began to comb her hair, from which fell pearls and garnets in handfuls, and at the same time a cloud of flowers came from her mouth and at her feet there lay a Syrian carpet of lilies and violets.

The King called Ciommo and asked him if he knew the beautiful girl. Ciommo, recognising his sister, ran to embrace her, and in the presence of the King heard all the story of Troccola's treachery, and how the envy of that ugly old pest had driven this fair flame of love to dwell beneath the waters of the sea.

Words cannot describe the joy of the King at finding so fair a jewel; turning to her brother, he said that with good reason he had praised her so much, and that he found her two-thirds more beautiful even than he had described, so that he deemed her more worthy to become his wife if she would deign to accept his sceptre and kingdom.

"Oh, would that Sol in Leo would grant it, and that I might come and serve you as the slave of your crown!" replied Marziella. "But do you not see this chain of gold fastened to my foot? With this the siren holds me prisoner, and if I take too much air and stay too long on the shore she drags me back to the rich slavery in which I am held by a golden chain."

"What remedy could there be," said the King, "which would free you from the clutches of this siren?"

"The remedy would be to sever the chain by filing it silently and to slip me out of it," answered Marziella.

"Wait till to-morrow morning," said the King, "and I will come, prepared with the tool, and will carry you back with me to my home, where you shall be my right eye, the child of my heart, and the entrails of my soul."

And, touching hands as an earnest of their love, she went back into water and he into fire—into such fire that he had not a moment's rest from it the whole day. And when that black hag, Night, came out to dance the tubba-catubba[12] with the stars, he did not close his eyes, but ruminated with the jaws of his memory the beauties of Marziella, reviewing all the marvels of her hair, the miracle of her mouth and the bewilderment of her feet; and testing the gold of her charms on the touchstone of his judgment, he found it was twenty-four carat gold. He cursed Night for tarrying so long at the embroidery she was making with the stars, and he cursed the Sun for not coming sooner with his load of light, and that he might enrich his house with the longed-for wealth, that he might bring back to his room the mine of gold-producing pearls, the pearl-shell from which flowers sprang.

But whilst he was thus lost in a sea of thoughts, thinking of her who dwelt in the sea, behold the sappers of the Sun appeared to make smooth the road along which he must pass with the army of his rays. Then the King dressed himself and went, in company with Ciommo, to the sea-shore. And here, when Marziella came up from the waves, with the file he had brought, and with his own hand, he severed the chain from the foot of his beloved, though by this very act he was forging a still stronger chain for his own heart. Setting her on the saddle behind him—she who already rode in his heart—he set off for the royal palace, where Marziella found, by the King's command, all the most beautiful ladies of the country waiting to receive her and to honour her as their mistress.

At the festival which took place when the King married Marziella, Troccola was thrown into the flames amongst the many barrels to which they set fire for the illuminations. In this way she paid the penalty of her treachery to Marziella. Lucida, who was sent for, came to the court and lived in princely fashion with Ciommo; but Puccia was driven out of the kingdom to wander about as a beggar; because she would not sow a little cake she now reaped the reward of always being in want of bread, for :

He who feels no pity will find no pity.

Notes

1. *Pizelle*, the Neapolitan name for a certain kind of little cake, can be traced in other parts of Italy in *pizzerie* and *pizze alla napoletana*.

2. *Passava battaglia*, which in Italian, as well as in Neapolitan, means "to surpass" or "conquer."

3. A metaphor taken from the ring game.

4. Text: *dotti* for *ti do*. On the subject of words suggested by the sound of bells, see Pitre, *Bibl.*, Vol. XIV. pp. 408–12, and in Tuscan, Nerucci, in *Arch. per lo studio delle tradizioni popolari*, Vol. III. p. 295. In French see the comments on *Pantagruel*, III, 27, where reference is made to the "sayings" of the bell of varenals.

5. Doctors used at that time, as is known, to go about on mules surrounded by their assistants or apprentices on foot.

6. Mercury was used as a remedy for head lice; in this case the quantity would have proved too much for the ointment!

7. "Sinneco de Chiunzo," says Basile in the First eclogue of the *Muse napolitane*, was a personage who thought a great deal of himself. A mountain near Tramonti was called Chiunzo, and this name gave rise to proverbial sayings: see Amalfi, *Tradizione ed usi nella penisola sorrentina* (Palermo, 1880), p. 128. See also Fasano, *Gerusalemme liberata*, XV, 63.

8. Either the Ricciardo or the Maddalena bridge: see Vol. I. p. 248 n[3].

9. Liebrecht in his notes (Vol. II, p. 258) says he cannot understand why these animals should be the enemies of truth and an annoyance to witnesses; but what they were can easily be guessed from the name which explains the author's ingenious pun. [This I take to be the same pun as we had at the end of Day II. Tale 7 (See note in Vol. I, p. 189 n[1]). The "little animal" must have been the crab-louse *(Phthirius pubis)*. If so, the pun is not apt, because the head-louse, or nit *(Pediculus capitis)* is never found on the body—but perhaps lice were less particular in Basile's day!]

10. Venus.

11. "Capipopoli," leaders of the populace, were well known to the Neapolitans. One of these was the Fucillo, who was strangled by the order of the viceroy Pietro di Toledo and then exhibited to the gaze of insurgents (See *Arch. stor. nap.*, Vol XV. pp. 593 *et seqq.*). There were later some who agitated in the time of the viceroy Ossuna, and were the forerunners of Masaniello.

12. Another allusion to the dance of the "Sfessania."

Day IV. Tale 7.—This tale contains the "True bride" *motif*, of which many versions are found in Italy and elsewhere. . . .

The tale resembles Grimm 135; while in Grimm 24 we have the beautiful girl who is polite, and the ugly one that is rude. . . .

See also Kohler, *Kleine Schriften*, Vol. I. pp. 62, 125; and Bolte and Polivka, Vols. I. p. 215, and III. p. 88.

N. M. PENZER

The Frame-Story*

In this section of Appendix B we shall consider very briefly the nature and use of a Frame-story. The subject is one that has not yet been scientifically treated. It is generally agreed that the idea of stringing together a series of stories by means of one Main Story is of Eastern origin, that the idea gradually travelled westwards, was used by Boccaccio in his *Decamerone,* and subsequently by the lesser Italian novelists of the fifteenth and sixteenth centuries.

It is impossible, however, to dismiss the subject as easily as that, for there are many queries that still remain unanswered. In the first place, then, we must ask ourselves whether the Frame-story was a device peculiar to the East or if it is possible to trace its use in European collections in no way dependent on Oriental sources.

We have no definite proof that Boccaccio *did* get the idea from the East. He knew no Arabic, and the *Arabian Nights* was unknown to Europe till the beginning of the eighteenth century. It is quite possible that his wish in some way to introduce Fiammetta into the *Decamerone* was sufficient to prompt the creation of the Frame-story that he adopted. At the same time, there were several collections of stories obtainable in Italy in the fourteenth century which did contain a Frame-story, *e.g.* the earliest complete collection of Oriental tales known to the Western world—the *Disciplina Clericalis* of Peter Alphonse. We might also mention the *Dialogus Miraculorum* of Caesarius of Heisterbach (c. 1230) and the *Gesta Romanorum* which made its appearance about the end of the thirteenth century. Now, in the case of Caesarius, we have an

* By N. M. Penzer in *The Pentamerone of Giambattista Basile,* translated from the Italian of Bendetto Croce, ed. by N. M. Penzer, 2 vols., London: E. P. Dutton and Company, 1932.

interesting proof of the individual use of practically the same kind of Frame-story as was used in a very old collection of Indian tales entirely unknown to Europe until the last century. I refer to the *Jataka*. In this famous collection, dating back to the third century B.C., the Buddha is represented as telling in the first place a "Story of the Present," followed by a "Story of the Past," which explains to his followers the reasons for the incidents in the "Story of the Present." It usually points a moral, and in this respect resembles the "Exempla" of mediaeval times.

In the same way Caesarius invented a Frame in the form of a dialogue in which the Novices seek light on a present-day matter, whereupon the Master explains it by telling a story. This is repeated just as in the *Jataka*.

Turning to our own country, we may well ask if Chaucer's Frame-story was his own invention. Certainly he may have copied the idea from Boccaccio or have read any of the collections with some kind of a Frame then in manuscript form. But here again we are reduced to guesswork and can give no definite proofs one way or the other. Bearing these facts in mind, then, it would seem unwise to jump to the conclusion that the Frame-story was the invention of the East and of the East alone.

In the second place, we must consider *the reason* for the Frame-story. Was it just a clever literary trick, introduced to present the collection as a closely-knit whole; or has it some more practical meaning?

Let us examine a few of the best-known Sankskrit collections and see what forms the Frame takes. In the world-famous *Panchatantra*, composed some time during the first 500 years A.D., the King, Amarasakti, is in despair at the appalling ignorance of his three sons. A wise Brahman, named Vishnu-sarman, undertakes to make them completely versed in the

science of polity within the space of six months. This he does
by the means of stories arranged into five separate Books.
Success crowns his efforts, and everyone is happy. Each Book,
however, has a distinct Frame-story of its own enclosing fifteen,
four, ten, one, and two tales respectively. These Frame-stories
reappear continually, so that we have no chance of forgetting
that the other tales are only secondary, and merely introduced
as examples to explain some point or other. But in the case of
the chief Frame-story, matters are different, and we hear no
more of Vishnusarman. Thus the *Panchatantra* provides two
varieties of Frame-story, neither of which resembles the form
adopted by Boccaccio, where the company reappears after
each group of ten tales told by one of them. A point we should
not miss is that the scheme of Boccaccio was simple, whereas
most of the Eastern ones are more elaborate and original.
Take, for instance, the *Dasakumaracharita* of Dandin (c. A.D.
650). Here the ten princes become lost, and when they are
reunited, each relates his adventures. Thus a unity to the
collection is cleverly established. But much more elaborate is
the Frame of the *Vetalapanchavimsati,* or *Twenty-five (tales)
of a Vetala* (or Vampire). King Trivikramasena receives daily
a fruit from an ascetic, and by pure chance discovers that each
contains a jewel. In return for this, the King promises to help
the ascetic. Consequently he goes to the cemetery and attempts
to remove the dead body of a man which the ascetic wants for
some reason or other. The King, however, discovers that the
body is hanging on a tree and tenanted by a demon. After
some trouble he takes it off on his shoulder, whereupon the
Vetala begins telling a story that ends with a question, but as
soon as the King tries to reply to it, the Vetala drops from his
shoulder, and is once more on the tree. Again the King fetches
it and commences his journey, but again it tells a story with a
question. This happens twenty-four times, till finally the King

does *not* speak, and the Vetala is in the power of the King. The same Frame-story also occurs in the *Vikrama-charita* (see Edgerton's fine edition, Harvard University Press, 2 vols., 1926), another of the Vikram cycles of tales dating back to the eleventh century A.D.

Finally we can glance at Somadeva's *Katha sarit sagara* (edited by myself in 10 vols., 1924–28, as the *Ocean of Story*). This mighty collection has for its Frame the History of Udayana, King of Vatsa, and his son Naravahanadatta. Unlike many other Frames, it is not a short introductory tale, but is a portion of the great cycle of Udayana legends known throughout India at the beginning of the Christian era, and adopted by Gunadhya about A.D. 500 in his *Brhatkatha,* the lost original of Somadeva's version (as well as of those of two other authors, Budhasvamin and Kshemendra). Somadeva has used the story of Udayana to introduce all his mass of sub-stories by making the chief characters in it relate tales to enliven the journey of the King or to help dissipate his worries. Thus it runs throughout the work, and, except when whole cycles of stories are introduced, is always in evidence. This, again, is quite unlike the forms taken by the Frame-stories in European collections. It is of considerable interest to note that the *Ocean of Story* contains (Vol. V. pp. 120 *et seqq.*) an early version of the tale that in later years was to appear as part of the Frame to the *Thousand Nights and a Night.* The full history of this great Moslem collection still remains to be written, although the researches of my friend Rev. D. B. Macdonald have done much to clear the ground. As the great French folklorist Cosquin has shown ("Le Prologue, Cadre des milles et une Nuits," *Revue Biblique,* Jan.-April 1909, and *Etudes Folkloriques,* 1922, pp. 265–347), each of the three distinct elements in the Frame of the *Nights* is of Indian origin. After leaving India it was first all used as the Frame to the

Persian *Hazar Afsana,* or "The Thousand Stories." From this an Arabic version was made, and finally stories of Arabic origin took the place of the Persian ones, but the original Frame remained practically unchanged. And this is the well-known story of King Shahryar and the Wazir's daughter Shahrazad, who saved her life by leaving her stories unfinished each night and so rousing the curiosity of the King. It is quite possible that this *motif* helps us to see why the Frame-story is such a favourite in the East, and why its creation must be due to conditions that could never arise in our colder latitudes. Just as Shahrazad was able to keep the King continually interested by her cleverly constructed Frame-story, so the Eastern story teller could ensure a regular audience in the market-place from day to day. Then, another point, no limit was fixed on the number of tales a Frame was to contain, and the story-teller could add or subtract at will. Thus he would vary his tales as occasion demanded. At times the Indian story-teller would travel with his stock-in-trade to the great annual festivals held at Kausambi and Ujjayini, where there would be plenty of opportunity to exhaust his collection. Thus different versions of a well-known cycle of tales would become known in different localities. At times such a collection, or part of one, would be taken westwards with a returning caravan. In most cases the Frame would be remembered, but many of the sub-stories would be forgotten. But others could easily be substituted. This is, as a matter of fact, what actually happened, as the history of the collection known at the *Book of Sindibad* shows.

And so we can more fully appreciate the importance and uses of the Frame-story in the East. With Boccaccio, as with Chaucer, it was merely a clever and charming way to present their collections. Why need we assume that the idea was taken from the East, where the Frames were so elaborate? In conclusion, we must not forget an important fact—Sanskrit literature was unknown to Europe until the beginning of the nineteenth century!

As to Basile, we cannot but conclude that he derived the form of the Frame-story used in his *Il Pentamerone* direct from Boccaccio. It may be that he did not know Straparola, but ignorance of Boccaccio was, of course, impossible.

At the same time, Basile's Frame-story is quite elaborate, and contains, as we have seen, several important *motifs* that in after years were to have a long history in European Marchen.

GESTA ROMANORUM

Of Chastity*

The Emperor Gallus employed a singularly skilful carpenter in the erection of a magnificent palace. At that period, a certain knight lived who had a very beautiful daughter; and who, perceiving the extraordinary sagacity of the artificer, determined to give him the lady in marriage. Calling him, therefore, he said, "My good friend, ask of me what you will; so that it may be possible, I will do it, provided you marry my daughter." The other assented, and the nuptial rites were celebrated accordingly. Then the mother of the lady said to the carpenter, "My son, since you have become one of our family, I will bestow upon you a curious shirt. It possesses this singular property, that as long as you and your wife are faithful to each other, it will neither be rent nor worn, nor stained. But if—which Heaven forbid!—either of you prove unfaithful, instantly it will lose its virtue." The carpenter, very happy in what he heard, took the shirt, and returned great thanks for the gift.

A short while afterward, the carpenter being sent for to superintend the building of the emperor's palace, took with him the valuable present which he had received. He continued absent until the structure was complete; and numbers, observing how much he laboured, admired the freshness and spotless purity of his shirt. Even the emperor condescended to notice it, and said to him, "My master, how is it that in despite of your laborious occupation, and the constant use of your shirt, it still preserves its colour and beauty?" "You must know, my Lord," said he, "that as long as my wife and I continue faithful to each other, my shirt retains its original whiteness and

* *Gesta Romanorum*, translated by Charles Swan, revised by Wynnard Hooper, London: George Bell & Sons, 1877. "Of Fidelity" also from *Gesta Romanorum*.

172

beauty; but if either of us forget our matrimonial vows, it will
sully like any other cloth." A soldier, overhearing this, thought
within himself, "If I can I will make you wash your shirt."
Wherefore, without giving any cause of suspicion to the carpenter, he secretly hastened to his house, and solicited his wife
to dishonour. She received him with an appearance of pleasure, and seemed to be entirely influenced by the same feelings.
"But," added she, "in this place we are exposed to observation;
come with me, and I will conduct you into a private chamber." He followed her, and closing the door, she said, "Wait
here awhile; I will return presently." Thus she did every day,
all the time supplying him only with bread and water. Without regard to his urgency, she compelled him to endure this
humiliating treatment; and before long, two other soldiers
came to her from the emperor's court, with the same evil
views. In like manner, she decoyed them into the chamber,
and fed them with bread and water.

The sudden disappearance, however, of the three soldiers
gave rise to much inquiry; and the carpenter, on the completion of his labours, received the stipulated sum, and returned
to his own home. His virtuous wife met him with joy, and
looking upon the spotless shirt, exclaimed, "Blessed be God!
our truth is made apparent there is not a single stain upon the
shirt." To which he replied, "My beloved, during the progress
of the building, three soldiers, one after another, came to ask
questions about the shirt. I related the fact, and since that time
nothing has been heard of them." The lady smiled, and said,
"The soldiers respecting whom you feel anxious thought me
a fit subject for their improper solicitation, and came hither
with the vilest intent. I decoyed them into a remote chamber,
and have fed them with bread and water." The carpenter,
delighted with this proof of his wife's fidelity, spared their lives,

and liberated them; and he and his wife lived happily for the rest of their lives.

Application

My beloved, the emperor is God; the palace is the human heart. The knight who married his daughter to the carpenter is Christ; the carpenter is any good Christian, and the mother is the Church. The shirt is faith; and three soldiers are pride, lusts of the eyes, and lusts of the heart.

Of Fidelity

The subject of a certain king fell into the hands of pirates, and wrote to his father for ransom. But the father would not redeem him; so the youth wasted away in prison. Now, he who detained him in chains had a daughter of great beauty and virtue. She was at this time in her twentieth year, and frequently visited the young man with the hope of alleviating his griefs. But he was too disconsolate to hearken. It one day fell out that, while the damsel was with him, the youth said to her, "Oh, that you would try to set me free, kind maiden." She replied, "But how am I to effect it? Thy father, thine own father, will not ransom thee; on what ground then should I, a stranger, attempt it? And suppose that I were induced to do so, I should incur the wrath of my parent, because thine denies the price of thy redemption. Nevertheless, on one condition thou shalt be liberated." "Kind damsel," returned he, "impose what thou wilt; so that it be possible, I will accomplish it." "Promise, then," said she, "to marry me, whenever the opportunity may occur." "I promise," said the youth, joyfully, "and plight thee a faith that shall never be broken." The girl straightway set him free from his bonds, without her father's knowledge, and fled with him to his own country. When they arrived, the father of the youth welcomed him, and said, "Son, I am overjoyed at thy return; but who is the lady under thy escort?" He replied, "It is the daughter of a king, to whom I am bethrothed." The father returned, "On pain of losing thy inheritance, I charge thee, marry her not." "My father," exclaimed the youth, "what hast thou said? My obligations to her are greater than they are to you; for when imprisoned and fettered by my enemy, I implored you to ransom me; but you would not. Now, she not only released me from prison, but from deadly peril—and, therefore, I am resolved to marry her." The father answered, "Son, I tell thee that thou canst not confide in her, and consequently ought not to espouse her. She deceived her own father, when she liberated thee from prison; for this did her father lose the price of thy ransom. Therefore, I am of opinion that thou canst not confide in her, and consequently ought not to espouse her. Besides, there is another reason. It is true she liberated thee, but it was for the gratification of her passions, and in order to oblige thee to marry her. And, since an unworthy passion was the source of thy liberty, I think that she ought not to be thy wife." When the lady heard such reasons assigned, she answered, "To your first objection, that I deceived my own parent, I reply that it is not true. He deceives who takes away or diminishes a certain good. But my father is so rich that he needs not any addition. When, therefore, I had maturely weighed this matter, I procured the young man's freedom. And if my father had received a ransom for him, he had been but little richer; while you would have been utterly impoverished. Now, in acting thus, I have served you, who refused the ransom, and have done no injury to my parent. As for your last objection, that an unworthy passion urged me to do this, I assert that it is false. Feelings of such nature arise either from great personal beauty, or from wealth, or honours; or finally, from a robust appearance. None of which qualities your son possessed. For imprisonment had destroyed his beauty; and he had not sufficient wealth even to effect his liberation; while much anxiety had worn away his strength, and left him emaciated and sickly. Therefore, compassion rather persuaded me to free him." When the father had heard this, he could object nothing more. So his son married the lady with very great pomp, and closed his life in peace.[1]

Application.

My beloved, the son captured by pirates is the whole human race, led by the sin of our first parent into the prison of the devil—that is, into his power. The father who would not redeem him is the world, which aids not man's escape from the evil one, but rather loves to detain him in thraldom. The

---

[1] The deliverance of the youth by the lady resembles the 236th Night of the Arabian Tales.—The *Gest* is mentioned by Warton as the *second* tale in his analysis; and two or three other variations occur. What edition he followed I know not. I have examined five. The sentiment conveyed by this tale (p. 9), that she who has deceived her father will deceive her husband, is thus expressed by Shakespeare:—

> "Look to her, Moor; have a quick eye to see;
> She has deceived her father, and may thee."
>
> *Othello,* Act i. Sc. 3.

In an 18mo edition of the *Gesta Romanorum,* published at Leyden, 1555, there is prefixed to the fourth tale, by way of argument, the following remarkable passage: "Justitia nempe et misericordia Deorum maximè est: *ad quos non possumus expeditius et proprius accedere, quàm his ducibus."* This is *literally* what Shakespeare makes Portia observe in the *Merchant of Venice"*—

> "But Mercy is above this sceptered sway,
>
> *   *   *   *   *
>
> It is an attribute of God Himself;
> And earthly power doth then show likest God's,
> When mercy seasons justice."—Act iv. Sc. 1.

daughter who visited him in prison is the Divinity of Christ united to the soul; who sympathized with the human species— and who, after His passion, descended into hell and freed us from the chains of the devil. But the celestial Father had no occasion for wealth, because He is infinitely rich and good. Therefore Christ, moved with compassion, came down from heaven to visit us, and took upon Himself our form, and required no more than to be united in the closest bonds with man. So *Hosea* ii : "I will marry her to me in faithfulness." But our father, the world, whom many obey, ever murmurs and objects to this. "If thou unitest thyself to God, thou shalt lose my inheritance"—that is, the inheritance of this world; because it is "impossible to serve God and mammon." *Matt.* vi. : "He who shall leave father, or mother, or wife, or country for my sake, he shall receive an hundredfold, and possess everlasting life." Which may Jesus Christ, the Son of the living God, vouchsafe to bestow upon us; who with the Father, and the Holy Ghost, liveth and reigneth for ever and ever. Amen.

THOMAS HARDY

The Discovery*

The distant light which Eustacia had cursorily observed on leaving the house came, as she had divined, from the cottage-window of Susan Nunsuch. What Eustacia did not divine was the occupation of the woman within at that moment. Susan's sight of her passing figure earlier in the evening, not five minutes after the sick boy's exclamation, 'Mother, I do feel so bad!' persuaded the matron that an evil influence was certainly exercised by Eustacia's propinquity.

On this account Susan did not go to bed as soon as the evening's work was over, as she would have done at ordinary times. To counteract the malign spell which she imagined poor Eustacia to be working, the boy's mother busied herself with a ghastly invention of superstition, calculated to bring power-lessness, atrophy, and annihilation on any human being against whom it was directed. It was a practice well known on Egdon at that date, and one that is not quite extinct at the present day.

She passed with her candle into an inner room, where, among other utensils, were two large brown pans, containing together perhaps a hundredweight of liquid honey, the produce of the bees during the foregoing summer. On a shelf over the pans was a smooth and solid yellow mass of a hemi-spherical form, consisting of beeswax from the same take of honey. Susan took down the lump, and, cutting off several thin slices, heaped them in an iron ladle, with which she returned to the living-room, and placed the vessel in the hot ashes of the fireplace. As soon as the wax had softened to the plasticity

* From *The Return of the Native* by Thomas Hardy, copyright 1922 by Harper & Brothers. Reprinted in Harper's Modern Classics, New York, 1922.

of dough she kneaded the pieces together. And now her face became more intent. She began moulding the wax; and it was evident from her manner of manipulation that she was endeavouring to give it some preconceived form. The form was human.

By warming and kneading, cutting and twisting, dismembering and rejoining the incipient image she had in about a quarter of an hour produced a shape which tolerably well resembled a woman, and was about six inches high. Meanwhile she took the candle and went upstairs to where the little boy was lying.

'Did you notice, my dear, what Mrs. Eustacia wore this afternoon besides the dark dress?'

'A red ribbon round her neck.'

'Anything else?'

'No—except sandal-shoes.'

'A red ribbon and sandal-shoes," she said to herself.

Mrs. Nunsuch went and searched till she found a fragment of the narrowest red ribbon, which she took downstairs and tied round the neck of the image. Then fetching ink and a quill from the rickety bureau by the window, she blackened the feet of the image to the extent presumably covered by shoes; and on the instep of each foot marked cross-lines in the shape taken by the sandal-strings of those days. Finally she tied a bit of black thread round the upper part of the head, in faint resemblance to a snood worn for confining the hair.

Susan held the object at arm's length and contemplated it with a satisfaction in which there was no smile. To anybody acquainted with the inhabitants of Egdon Heath the image would have suggested Eustacia Yeobright.

From her work-basket in the window-seat the woman took a paper of pins, of the old long and yellow sort, whose heads were disposed to come off at their first usage. These she began to thrust into the image in all directions, with apparently excruciating energy. Probably as many as fifty were thus inserted, some into the head of the wax model, some into the shoulders, some into the trunk, some upwards through the soles of the feet, till the figure was completely permeated with pins.

She turned to the fire. It had been of turf; and though the high heap of ashes which turf fires produce was somewhat dark and dead on the outside, upon raking it abroad with the shovel the inside of the mass showed a glow of red heat. She took a few pieces of fresh turf from the chimney-corner and built them together over the glow, upon which the fire brightened. Seizing with the tongs the image that she had made of Eustacia, she held it in the heat, and watched it as it began to waste slowly away. And while she stood thus engaged there came from between her lips a murmur of words.

It was a strange jargon—the Lord's Prayer repeated backwards—the incantation usual in proceedings for obtaining unhallowed assistance against an enemy. Susan uttered the lugubrious discourse three times slowly, and when it was completed the image had considerably diminished. As the wax dropped into the fire a long flame arose from the spot, and curling its tongue round the figure ate still further into its substance. A pin occasionally dropped with the wax, and the embers heated it red as it lay.

OLIVER LA FARGE

Laughing Boy*

1. The dance of the second night was much like that of the first, although perhaps a little less exuberant. He entered once more into the river of song, and was happy, yelling his head off, save that he kept on being conscious of that girl. While she was dancing, he would forget about her, but when he saw her looking for another partner, he would be uneasy until she had made her choice. He noticed that she did not dance with Red Man. Halfway between midnight and dawn, the women having departed, he fell out, to sleep by a fire.

They rode down to Ane'e Tseyi that day, where the dance of the final night would be held. He rode behind Jesting Squaw's Son's saddle, leading the mare. He hoped they would find a place with some grass for the animal, and reflected that in any case, now, he could afford to buy corn. The long, hot ride, hot sun, hot wind, unrelieved, weighed on them somewhat, combining with lack of sleep to make limbs sluggish and eyes heavy. It was a relief to ride into the narrow cañon of their destination, to rest in a strip of afternoon shade. Laughing Boy took the horses down to the windmill for water, and staked them out in a corner where uncropped spears of grass stood singly, each inches from the next, in brown sand. A beaten track toward an oak tree and a break in the rock caught his eye. A spring, perhaps.

He followed it. Behind the oak, currant bushes grew in a niche of red rock like the fold of a giant curtain. At the back was a full-grown, lofty fir. A spring, surely. Behind the fir a cleft opened at shoulder height into transparent shadow. The footholds were worn to velvety roundness in the sandstone; at

* From *Laughing Boy* by Oliver La Farge, copyright 1929 and 1957 by Oliver La Farge.

one side a pecked design showed that long before the Navajos had swooped upon the land, a people of an elder earth had known this entrance. Laughing Boy climbed lightly in.

It was a stone-lined pocket, scarce twenty feet across, narrower at the top. One went forward along a ledge at one side, shouldering against young aspens, then slid down a rock face into a curving bowl, with a seep at one lip from which silent water oozed over moss and cress into the bottom. Spears of grass grew in cracks. By the tiny pool of water in the bowl was a square of soft turf with imprints of moccasins. He squatted there, leaning back against the rock. Here was all shade and peace, soft, grey stone, dark, shadowed green, coolness, and the sweet smell of dampness. He dabbled his hands, wet his face, drank a litle. He rolled a cigarette with crumpled cigar tobacco. This was good, this was beautiful.

Away above, the intolerant sky gleamed, and a corner of cloud was white fire. His eyes shifting lightly, the edge of the rocks above took on a glowing halo. He amused himself trying to fit it back again, to get the spot the cloud made back against the cloud, playing tricks with his half-closed eyelashes that made things seem vague.

"*Ahalani!*" The two-toned greeting came from a voice like water.

He returned to himself with a start, Slim Girl stood poised on the edge of the bowl, above his shoulder, water-basket in hand.

"*Ahalani, shicho.*" Dignified, casual.

"Move over, wrestler, I want to come down."

He observed her small feet in their red, silver-buttoned buckskin, sure and light on the rocks as a goat's. She seemed to be hours descending. She was business-like about filling the basket, but she turned utilitarian motions into part of a dance.

Now she knelt, not two feet from him, taking him in with the long, mischievous eyes that talked and laughed.

She is a butterfly, he thought, or a humming-bird. Why does she not go away? I will not go—run away from her. He thought, as he tried to read her face, that her slimness was deceptive; strength came forth from her.

"Now, for ten cents, I go."

He blinked. "I save that to get rid of you to-night, perhaps."

"I do not dance to-night. There is trouble, a bad thing. I come from far away."

He thought he had better not ask questions. "Tomorrow there will be horse-racing, a chicken-pull, perhaps."

"And you have a fine horse to race, black, with a white star and a white sock." He grunted astonishment. She smiled. "You are a good jeweller, they say. You made that bow-guard. You sold Red Man's belt to the American, they say, for sixty-five dollars."

"You are like an old wife, trying to find out about everything a man is doing."

"No, I am not like an old wife."

They looked at each other for a long time. No, she was not like an old wife. Blood pounded in his ears and his mouth was dry. He pulled at the end of his dead cigarette. At length,

"You should stay for the racing. There will be fine horses, a beautiful sight."

"I shall stay, perhaps."

Her rising, her ascent of the rock, were all one quick motion. She never looked back. He stayed, not exactly in thought, but experiencing a condition of mind and feeling. Loud laughter of women roused him, to pass them with averted eyes and go forth dazed into the sunlight.

2.   The last night of the dance was a failure for Laughing Boy, for all its ritual. He tried to join the singing, but they

were not the kind of songs he wanted; he tried to concentrate
on the prayer that was being brought to a climax, but he
wanted to pray by himself. He quit the dance, suddenly very
much alone as he left the noise and the light behind him,
strongly conscious of himself, complete to himself. He followed
a sheep trail up a break in one cañon wall, to the rim, then
crossed the narrow mesa to where he could look down over the
broad Ties Hatsosi Valley, a great pool of night, and far-
distant, terraced horizon to mesas against the bright stars, cool,
alone, with the sound of the drumming and music behind him,
faint as memory. This also was a form of living.

He began to make up a new song, but lost interest in it, feeling too centered upon himself. He sat noticing little things,
whisper of grass, turn of a leaf—little enough there is in the
desert at night.

Yota zhil-de tlin-sha-igahl . . .

His song came upon him.

> *A-a-a-aine, aine,*
> I ride my horse down from the high hills
>   To the valley, *a-a-a.*
> Now the hills are flat. Now my horse will not go
>   From your valley, *a-a-a.*
> *Haineya, aine, o-o-o-o.*

Slim Girl sat down beside him. His song trailed off, embar-
rassed. They rested thus, without words, looking away into the
night while contemplation flowed between them like a current.
At length she raised one hand, so that the bracelets clinked.

"Sing that song."

He sang without effort. This was no common woman, who
ignored all convention. The long-drawn *"Haineya, aine,*

o-o-o-o," fell away into the lake of darkness; silence shut in on them again.

On the heels of his song he said, "My eldest uncle is here. I am going to speak to him to-morrow."

"I should not do that if I were you."

He rolled a cigarette with careful movements, but forebore to light it. Again they sat watching the motionless stars above the shrouded earth. No least breeze stirred; there were no details to be seen in the cliffs or the valley, only the distant silhouettes against the sky. A second time her hand rose and her bracelets clinked, as though speech unannounced would startle the universe.

"You are sure you are going to speak to your uncle, then?"

"Yes." The second self that is a detached mentor in one's mind recognized that he would never have talked this way with any other woman. Etiquette had been left behind down in the narrowness of Ane'c Tscyi.

"Perhaps you will listen to what he says, I think; perhaps you will not. Perhaps your mind is made up now."

"I am thinking about what I intend to do. I shall not change."

"We shall see then. Good-bye."

She rose like smoke. He called a startled "Good-bye," then began to follow at a distance. He stopped at the rim of the cañon, where the noise of singing that welled up from below passed him by as he stood watching her dark form, down to the bottom, along by the grove where his camp was, and beyond into the shadows.

He went back to the far edge of the mesa. He did not want to sleep, not ever again.

> Now with a god I walk,
> Now I step across the summits of the mountains,
> Now with a god I walk,

> Striding across the foothills.
> Now on the old age trail, now on the path of
> beauty wandering.
> In beauty—*Hozoji, hozoji, hozoji, hozoji.*

The deep resonance of the prayer carried his exaltation through the land. Then he began to analyse her words, finding in them nothing save unconventionality, no promise, and his own he found laggard and dull. Was she playing with him, or did she mean all he read into her brevity? Was she thus with other men?

> I ride my horse down from the high hills
> To the valley, *a-a-a* . . .

He was up and down, restless, no longer on the path of beauty, yet tormented by a new beauty. Far away, high-pitched, he heard the faint *"Yo-o galeana, yo-o galeana,"* and the thudding drum. He walked to and fro. My mind is made up, I shall make things as they should be. Now with a god I walk— or is it a game, looseness?

Suddenly he fled to sleep for refuge, rolling in his blanket by a high place under thickly clustered, brilliant, unhelpful stars, falling asleep with the feeling of vastness about him and clean gracious silence.

3.   He woke to a feeling of expectation, and made his Dawn Prayer with all the gladness that his religion prescribed. He could not wait to see his uncle and have the matter settled before they went to the trading post for the races. At the same time, his own certainty told him that his eldest uncle, his mother, and all her kin were only wanted to ratify a decision already made. What was, was; he would announce what he wanted to do, not ask for permission.

Now he stood on the rim above the cañon, bathed in sunlight, while below him in thick, visible shadow unimportant people moved, horses stamped, smoke rose from tiny fires.

His uncle was staying down by the trading post with Killed a Navajo. He started off without breakfast, leading the pony, and sorely tempted to mount and gallop those few miles, but the thought of the race and the pleasure of winning restrained him. I'll win for Slim Girl, he thought with a smile, and burst into song, lustily pouring forth keen delight from tough lungs over the empty flat. The dusty walk and hot sun, the heat that lay over the baked adobe and the dull sage-brush, troubled him not at all. The bleak, grey parts of the desert have a quintessential quality of privacy, and yet one has space there to air one's mood. So Laughing Boy sang loudly, his horse nosed his back, a distant turtle-dove mocked him, and a high-sailing, pendent buzzard gave him up as far too much alive.

Killed a Navajo's hogahn was well built, of thick-laid evergreens over stout piñon poles. Looking in through the wide door one was conscious of cool darkness flecked with tiny spots of light, a central brilliance under the smoke-hole, vague outlines of reclining figures, their feet, stretched towards the centre, grotesquely clear. He stood in the doorway. Some one spoke to him, "Come in." He shook hands all round. They offered him a little coffee, left over from breakfast, and tobacco. He made himself comfortable on the sheepskins beside his uncle in the place of honour.

One by one the family went about their work; the children to tend the sheep, Killed a Navajo down to the store where he did odd jobs, and was needed to-day for distributing free food, his younger wife to preparing a meal for the many guests expected that day, his first wife to weaving, outside. Laughing Boy's cigarette smoke went up in shadow, was caught in a pencil of sunlight, disappeared, and gleamed once again before it seeped through the roof. A suggestion of a breeze rustled the green walls. He studied his uncle's face—big and massive, with heavy, high-bridged nose and deep furrows enclosing the wide sure mouth. Under the blue turban wisps of hair showed a little grey. Across his cheek-bone ran the old scar from which he took his name, Wounded Face. It was an old eagle's head. Laughing Boy was a little afraid of it.

"My uncle."

"Yes, my child." The old-fashioned, round silver earrings shimmered faintly.

"I have been thinking about something."

They smoked on. A black-and-white kid slipped in the door, leaped up and poised itself on the cantle of a saddle. Outside was a rhythmic thump-thump-thump of a weaver pounding down the threads in her loom. A distant child laughed, some one was chopping wood—sounds of domesticity.

"I have been thinking about a wife."

"You are old enough. It is a good thing."

He finished his cigarette.

"You know that Slim Girl? The one who wears so much hard goods? She danced the first two nights."

"She is a school-girl." The tone was final. "She was taken away to that place, for six years."

"That is all right. I like her."

"That is not all right. I do not know how she came to be allowed to dance. They made her stop. Water Singer let her dance, but we stopped him. She is bad. She lives down by the railroad. She is not of the People any more, she is American. She does bad things for the Americans."

"I do not know what you mean, but I know her, that girl. She is not bad. She is good. She is strong. She is for me."

"You come from away up there; you do not know about these things. Nor do you know her. What is her clan?"

"I do not know."

"Well? And what makes you think you can go out and pick a wife for yourself like this? The next thing I know, you will jump into the fire. I tell you, she is all bad; for two bits she will do the worst thing."

Laughing Boy sat up suddenly. "You should not have said that, you should not have thought it. Now you have said too much. I hope that bad thing follows you around always. Now you have said too much. Ugh! This place is too small for me!"

He ran outside. He needed space. People were beginning to arrive; there was laughing and shouting around the trading post. He went off rapidly to get by himself, too proud to run before people. His mind was boiling; he wanted to hit something, he was all confused. This way he went on until at last he reached a small butte that offered protection. He tore around the corner.

Slim Girl was walking towards him, cool and collected. Her brows rose in surprise as she stopped. He came up to her uncertainly.

"Sit down; there is shade here." They faced each other. "You have seen your uncle."

His hand fell forward in the gesture of assent.

"And he spoke to you."

"He said bad things. I am angry with him."

"And towards me?"

"You came here on purpose to meet me."

"Yes; I knew that when you had seen your uncle, you should see me soon."

"What my uncle said will stay with him. He has made a bad thing, it will follow him. The track of an evil thought is crooked and has no end; I do not want it around me; I do not keep it going. I have only good thoughts about you."

"Your mother will never send some one to ask for me. You must just come with me."

"Wait; what is your clan?"

"I am a Bitahni; and you?"

"Tahtchini; so that is all right. But I have nothing to give your mother, only one horse."

"I have no parents; they died when I was at school. I belong to myself. All this"—she raised the necklaces, turquoise, coral, white shell and silver, one by one, then let them fall back together—"is mine. All this"—she touched her rings, and shook her braceleted wrists—"and much more is mine. They left it for me. Now I do a little work for the missionary's wife there at Chiziai; she pays me money, so I grow richer. I shall give you silver to make jewelry, and I shall weave, and you shall have fine horses. You can make money with them, and we shall be rich together."

The long, talking eyes looked into his now, with nothing hidden. He felt her strength, this woman who could talk so straight, who made the direct road seem the only sensible one. It ceased to be strange that they sat and talked about love, while elopement became obvious and commonplace in a scheme of things the whole of which was suddenly miraculous.

After a while she said, "We shall go to-night, after the races."

He reflected. "No, I came here to gamble. I told Red Man I would play against him. If I do not do it, he will say I am afraid."

"He is crooked; he will take your money."

"That makes no difference; I cannot back down now. If I let this go because I was afraid to lose, what would I be? If I refused because of you, what kind of a man should I be for you?"

He saw that he had spoken well.

"It will be time for the races soon; you must go. I go the other way round."

He was in a new and more profound daze returning, but yards that had seemed like miles were passed as inches. He floated over the ground, he was a walking song.

HERMAN MELVILLE

The Booble-Alleys of the Town*

In the evening, especially when the sailors are gathered in great numbers, these streets present a most singular spectacle, the entire population of the vicinity being seemingly turned into them. Hand-organs, fiddles, and cymbals, plied by strolling musicians, mix with the songs of the seamen, the babble of women and children, and the groaning and whining of beggars. From the various boarding-houses, each distinguished by gilded emblems outside—an anchor, a crown, a ship, a windlass, or a dolphin—proceeds the noise of revelry and dancing; and from the open casements lean young girls and old women, chattering and laughing with the crowds in the middle of the street. Every moment strange greetings are exchanged between old sailors who chance to stumble upon a shipmate, last seen in Calcutta or Savannah; and the invariable courtesy that takes place upon these occasions, is to go to the next spirit-vault, and drink each other's health.

There are particular paupers who frequent particular sections of these streets, and who, I was told, resented the intrusion of mendicants from other parts of the town.

Chief among them was a white-haired old man, stone-blind; who was led up and down through the long tumult by a woman holding a little saucer to receive contributions. This old man sang, or rather chanted, certain words in a peculiarly long-drawn, guttural manner, throwing back his head, and turning up his sightless eyeballs to the sky. His chant was a lamentation upon his infirmity; and at the time it produced the same effect upon me, that my first reading of Milton's

* From *Redburn* by Herman Melville, copyright 1957 by Doubleday & Company, Inc., Garden City, New York. "A Sailor a Jack of all Trades" also from *Redburn*.

Invocation to the Sun did, years afterward. I can not recall it all; but it was something like this, drawn out in an endless groan—

"Here goes the blind old man; blind, blind, blind; no more will he see sun nor moon—no more see sun nor moon!" And thus would he pass through the middle of the street; the woman going on in advance, holding his hand, and dragging him through all obstructions; now and then leaving him standing, while she went among the crowd soliciting coppers.

But one of the most curious features of the scene is the number of sailor ballad-singers, who, after singing their verses, hand you a printed copy, and beg you to buy. One of these persons, dressed like a man-of-war's-man, I observed every day standing at a corner in the middle of the street. He had a full, noble voice, like a church-organ; and his notes rose high above the surrounding din. But the remarkable thing about this ballad-singer was one of his arms, which, while singing, he somehow swung vertically round and round in the air, as if it revolved on a pivot. The feat was unnaturally unaccountable; and he performed it with the view of attracting sympathy; since he said that in falling from a frigate's mast-head to the deck, he had met with an injury, which had resulted in making his wonderful arm what it was.

I made the acquaintance of this man, and found him no common character. He was full of marvelous adventures, and abounded in terrific stories of pirates and sea murders, and all sorts of nautical enormities. He was a monomaniac upon these subjects; he was a Newgate Calendar of the robberies and assassinations of the day, happening in the sailor quarters of the town; and most of his ballads were upon kindred subjects. He composed many of his own verses, and had them printed for sale on his own account. To show how expeditious he was at this business, it may be mentioned, that one evening on leaving the dock to go to supper, I perceived a crowd gathered about the *Old Fort Tavern;* and mingling with the rest, I learned that a woman of the town had just been killed at the bar by a drunken Spanish sailor from Cadiz. The murderer was carried off by the police before my eyes, and the very next morning the ballad-singer with the miraculous arm, was singing the tragedy in front of the boarding-houses, and handing round printed copies of the song, which, of course, were eagerly bought up by the seamen.

A Sailor a Jack of all Trades

As I began to learn my sailor duties, and show activity in running aloft, the men, I observed, treated me with a little more consideration, though not at all relaxing in a certain air of professional superiority. For the mere knowing of the names of the ropes, and familiarizing yourself with their places, so that you can lay hold of them in the darkest night; and the loosing and furling of the canvas, and reefing topsails, and hauling braces; all this, though of course forming an indispensable part of a seaman's vocation, and the business in which he is principally engaged; yet these are things which a beginner of ordinary capacity soon masters, and which are far inferior to many other matters familiar to an *"able seaman."*

What did I know, for instance, about *striking a top-gallant-mast,* and sending it down on deck in a gale of wind? Could I have *turned in a dead-eye,* or in the approval nautical style have *clapt a seizing on the main-stay?* What did I know of *"passing a gammoning," "reiving a Burton," "strapping a shoe-block," "clearing a foul hawse,"* and innumerable other intricacies?

The business of a thorough-bred sailor is a special calling, as much of a regular trade as a carpenter's or a locksmith's.

Indeed, it requires considerably more adroitness, and far more versatility of talent.

In the English merchant service boys serve a long apprenticeship to the sea, of seven years. Most of them first enter the Newcastle colliers, where they see a great deal of severe coasting service. In an old copy of the Letters of Junius, belonging to my father, I remember reading, that coal to supply the city of London could be dug at Blackheath, and sold for one half the price that the people of London then paid for it; but the Government would not suffer the mines to be opened, as it would destroy the great nursery for British seamen.

A thorough sailor must understand much of other avocations. He must be a bit of an embroiderer, to work fanciful collars of hempen lace about the shrouds; he must be something of a weaver, to weave mats of rope-yarns for lashings to the boats; he must have a touch of millinery, so as to tie graceful bows and knots, such as *Matthew Walker's roses,* and *Turk's heads;* he must be a bit of a musician, in order to sing out at the halyards; he must be a sort of jeweler, to set dead-eyes in the standing rigging; he must be a carpenter, to enable him to make a jurymast out of a yard in case of emergency; he must be a sempstress, to darn and mend the sails; a ropemaker, to twist *marline* and Spanish foxes; a blacksmith, to make hooks and thimbles for the blocks; in short, he must be a sort of Jack of all trades, in order to master his own. And this, perhaps, in a greater or less degree, is pretty much the case with all things else; for you know nothing till you know all; which is the reason we never know anything.

A sailor, also, in working at the rigging, uses special tools peculiar to his calling—*fids, serving-mallets, toggles, prickers, marlingspikes, palms, heavers,* and many more. The smaller sort he generally carries with him from ship to ship in a sort of canvas reticule.

The estimation in which a ship's crew hold the knowledge of such accomplishments as these, is expressed in the phrase they apply to one who is a clever practitioner. To distinguish such a mariner from those who merely *"hand, reef, and steer,"* that is, run aloft, furl sails, haul ropes, and stand at the wheel, they say he is *"a sailor-man;"* which means that he not only knows how to reef a topsail, but is an artist in the rigging.

ROBERT A. GEORGES

Silone's Use of Folk Beliefs*

There is a dearth of literary criticism about the novels of Ignazio Silone. Those articles and reviews which have appeared sporadically emphasize political doctrines with which Silone has been in sympathy. He is regarded foremost as a political novelist, and his works are interpreted to support this viewpoint.[1]

In addition to this justifiable concern with Silone as communist or Silone as socialist, some critics and reviewers have given at least secondary consideration to his style and artistic development.[2] Significant in any evaluation of Silone as an artist is an analysis of his character presentation, particularly of the *cafoni*, or landless peasants, with whom he is primarily concerned. It is through his depiction of their mores and their everyday lives that Silone captures the peasant mentality. "In his description of the Italian peasants," wrote James T. Farrell, "there is revealed a whole cultural pattern with its background of superstitions, and the effect of this cultural pattern on the mind of the peasantry."[3]

The peasants about whom Silone writes are not romanticized stereotypes, but rather a secluded group from the Abruzzi region in the heart of Italy. There are no great cities in this inaccessible mountain area whose inhabitants have lived in isolation for centuries. "It's a sober folk of feudal traditions, hardworking, taciturn, and deeply religious," wrote one reviewer of a Silone novel.[4]

The Abruzzi, "where automobiles or tax-collectors arrived at their own risk, and the priest came once a year (if at all) on mule back,"[5] is the district in which Silone was born and

* By Robert A. Georges, *Midwest Folklore*, XII, No. 4 (Winter, 1962).

raised. Young Ignazio's contacts with the *cafoni* are described by George Woodcock :

> As a child Silone moved among the poor peasants, went to school with their children, and came early to understand and love them. This love of the poor has remained with him throughout his life, has dominated his actions and given his writings their outstanding quality of sympathy for human suffering.[6]

Silone himself admitted the importance of the Abruzzi and its people for his writing :

> There was a point in my rebellion where hatred and love coincided; both the facts which justified my indignation and the moral motives which demanded it stemmed directly from the district where I was born. This explains, too, why everything I have happened to write up to now, and probably everything I shall ever write, although I have traveled and lived abroad, is concerned solely with this same district or more precisely with the part of it which can be seen from the house where I was born—not more than thirty or forty kilometers on one side or the other.[7]

Not only was Silone well acquainted with the Abruzzi *cafoni* from his earliest days, but he also felt that people like them needed to be the subject for writers. Commenting in 1937 on why literature is not popular in Italy, he said :

> The answer is easy; it is that Italian literature does not come from the people but has always been an upper-class product. Italian literature has been a literature of nobles, courtiers, priests, monks, and in our century professors. It was originally developed at the Sicilian Court, and it is still an apanage of the Middle School or of the Academy.[8]

He comments further in the same article that good novels are lacking in Italian literature because of novelists' failure to

present great cross-sections of society.[9] Silone was in a position
to fill this need. He was from the people; he knew them and
their society. Most important of all, he knew their traditional
beliefs, an understanding and presentation of which is one of
the best indicators of his success. A consideration of the folk
beliefs of the *cafoni* in Silone's best known novel, *Bread and
Wine,* will show why he triumphs as a creative writer.

Most of the action of *Bread and Wine* takes place in the
village of Pietrasecca, "a collection of about sixty cracked and
grimy cottages."[10] and neighboring villages. Early in the novel,
Silone introduces the wise woman Cassarola, " a revolting hag
with a snub-nose and negroid blubber lips" (p. 54), who comes
from the mountain "with her herbs and badger's hair and
snakeskins against the evil eye" (p. 7).[11] Though her role is a
minor one, Cassarola appears throughout the novel as the
local witch, at one time offering Pietro Spina—alias the priest
Don Paolo—magic herbs for his cough (p. 54),[12] at another
time predicting war and pestilence as a result of the appearance of a yellow comet in the sky (p. 161). She is feared by
the peasants and at the same time respected for her advice and
patronized for her wares. Like wise women in so many European villages, she is an integral part of the community.

Don Paolo sees evidence of various folk beliefs on his way
to Pietrasecca and during his stay there. Outside the Girasole
Hotel at Fossa dei Marsi, he observes the young men sitting
around "dozing, with extinguished cigarette stumps in their
mouths, with their trousers half unbuttoned, looking as if they
were dead" (p. 38). When one of them spots Don Paolo,
however, there is immediate action :

> At the sight of the strange priest he [one of the men playing
> cards] gave the sign against the evil eye.
> "Iron ! Iron !" he called out.

The sleepers awakened, and everyone hastened to find some iron object to touch. Those who were last put their hands into their left trousers pockets. Don Paolo was well acquainted with this rite (p. 38).[13]

Shortly after his arrival in Pietrasecca, Don Paolo inquires about a cow's skull with two great curved horns planted at the top of the inn. Matalena, the innkeeper, replies: "It's a protection against the evil eye . . . but it's no good as a protection against anything else. The only thing it protects you against is the evil eye." (p. 49). Ox horns fixed to the outsides of houses and cottages in the neighboring village of Lama dei Marsi serve an identical function (p. 42).[14]

Other less obvious precautions are taken against the feared glance. "One man wore a piece of snake skin in his hatband against the evil eye; another had some badger's hair tied to his watch chain." (p. 222).[15] Amulets and charms are not used alone, however. When Magascià is taking Don Paolo to Pietrasecca, they pass a family of poor peasants.

"How the crops?" Magascià asked the man on the donkey.

"Bad, very bad," was the answer.

"That means he'll have a good harvest," Magascià whispered in the priest's ear.

"Then why did he say the opposite?"

"To save himself from the evil eye, of course," said Magascià (pp. 41–42).[16]

Despite precautions against the evil eye, there are instances in the novel when unexplainable happenings are believed to result from its power. Matalena attributes the 1915 earthquake to the evil eye and fears it so much that she remains buried in the ruins of her house for several days rather than permit rescuers to dig her out (pp. 49–50). She is also convinced that the bad eye caused the death of her late husband, who was run over by an automobile.

"I started weeping and wailing and crying that it was the evil eye that had got him because he had just been coming home to live in a new house. But the clerk insisted that it wasn't the evil eye, but an accident that might have happened to anybody. But it must really have been the evil eye. Of course priests say they don't believe in the evil eye, but if they really didn't believe in it they wouldn't wear black" (p. 50).[17]

In at least one instance the results of the penetrating glance are even more mystical. Donna Evangelina, a student, had this experience :

"She went to Rome for the government party anniversary celebration, and the head of the government, you know whom I mean, seems to have looked at her. He was two hundred yards away ! Ever since Donna Evangelina has done nothing but talk of the devastating glance that penetrated her from two hundred yards' distance. It made the poor girl pregnant" (p. 63).[18]

The entire evil eye complex, so widespread in the Mediterranean area in particular, is used by Silone throughout *Bread and Wine* to provide insight into the values and beliefs of his characters. It is their gullibility and conservatism which make Don Paolo's role difficult when he tries to excite the peasants to action against the existing government.

Beliefs other than those connected with the evil eye are also found throughout *Bread and Wine*. During an unusually severe storm, certain acts are performed as a matter of course :

Kettles were put outside the house upside down, and mothers exposed their babies in swaddling clothes at the windows. These rites were designed to beseech pity of the supernatural powers. But they had no pity. The violence of the storm did not abate (p. 73).

Several local legends are also included in the novel to

emphasize the kinds of lore which the *cafoni* readily accepted.
Magascià tells Don Paolo this tragic place legend :

> "That is where my brother went over with his cart," said
> Magascià. "He was coming back from Fossa with salt and
> tobacco, at night. The Evil One suddenly appeared before
> him at this spot. He had no time even to make the sign of the
> Cross. The mule reared and plunged to the left to avoid the
> Evil One, and fell over the precipice." (p. 44).[19]

A house built by the Colamartini family of Pietrasecca was
taken over by "the souls of the damned . . . and no one has
ever been able to live in it. Everyone in the valley calls it the
refugium peccatorum" (p. 44).[20] Even a local religious legend
illustrates the peasants' deeply rooted superstitions :

> "That is a chapel to Our Lady of the Roses, and it com-
> memorates an ancient miracle," he [Magascià] said. "One
> year roses bloomed and cherries ripened and sheep lambed
> in January. Instead of rejoicing the people were terrified.
> Did not all those blessings portend some great disaster? Sure
> enough, that summer the cholera came."
> "Why was the chapel built?" the priest asked.
> "To keep Our Lady quiet," Magascià replied. "And this
> year's a good year, too," he went on. "Not for me, of course.
> I mean for others, for most people. Who knows what mis-
> fortunes are in store ?" (p. 42).[21]

While there is an implied moral in the local legends mentioned above, there are other tales in *Bread and Wine* which
are told expressly for didactic purposes. Scitàp, a repatriated
Italian-American, relates such a tale to illustrate his professed
belief that one must sell his soul to live well :

> "Once upon a time a big devil lived in a cave, clothed all in
> black, with a top-hat and his fingers full of rings, like a
> banker. Three peasants went to him and asked : 'What must
> we do to live well, without working?' The devil said : 'Bring

me a soul, a living soul.' The peasants went away, took a cat, wrapped it up just like a new-born baby, and took it to the devil. 'Here is a soul, a really innocent soul,' they said. In return the devil handed them a book which gave all the directions for living well without working. But while they were going away with it the cat started miaowing. The devil discovered he had been tricked. The magic book disappeared in flames in the men's hands. A cat's no good. You need a soul, a real soul" (p. 88)."

In another instance a father apprehends his son for whistling and smoking while the two are trying to push their cart out of the mud. When Don Paolo intervenes on the son's behalf, indicating that whistling is not a sin, the angry father relates a tale of the Giant Orlando to illustrate his point that "To get any return from work, you have to suffer and sweat blood" (pp. 74–75). These and other tales are told leisurely by their raconteurs. They are used by Silone to develop a picture of the peasants, a people who cannot rally to action as a result of their inability to shake off these traditional fears and doubts.

In *Bread and Wine,* then, as well as in his other novels, Silone presents a people "whose wisdom was summed up in a few proverbs passed down from generation to generation" (p. 168), a people among whom "a joke or a funny story lasts for many years, and passes from father to son and is repeated an endless number of times, always in the same way" (p. 168), a people who talk only "of calamities, famines, the cholera, hangings, and saintly miracles" (p. 166). For while Silone is able to show the *cafoni's* inability to act or change quickly in other ways, it is through his description of their folk beliefs that he captures those aspects of the peasant mentality difficult to depict otherwise. Only a writer familiar with such traditional beliefs *can* draw on them. And only a writer who exercises discretion can present them effectively.

Silone demonstrates in his novels that folk beliefs can be an integral part of creative writing and can contribute to the development of the central theme. "For him," wrote Michael Harrington, "the peasant is not a literary convention, a negative deduction from the real or supposed inadequacies of the worker; for him, the peasant is reality."[23]

Notes

1. See, for example, "Ignazio Silone," in Harry Slochower, *No Voice Is Wholly Lost . . . : Writers and Thinkers in War and Peace* (New York: Creative Age Press, 1945), pp. 62–69; and Ignazio Silone: Novelist of the Revolutionary Sensibility," in Nathan A. Scott, Jr., *Rehearsals of Discomposure* (New York: King's Crown Press, 1952), pp. 66–111.

2. The best overall article on Silone as a writer is R. W. B. Lewis, "Fiction and Power: Some Notes on Ignazio Silone," *Kenyon Review,* XVII (Winter, 1955), 23–41. Other significant treatments of various aspects of Silone's writing are James T. Farrell, "Ignazio Silone," *The Southern Review,* IV (Spring, 1939), 771–783; Edmund Wilson, "Two Survivors: Malraux and Silone," *Horizon,* XII (Oct., 1945), 245–256; George Woodcock, "Ignazio Silone," in *Focus Two,* ed. B. Rajan Andrew Pearse (London: Dennis Dobson Limited, 1946), pp. 39–55; Milano Paolo, "Silone the Faithful," in *The Arts at Mid-Century,* ed. Robert Richman (New York: Horizon Press, 1954), pp. 146–149; and A. Kingsley Weatherhead, "Ignazio Silone: Community and the Failure of Language," *Modern Fiction Studies,* VII (1961), 157–168.

3. Farrell, p. 776.

4. Thomas G. Bergin, "From Revolution to Freedom," *Saturday Review of Literature,* XXXV (Oct. 24, 1953), 62.

5. Lewis, p. 36.

6. Woodcock, p. 42.

7. *The God That Failed,* ed. Richard Crossman (New York: Bantam Books Edition, 1952), p. 86.

8. Ignazio Silone, "On Italian Literature and Other Things," *London Mercury,* XXXV, No. 207 (Jan., 1937), 290.

9. *Ibid.,* p. 293.

10. Ignazio Silone, *Bread and Wine,* tr. Gwenda David and Eric Mosbacher (New York: Signet Books Edition, 1946), p. 44. All page number references to the novel are to this edition.

11. The best overall treatment of the widespread belief in the evil eye is still Frederick Thomas Elworthy, *The Evil Eye: The Origins and Practices of Superstition* (London: John Murray, 1895). A more recent work is Edward E. Gifford, Jr., *The Evil Eye: Studies in the Folklore of Vision* (New York: The MacMillan Company, 1958), a less scholarly and greatly popularized treatment.

An excellent work dealing specifically with the folk traditions of the Italian Abruzzi region and mentioning the evil eye *passim* is Estelle Canziani, *Through the Apennines and the Lands of the Abruzzi: Landscape and Peasant Life* (Cambridge: W. Heffer & Sons Ltd., 1928). For a discussion of the use of badger's hair as a protection against the evil eye, see Canziani, pp. 2, 7.

12. See Stith Thompson, *Motif-Index of Folk-Literature* (Bloomington, Ind., 1955–58), Motif D978, "Magic Herbs."

13. Gifford states that "a modern method of protection against the

evil eye in Italy consists of touching some bit of iron" (p. 98). See Elworthy, pp. 221–225, for a general discussion of the use of iron against evil spirits.

14.   For the use of animal horns for protection against the evil eye, see Elworthy, pp. 258–260, and Gifford, pp. 72–73. In the Abruzzi region specifically Canziani says: "In nearly every house, either over one of the doors, or on a shelf, or above the large, open fireplace, there are the horns of oxen . . . to keep away the evil eye." (p. 6).

15.   See note 11.

16.   The fear of boasting of one's good fortune goes back to ancient times when it was felt that the gods looked with envy upon man's achievements and prosperity. Elworthy states "Here in the west we have a common expression of the peasantry, which keeps alive and tersely expresses this firm belief. Any untoward event which has brought misfortune is described as 'a very wisht thing'" (p. 15). Even today the habit of knocking on wood when boasting of good fortune is widespread. See also Gifford, p. 55.

17.   See Thompson, Motif D2071.1.4, "Black as guard against Evil Eye."

18.   See Thompson, Motif T515, "Impregnation through glance." An informant from Athens, Greece, recently told me that there is a humorous expression in tradition in Athens which, freely translated, means, "Don't look at that girl like that; you'll make her pregnant."

In *Fontamara*, there is an incident in which Damià becomes paralyzed, and Maria Rosa attributes the paralysis to the evil eye, Ignazio Silone, *Fontamara*, tr.Harvey Fergusson II, (New York, 1960), p. 93. See Thompson, Motif D2072.1, "Magic paralysis by Evil Eye").

19.   The sign of the cross as a method of overpowering the devil is a recurring motif in folklore. See Thompson, Motif G303.16.3.4, "Devil made to disappear by making the sign of the cross." Many cures for the evil eye even today involve making the sign of the cross on the afflicted person. See Elworthy, Chapter VIII, pp. 277–292. For the use of the sign of the cross for curing the evil eye among immigrant Americans (including Italian-Americans), see Louis C. Jones, "The Evil Eye among European-Americans," *Western Folklore*, X (Jan., 1951), 11–25.

20.   See Thompson, Motif E281, "Ghosts haunt house."

21.   This tale is interesting since the resulting cholera is attributed to the Virgin Mary. It illustrates the common practice of attributing supernatural powers to religious personages.

22.   For the well-known folklore motif in this tale, see Thompson, Motif K219.6, "Devil gets an animal in place of a human being."

23.   Michael Harrington, "The Political Novel Today," *Commonweal*, LXIII, No. 4 (Oct. 28, 1955), 80.

3

Modern Collections and Studies

COLLECTION IS THE FOUNDATION FOR FOLKLORE STUDIES. Some nineteenth-century scholars fell into the error of reaching conclusions or formulating theories based on too few or non-typical examples of traditional arts and knowledge. Still others collected examples, but they failed to apply strict standards of accuracy to their materials. Studies in folklore involve the basic principles of collection, classification, and analysis which are to be found in any other systematic investigation.

In the twentieth century these activities have greatly improved through the use of mechanical recording devices, bibliographical aids, and regional or national archives devoted to the preservation and classification of folklore so that it may be studied as a living social and aesthetic process.

Collection, even with modern recording devices, may still fall short of the ideal if the collector is blind to the social context from which he has abstracted his material. Mere mechanical accuracy and laborious annotation cannot correct errors of interpretation or distortions, arising from ignorance of the social matrix which has yielded the collection. The merely technical approach, regardless of the technique used, comparative, bibliographical, structural, historical, or what have you, can be the least meaningful study of a particular selection. For a good statement on the pitfalls of collection and interpretation, examine carefully the article by MacEdward Leach in Chapter I.

The selections in this chapter reflect the trends in modern collection and study.

VANCE RANDOLPH

The Talking Turtle*

One time there was a fellow named Lissenbee, and the trouble was that he couldn't keep nothing to himself. Whenever anybody done something that wasn't right, Lissenbee would run and blab it all over town. He didn't tell no lies, he just told the truth, and that's what made it so bad. Because all the people believed whatever Lissenbee said, and there wasn't no way a fellow could laugh it off.

If he seen one of the county officers going to a woman's house when her husband was not home, Lissenbee would tell it right in front of the courthouse, and so there would be hell to pay in two families. Or maybe some citizens liked to play a little poker in the livery barn, but there wasn't no way to keep it quiet, on account of that goddam Lissenbee. And when the Baptist preacher brought some whiskey home, there was Lissenbee a-hollering before the preacher could get the keg out of his buggy. After while the boys was afraid to swipe a watermelon, for fear old blabbermouth Lissenbee would tell everybody who done it.

The last straw was the time Lissenbee found a turtle in the road. It was bigger than the common kind, so he stopped to look at it. The old turtle winked its red eyes, and it says, "Lissenbee, you talk too damn much." Lissenbee jumped four foot high, and then just stood there with his mouth a-hanging open. He looked all round, but there wasn't anybody in sight. "It must be my ears have went back on me!" says he. "Everybody knows terrapins is dumb." The old turtle winked its red eyes again. "Lissenbee, you talk too damn much," says the turtle. With that Lissenbee spun round like a top, and then he lit out for town.

* From *The Talking Turtle and Other Ozark Folk Tales* by Vance Randolph, copyright by Columbia University Press, New York.

209

When Lissenbee come to the tavern and told the people about the turtle that could talk, they just laughed in his face. "You come with me," says he, "and I'll show you!" So the whole crowd went along, but when they got there the old turtle didn't say a word. It looked just like any other turtle, only bigger than the common kind. The people was mad because they walked out there in the hot sun for nothing, so they kicked Lissenbee into the ditch and went back to town. Pretty soon Lissenbee set up, and the old turtle winked its red eyes. "Didn't I tell you?" says the turtle. "You talk too damn much."

Some people around here say the whole thing was a joke, because it ain't possible for a turtle to talk. They claim some fellow must have hid in the bushes and throwed his voice, so it just sounded like the turtle was a-talking. Everybody knows that these medicine-show doctors can make a wooden dummy talk good enough to fool most anybody. There was a boy here in town that tried to learn how out of a book, but he never done no good at it. The folks never found nobody in these parts that could throw his voice like that.

Well, no matter if it was a joke or not, the story sure fixed old blabbermouth Lissenbee. The folks just laughed at his tales after that, and they would say he better go talk to the turtles about it.

* *Notes*

Told by Mr. George E. Hastings, Fayetteville, Ark., January, 1942. He got it from a student at the University of Arkansas. Cf. the "Talking Turtle" story reported by Allsopp, *Folklore of Romantic Arkansas*, 1931, II, 189–90; and W. A. Percy, *Lanterns on the Levee*, 1941, pp. 294–96. I published this item as "A Folktale from Arkansas" in the *Tennessee Folklore Society Bulletin* (XIX, 4 December, 1953, pp. 102–3). (Vance Randolph).

Reports of this story from English-speaking white informants are rare. The story is usually told by Negroes, and I believe it is of African origin. Nearly all versions retain the admonition that too much talk brings one to trouble. Negro texts with a talking turtle, terrapin, or cooter, have been reported by Parsons (*Journal of American Folklore*, XXX, 177, second version) from North Carolina; Fauset (*Journal of American Folklore*, XL, 263) from Alabama; B. A. Botkin (*Lay My Burden Down*, Chicago, 1945, p. 7) from an Oklahoma informant who had been a slave in Texas. Botkin (*Treasury of Southern Folklore*, p. 510) reprints the Mississippi text given by W. A. Percy (see above). Brewer (*Publications of the Texas Folklore Society*, X, 48–50) gives a Texas version with a talking bullfrog. In a footnote to Brewer's story, J. Frank Dobie gives a text in which a turtle plays a banjo and sings over and over, "Live in peace; don't tell all you see." This is surprisingly like the African version from the Gold Coast Colony given in adapted form by H. Courlander and G. Herzog (*The Cow-Tail Switch*, New York, 1947, pp. 65–71), which also has a singing and playing tortoise.

In the original form of this Gold Coast story the man is put to death when the tortoise refuses to perform publicly. This grim outcome to talking too much is also found in a closely related story, told in both Africa and America. In the Nupe version given by L. Frobenius and D. C. Fox (*African Genesis*, New York, 1937, pp. 161–62), a hunter finds a human skull and asks, "What brought you here?" The skull replies, "Talking brought me here." The hunter reports the talking skull to the king, who sends guards with him to kill the hunter if he can't prove his statement. When the skull remains obdurately silent, the hunter is killed. After the guard has left, the skull ironically asks the dead hunter's head the hunter's original question, "What brought you here?" The head replies, "Talking brought me here."

American Negro versions of this talking skull story have been published by Parsons (*Journal of American Folklore*, XXX, 176–77) from North Carolina; Fauset (*Journal of American Folklore*, XLI, 536–37) from Pennsylvania; and by Z. N. Hurston (*Mules and Men*, Philadelphia, 1935, pp. 219–20) from Florida. Dorson (*Western Folklore*, XIII, 256–58) gives a lengthy version from a Michigan Negro informant in which a rather verbose mule warns the Negro he talks too much. When he reports to his Boss that the mule talks, the Boss threatens to hang him just to scare him. Later the Negro overhears the Boss say the Negro is crazy and will have to be shot. The text is an odd combinaton of the talking turtle story with the popular humorous tale "All Things Talk." (Herbert Halpert).   ,

RICHARD DORSON

Utah Mormons*

A legendary history of Mormonism developed simultaneously with the factual history. The collective survival of the Saints
in itself amounted to a miracle. As they hewed their way
across the continent, the religious traditions gathered into a
dense volume of testimony: prophecies and visions, deliver-
ances and judgments, the healing of the faithful and the conversion of cynics. Joseph Smith and Brigham Young became
the center of glowing cycles, though all the elders possessed
spiritual gifts which formed the basis for legends. The inviol-
ability of the Book of Mormon furnished a theme for repeated
stories. Persecution by the Gentiles, who vilified, threatened,
and murdered the Saints all along their route to Zion, from
New York to Utah, set the stage for acts of providence. Nature
offered its hazards after the pioneers reached the Promised
Land. The best-known Mormon providence occurred in the
summer of 1848, when a plague of crickets descended on the
first grain planted in the Great Salt Lake valley by the Saints.
All efforts to dispel them proved fruitless, until miraculously
wave on wave of gulls from the lake hove into view and de-
voured the insects. Because the obligations of the church required young Mormon men to spend a year or two abroad in
a foreign country, ignorant of the language and untrained in
proselytizing, accounts of their spectacular successes in con-
verting cynical Gentiles passed into general Mormon tradition.

Mormon theology invited folklore of the supernatural with
its strong commitment to intuitive knowledge and extrasensory
experience. The church dogmas supported the reality of spirits
and miracles, the rewards for prayer and zeal, the genuineness
of inspiration, and the uniqueness of the Saints in the eyes of

* From *American Folklore* by Richard Dorson, copyright 1959 by
the University of Chicago.

the Lord. In the course of their pioneer history, Mormon families encountered innumerable situations when these articles of faith could be tested and confirmed.

One supreme legend arose soon after the establishment of the Church of Latter-Day Saints in Utah, which came to symbolize the whole Mormon experience. In time of distress, physical or spiritual, one, two, or three elderly strangers appeared at a Mormon home, or by the roadside, or even in the desert, proffering aid to a Saint. Only when they were gone, leaving perhaps a full larder behind, did the faithful realize that the three Nephites had given them succor. The ubiquitous three, who usually materialized singly, devoted their powers to humble individual cases, making no attempt to interfere with divinely foreordained persecutions and martyrdoms.

The year 1855 marks the emergence of the Nephite tradition. In a sermon before a conference of Saints, Apostle Orson Pratt declared "how pleasing—how glorious it would be, could we see those three old Nephites whose prayers have ascended up, for something like 1800 years, in behalf of the children of men in the last days, and have them return to their old native land . . . . Do you suppose that these three Nephites have any knowledge of what is going on in this land? They know all about it; they are filled with the spirit of prophecy. Why do they not come into our midst?"

These three Nephites familiarly referred to by the apostle appear in the Book of Mormon, whose plates Joseph Smith received from the angel Moroni. The race of Nephites sprang from the followers of Nephi, son of Lehi, a good man who sailed from Jerusalem for South America six centuries before the birth of Christ. After his resurrection, Christ visited the Nephites in the New World and preached to twelve chosen disciples. Nine asked to live seventy-two years, and enter heaven. To the others, however, Jesus granted everlasting life, transfigured them, and brought them to heaven. For three hundred years they ministered to the Jews and Gentiles on earth, and suffered extreme tortures, when they were withdrawn because of the wickedness of man. Meanwhile the fair and virtuous Nephites in South America had been pushed north into North America and there had been conquered by the dark and evil Lamanites, followers of Laman, the other son of Lehi, who are today known as the Indians. Moroni, the angel who delivered the Book of Mormon to Joseph Smith in 1827, had sealed the sacred record in A.D. 421, then in his human person, as the last Nephite historian.

Angels and spirits had visited Mormons in the years from 1827 to 1855, according to testimony of the church fathers. But after the sermon of Apostle Pratt dramatically invoking the three Nephites, the common folk in Utah began to perceive the transfigured ones. Instances multiplied, reaching a peak between 1875 and 1900 and gradually dwindling, until after 1925 only scattered experiences are reported, although the Nephites still appear. In the pioneer period of Mormon settlement, the Nephites brought food to the hungry and healed the sick, but as the communities prospered, their mission changed, and they turned to bringing spiritual messages. With the church now so successfully established there is less work for the Nephites. As one elderly woman explained, "Things are so easy for us now that we don't have the need for those Nephites that we once had when we were pioneering and homesteading." However, appearances of the Nephites are now extended back in time, and Columbus is supposed to have encountered the Three.

The trio of Nephite legends most widely told and printed display a wide variety in circumstance. A professor at the University of Utah, Maud May Babcock, while riding through the Silver Lake country in Utah with a schoolteacher friend in 1900, found herself crawling with her horse on a jagged mountain peak covered with slippery shale. In her hopeless plight she prayed, and found herself with her horse on a path below the peak facing a courteous stranger, in Van Dyke beard and blue overalls, with clean white hands. He directed her back to camp and vanished. Miss Babcock's friend joined the Mormon church.

While helping erect a temple at Logan, Utah, in 1884, Brother Ballard sought for the genealogical information prerequisite to his performing services for his English ancestors. The day before the temple dedication, two elderly strangers thrust a newspaper into the hands of Ballard's daughters, telling them to take it posthaste to their father. He found it to be an English newspaper printed three days before, giving all the data he needed.

In the early days of Payson, Utah, a Mormon farmwife, living alone while her husband served his missionary term in Germany, saw an elderly stranger materialize at her remote doorstep. He requested something to eat. She wrapped bread in a cloth of peculiar pattern, and he disappeared. Several years later her husband related how, on that same day, when he was hungry and penniless in Germany, a stranger had thrust upon him a parcel of bread in a cloth of the same pattern, urging him to call at the post office, where indeed he found money waiting for him.

In all these accounts one special folk touch intrudes, the sudden disappearance of the strangers, a motif not sanctioned by the church but characteristic of other folktale cycles. The legend of the Three Nephites shows some affinity with that of the Wandering Jew, and of the myths about gods visiting mortals in disguise and requiting their hospitality, best known in the Greek tale of Philemon and Baucis. During the 1940's it became entangled with the contemporary legend of the Ghostly Hitch-hiker. Mormons driving in their car picked up a stranger who uttered mystic predictions that they would shortly transport a corpse and that the war would end in the following August. Both prophecies come true.

The traditions of the three Nephites belong exclusively to Mormonism. The bulk are placed in Utah, although the Nephites appear wherever Saints reside. All ethnic groups who belong to the church (they are chiefly Anglo-Scandinavian) share in the legend, but non-Mormons have no idea who or what the Nephites are.

BIBLIOGRAPHICAL NOTES

All students of American folklore appreciate the splendid treatment of Mormon folk traditions by Austin E. and Alta S. Fife in *Saints of Sage and Saddle* (Bloomington, Ind., 1956). . . . Important individual articles by Austin Fife are "The Legend of the Three Nephites among the Mormons," *Journal of American Folklore*, LIII (1940), 1–49; "Popular Legends of the Mormons," *California Folklore Quarterly*, I (1942), 105–25; . . . A fascinating study is Hector Lee, *The Three Nephites: The Substance and Significance of the Legend in Folklore* (Albuquerque, 1949).

RAPHAEL PATAI

Jewish Folklore and Jewish Tradition*

i

Fifteen years ago in a programmatic paper, "Problems and Tasks of Jewish Folklore and Ethnology,"[1] I expressed the hope that the study of folklore of present-day Jewish communities would receive the highest priority within the general field of Jewish learning. The years which have elapsed since then have brought no realization of this hope. While the great ethnic upheavals in the life of the post-Nazi remnant of the Jewish people hastened the oblivion of the living folklore of the Jewish communities, the study of Jewish folklore progressed at a snail's pace. In Israel itself, after five years of struggling for existence in the face of overwhelming odds, the Palestine (later : Israel) Institute of Folklore and Ethnology and its journal *Edoth* became war casualties. Thus the few students of folklore in the new state remained without the stimulus of a scientific forum. Outside Israel, no periodical publication devoted to Jewish folklore has existed since 1925, when Max Grunwald's *Jahrbuch für jüdische Volkskunde* was suspended. In regional and general folklore journals, Jewish folklore has figured very meagerly.

Only two articles dealing with Jewish folklore have appeared in the *Journal of American Folklore* since the publishing of "Problems and Tasks of Jewish Folklore and Ethnology."[2] "Folklore Research in North America" (the "Report of the Committee on Research in Folklore in North America in 1945 and 1946")[3] contained individual reports on studies in

* "Jewish Folklore and Jewish Tradition," by Raphael Patai. In *Studies in Biblical and Jewish Folklore,* edited by Raphael Patai, Francis Lee Utley, and Dov Noy. Indiana University Press (Folklore Series Vol. 51), Bloomington, 1960.

217

American Regional, German-American, Spanish-American, Afro-American, and American-Indian folklore; but there was no report on Jewish folklore, in spite of the fact that a great deal of the activity of the Yiddish Scientific Institute (Yivo) was devoted to these studies. With whomever the fault lies—and it seems that lack of interest on the part of Jewish folklorists is to a great extent responsible—the facts are that Jewish folklore has not figured so prominently in American folklore research as have several other bodies of folklore and that the study of American Jewish folklore has not been so integral a part of American folklore research as the study of the folklore of other nationalities in this country.

ii

The great ethnic upheavals referred to above, including the establishment of the state of Israel and the large-scale "ingathering of the exiles," have brought about in the objective circumstances of the Jewish people a number of significant changes which are not only limiting but also contributing factors in the study of Jewish folklore. These changed circumstances, coupled with the recent advances in the world-wide effort of systematic folkloristic study, call for a re-examination and restatement of the scope of Jewish folklore. Let us begin with a glance at the reasons given in the *Standard Dictionary of Folklore, Mythology, and Legend*[4] for excluding Jewish folklore from its series of excellent survey articles which outline the folklore of several important culture groups in the world.[5] As stated in Theodore Gaster's article on Semitic folklore, "modern Semitic folklore, including especially that of the Arabs and Jews, has been excluded, on the grounds that much of it is due to direct borrowings from other peoples and can therefore not be described as distinctive."[6]

This statement raises two immediate questions concerning Jewish folklore. First, is it justifiable to include the folklore of the Jews under "modern Semitic folklore"? The only legitimate definition of "Semitic folklore" is the one correctly given in Dr. Gaster's article : "the folklores of the people who spoke (or speak) Semitic languages." While this definition enables us to include under "modern Semitic folklore" the folklore of those Jewish communities whose colloquial speech belongs to the Semitic language family (such as the Jews of the Arab lands, of Kurdistan, and of Ethiopia), it excludes the folklore of the great majority of the Jews whose speech has until very recently been Yiddish, that is Judaeo-German, and whose folklore by the same token would have to be included in Germanic folklore. The same linguistic classification would commit us to include the folklore of the Persian, Afgan, and Bokharan Jews under Iranian, rather than under Semitic, folklore. It thus becomes evident that contemporary Jewish folklore as a whole cannot be regarded as a subdivision of "modern Semitic folklore."

The second question is whether it was justifiable to omit from the *Dictionary* a survey article on Jewish folklore "on the grounds that so much of it is due to direct borrowings from other peoples and can therefore not be described as distinctive."

No one familiar with Jewish folklore would deny that "much of it is due to direct borrowings from other peoples." This is true, however, of the folklore of practically every people, even of those who have lived until recently in relative isolation. A comparative study of the total folklore inventory of a culture (if such were available) would inevitably lead to the conclusion that only a very small part of it is, beyond any doubt, not "due to direct borrowings." Incidentally, the instrumentality of the Jews in these processes of borrowing, and especially in the transmission of folklore from the East to the West, is being more and more clearly recognized.

It would seem, moreover, that the distinctiveness of a body of folklore is not contingent upon the amount of borrowing characterizing it. Consequently, it does not follow that a folklore much of which "is due to direct borrowing from other peoples" can on this count "not be described as distinctive." The amount of borrowing is usually determined with the help of the prevalent methods of folklore research by a study of motifs. But in addition to the more easily discernible, definable, and classifiable motifs contained in a piece of narrative folklore, the latter is also characterized by such traits as mood, flavor, spirit, and atmosphere. These traits may account for its distinctiveness even though its motifs and structure (i.e., its concrete content) may be borrowed. As Bascom has recently emphasized, "the problem of stylistic features of a body of folklore is regarded as of primary importance . . . as well as the analysis of tales in terms of plot, incident, conflict, climax, motivation, and character development."' In fact, much of the specifically Jewish character of Jewish folklore can be found precisely in these elements to which the usual classificatory techniques of motif analysis are not applicable.

iii

In addition to vitiating the argument on which the exclusion of modern Jewish folklore from the *Dictionary* was based, the above considerations demonstrate something definite about Jewish folklore itself. We recognize that the prevalent classification of folklore into subdivisions characterized by a common language and by residence in contiguous geographical territories is not applicable to the folklore of the Jews. In this respect, even the folklore of the Gipsies can be regarded as closer typologically to the folklore of other nations than to Jewish folklore. When we speak of Gipsy folklore, the reference is to folklore characterized by many local variants. Gipsies reflect the influence of several countries and adhere to different religions (there are Catholic and Protestant as well as Moslem Gipsies), but they utilize everywhere the same linguistic medium : the common and ancient Gipsy language rooted in Sanskrit and closer to Hindustani than to any other living tongue.[8] In contrast, the unifying characteristic of Jewish folklore is not the language it utilizes but the common religious tradition underlying it.

Another people whose culture is occasionally pointed out as manifesting certain analogies to the Jews are the Armenians. Like the Jews, the Armenians live in many different countries and cherish everywhere the traditions of their common origin and history. But the Armenians, unlike the Jews, have preserved until very recently their Armenian language. Again, unlike the Jews, the Armenians are split into two mutually intolerant religions, one represented by the Armenian Orthodox Church and the other by the Armenian Catholic Church.

iv

Since Jewish folklore is obviously the folklore of the Jews, the temporal and spatial extent of its subject matter must be co-extensive with the duration of Jewish history and the spatial dispersion of the Jewish people. This much is evident. But, in addition, the Jews were throughout their long history a literate people who developed at an early date the habit of committing to writing whatever they regarded as important in their oral traditions. As a result, the history of Jewish folklore is characterized, in each epoch, by a continuous process of lifting out considerable bodies of folklore from the stream of oral tradition and freezing them in written form. This process started with the earliest documents incorporated in the Hebrew Bible, in which the narrative element is fascinating both in the uniqueness of its style and spirit and in the incomparable interest of its motifs and content. The process continued through the early post-Biblical literature of the Apocrypha, in which, incidentally, the polyglot character of Jewish folklore—initially indicated in some of the late books of the Biblical canon itself—is first fully manifested; then branched off into the Greek writings of the Jewish Hellenists, of whom Philo of Alexandria and Josephus Flavius are the classical exponents; and culminated—still in antiquity—in the "great sea" of Talmudic literature which sprang up in Palestine and then flourished simultaneously there and in Babylonia.

With the spatial spread of the Diaspora from ancient times onward, the originally unified Jewish tradition branched out into more and more independent branches. Hebrew and Aramaic remained the principal languages of literary expression, but Arabic, Persian, Ladino, and Yiddish soon appeared. Everywhere, however, the same process continued : oral traditions found their way into writing which, irrespective of their main intent, became repositories of the folksong of their age without detracting from the stream of oral, living, folk tradition, which continued undiminished century after century. The history of Jewish folklore therefore illustrates in detail B. A. Botkin's generalization that "The transference of oral tradition to writing and print does not destroy its validity as folklore but rather, while freezing or fixing its form, helps to keep it alive and to define it among those to whom it is not native or fundamental."[9]

Consider as an example the rich harvest of books of customs, or better, one of their subvarieties, the collections of magical or religio-magical prescriptions used in obtaining benefits and preventing or curing ills. The earliest example of these within Hebrew tradition is contained in the book of Genesis (in the story of Rachel and the mandrakes). Talmudic literature contains many such examples, but even more are found in Jewish literature of the Middle Ages and in later periods down to the 19th century.

In spite of the many outside influences that it absorbed and the changes that it underwent in many localities and in the course of many centuries, the specifically Jewish component in the folk life of the Jews everywhere is ultimately based on Talmudic or Biblical origins. Single customs cannot in every instance be traced back to the Talmud or the Bible, but in Biblical, and even more so in Talmudic times, a tendency developed among the Jewish people to conduct their entire lives, from the cradle to the grave, and including all daily and periodic activities, in conformity with explicit or implicit rules (these latter contained either in the Writ or in oral tradition and known as *Halakha,* a term covering the normative part of all Jewish tradition). This religious oral tradition became the main molding force of Jewish life, with all its customs and usages.

With the passage of centuries in post-Talmudic times the reliance on rules not only continued but became more pronounced, creating the need for repeated recapitulations of the Law in a series of codes once every few generations.[10] Thus a considerable part of Jewish literature in the Middle Ages consisted of collections of rules of conduct, of *do's* and *don'ts,* which, although extending into all walks of life, had an essentially religious character and derived their binding force from the Bible and the Talmud as the ultimate sources of authority. The number of these codes increased, and the latest one, the

Shulhan 'Arukh, was provided with commentaries. Also, handy compendia, based on the *Shulhan 'Arukh* and giving its essential rulings in brief form, were prepared. Thus the habit of looking for guidance in a handbook became widespread, and supplemental handbooks containing collections of customs *(minhagim)* and other handbooks containing remedies and prescriptions were compiled both in Europe and in the Orient, first in handwriting, then in print. So many of these collections were prepared that one would expect much or all of the oral traditions to have been absorbed into the written word; but instead the exact opposite seems to have been true. In fact, the more that is committed to writing in any age and place, the richer the oral tradition that continues to flow thereafter. Therefore, much as the student of Jewish folklore may be enthralled by the wealth of manuscript and printed collections of customs, remedies, and prescriptions dating from past centuries, he finds himself in a world of even greater unexplored riches when he turns to the living lore of any Jewish community still anchored in its traditions.

The quasi-religious character of these books of customs and remedies is attested to by the fact that they were compiled, copied, printed, and used by Jews whose entire life was dominated by religious tradition as embodied in the first place in the religious codes. Scrupulous fulfillment of all the most minute rules of the *Shulhan 'Arukh* went hand in hand with unquestioning belief in the binding force of local custom and in the efficacy of the prescriptions collected in books of remedies. Law and lore were followed together for centuries, until, with the onset of the Enlightenment, they were both questioned and in many places, both discarded.

In certain specific details occasional contradictions can be discovered between the local tradition and, especially, the instructions contained in the remedy books, on the one hand,

and the hard and fast rulings of the officially sanctioned codes of conduct, on the other. In most cases these contradictions went unnoticed, but whether noticed or not, the old Talmudic observation that custom is stronger than law was confirmed again and again.

V

While living Jewish custom and its repositories are thus the outgrowth of the *Halakha,* Jewish tales, legends, fables, parables, and other types of folk literature go back to the narrative parts of the Bible and to the second main component of Talmudic literature, the so called *Agada,* which also includes ethical teachings. In one of the varieties of the Talmudic *Agada* a superstructure of legends and tales was built upon the concise Biblical foundations. In post-Talmudic times, the development of Jewish legend and tale shows a close parallel to that of Jewish custom and usage. On the one hand, the legend material was excerpted from the Talmud and the Midrashim and published in separate volumes, such as the *'Ein Y a' gov* (c. 11th century) and the *Yalqut Shim'oni* (13th century). On the other hand, an independent literature grew up consisting of collections of tales and legends which either follow the narrative portions of the Bible (e.g., the *Sepher Hayashar* in the 12th century) or deal with non-Biblical themes and show traces of outside influences to varying degrees. An important variety in this latter category is the collections of fables (e.g., the *Mishle Shu'alim,* or Fox Fables, of Berekhya ben Natronai Hanaqdan in the 13th century) which continue a trend found in the Talmud and even earlier in the Bible itself (e.g., Yotham's fable, Judges 9 : 8–15).

Like Jewish folk custom, the Jewish folktale also retained its close affiliation with Jewish religion, both being regarded as manifestations of Jewish tradition, which in its totality has always remained inseparable from Jewish religion and its cornerstone, the Five Books of Moses. Again, as in the case of Jewish folk custom, however much of this originally unwritten literature was being put to writing, more of it remained to be orally transmitted down to the time when the Enlightenment began to make its inroads upon Jewish traditional life in Europe. In the Orient, both custom and oral literature remained intact for several additional generations, until in our day the "ingathering" of several Oriental Jewish Diasporas in Israel initiated the process of their assimilation to the secular, Western culture of the modern Jewish state, with its inevitable concomitant—the disappearance of folk traditions.

vi

Legends, myths, tales, and other types of unwritten literature function as sanctions of custom and belief. This general thesis is fully borne out by an examination of Jewish folklore. Indeed, the close interlacing of custom and legend, and their mutual interdependence, are characteristics of Jewish folklore that are found in all Jewish literary sources from the most ancient times down to the present day. The story of Jacob's fight with the angel at the ford of Jabbok (Gen. 32) explains the origin of the name Israel and of the prohibition of eating the sinew of the thigh vein. The story of the levity committed by the men and women in the Temple of Jerusalem (Talmudic sources) explains the custom of separating the sexes during services.[11] The legend of the medieval martyr Rabbi Amnon explains the origin and the significance of the moving prayer *Un'tane Toqef*, recited on the New Year and on the Day of Atonement. The innumerable stories about the piety, the wisdom, and the miracles of Hassidic rabbis from the 18th century on, explain and motivate the veneration of their followers. And the equally colorful tales told to this day by Oriental Jews about their own miracle-working rabbis *(hakhams or moris)* motivate and sanction the custom of visiting the shrines of these holy men and of performing certain rites at their tombs.

As long as the customs and beliefs were part of the reality of the life of Jewish communities in the West or in the East, the survival of legends and tales was assured, for by providing a sanction for customs and beliefs, the legends and tales, too, constituted an integral part of the living religious culture of each community. Once the beliefs crumble under the influences of a modern, Western, secular atmosphere, and once the customs are no longer practiced for the same reason, or cannot be practiced because of the migration of the community into a new country (e.g., from Morocco, Yemen, or Iraq to Israel), the unwritten literature, having lost its function, is bound to be forgotten soon after.

vii

Several conclusions can be drawn from the foregoing remarks on folk custom and folk literature as the two main categories of Jewish folklore.

First, it seems evident that in the study of Jewish folklore it is possible to an even lesser degree than in other folklores to deal separately with folk custom on the one hand and with folk literature on the other. As an anthropologist, one agrees with the anthropological definition of folklore as "dependent on oral transmission" and thus including "myths, legends, tales, proverbs, riddles, the texts of ballads and other songs, and other forms of lesser importance, but not folk art, folk dance, folk music, folk costume, folk medicine, folk custom or

228   A FOLKLORE READER

folk belief."[12] But as a student of Jewish culture one knows that Jewish legends and tales can be studied only in the context of Jewish folk custom. If the scholarly consensus is that folk custom is not a legitimate object of study for the folklorist because it belongs to the realm of anthropology, then the Jewish folklorist must be an anthropologist as well in order to be able to study fully the inseparable oral and behavioral components of Jewish tradition.

Second, it has been found that modern Jewish folklore everywhere, as expressed in this two-in-one manifestation of the oral and the behavioral, is merely the surface appearance of an ore that goes deep down into the bedrock of Jewish tradition. No Jewish custom, or belief, or piece of unwritten literature can be fully understood and adequately studied without a thorough search of that vast accumulation of written literature in which so much of the Jewish tradition of past centuries has received a fixed form. A student of Australian folklore may have nothing to build on but the actually existing oral tradition of the tribe he studies. Methods developed for studying such "historyless" human groups are inadequate for studying the folklore of the Jews, who have been the "people of the book" for millennia.

Third, a few conclusions can be reached about the outside influences on Jewish folklore, of which there have been many in every age and in every place. The tradition-bound and religion-dominated character of Jewish life everywhere up to the Enlightment provided it with an extraordinary capacity for absorbing elements of foreign cultures. The life of a Jewish community under the aegis of its own religious tradition was one and indivisible. Religion was always ready, soon after something new appeared on the horizon, with its decisive reaction : whether to reject it at as *huqqat hagoy* (the law or custom of Gentiles) or to accept it, digest it, and make it part of the Jewish tradition. If the decision fell in the latter direction, a very short time later the non-Jewish origin of the trait was forgotten, and it acquired the same binding force, the same traditional sanction, as any traditional Jewish *minhag*. Or, if it was a tale or a fable or a legend, its acceptance meant that it had come to be regarded as a legitimate addition to the old Jewish storehouse of oral literature, and in this case, too, its non-Jewish origin was soon completely forgotten.

This tendency to incorporate foreign elements constitutes an additional challenge for the student of Jewish folklore. He must always be familiar with the results of general folklore studies, for Jewish folklore always contains non-Jewish elements and must be studied in its relation to them.

Finally—a warning. Israel the state and Israel the people have to be made aware of the acute danger of the total submergence of the folklore of the surviving Jewish communities in the new, nascent culture of Israel. In 1945 only the folklore of the European Jewish remnant seemed to be threatened with oblivion, while the folkore of the Oriental Jews, who in those days still lived in relative peace in their tradition-favoring Moslem environment, seemed to be safe for generations to come. Now, only fifteen years later, the danger of extinction is greater for the folk traditions of the Oriental Jews than for those of the European Jews. There are no more Jewish communities left in Yemen and Iraq; in other Oriental countries their number has been drastically reduced and their communal life broken down. In Israel, which in the last ten years has absorbed close to a half million Oriental Jews, the dominant atmosphere of Western society and culture is more unfavorable for the continued survival of Oriental folk traditions than it is for the continued existence of Western Jewish folklore.

Notes

1. Published in Hebrew as the introductory article of the journal *Edoth* (Jerusalem) I (Oct., 1945), No. 1, 1–12; and subsequently in an English translation in the *Journal of American Folklore*, II (1946), 25–39.

2. L. R. C. Yoffie, "Songs of the '12 Numbers' and the Hebrew Chant of Echod Mi Yodea," JAF, LXII (1949), 382–411; Ruth Rubin, "19th Century Yiddish Folksongs of Children in Eastern Europe," JAF, LXV (1952), 227–54.

3. Cf. JAF, LX (1947), 350–416.

4. Maria Leach (ed.), *Standard Dictionary of Folklore, Mythology, and Legend* (2 vols.; New York, 1949–50).

5. Europe and America are most fully covered, the former by survey articles dealing with Basque, Celtic, Estonian, European, Finnish, French, Germanic, Latvian, Lithuanian, Romany, Slavic, Spanish folklore; the latter by articles on African and New-World Negro, American, Mexican and Central American Indian, North American Indian, Pennsylvania Dutch, South American Indian and Spanish folklore (which includes Spanish America). Although even this coverage is far from complete (we miss, e.g., Hungarian and Balkan folklore), it is unquestionably much more adequate than the spotty coverage of the rest of the world. Asia is represented only by articles on Chinese folklore, Indian and Persian folklore and mythology, Japanese folklore and Semitic folklore (the latter confined to a discussion of the ancient Near East). Oceania and Australia are discussed in four articles, while Africa is summarily dealt with in an article which includes also New-World Negro Folklore. The folklore of the contemporary Middle East (which comprises the rich, though insufficiently explored, folklore of Iran, Turkey and the Arab lands) is excluded altogether, as is Jewish folklore.

6. Cf. II, 981.

7. William R. Bascom, "Folklore and Anthropology," JAF, LVI (1953), 289.

8. Cf. *Standary Dictionary of Folklore*, II, 953.

9. *Ibid.*, I, 398.

10. The Mishna (c. A.D. 200); the Babylonian Talmud (c. 500); the code of Yitzhaq Alfasi (1013–1103); the code of Maimonides (1135–1204); the code of Jacob ben Asher (c. 1269–1343); the *Shulhan 'Arukh* of Joseph Caro (1488–1575).

11. Cf. Raphael Patai, *Man and Temple in Ancient Jewish Myth and Ritual* (Edinburgh, 1947).

12. Bascom, *op. cit.*, p. 285. Cf. also Bascom's subsequent discussion of the scope of folklore in his paper, "Verbal Art," JAF, LXVIII (1955), 245–52.

RUTH BENEDICT

Origin Tales and Stories of the Katchinas*

Uretsitī

They were living at White House, and all the people (of the world) called each other by relationship terms; they were brothers and sisters. Uretsiti, the mother of the pueblos, and Naotsiti, the mother of the Navahos, were sisters.

It was when they left White House that they began to have trouble. Naotsiti challenged Uretsiti to a contest. She said, "Whoever the sun shines on first shall be the greater," for she was taller than her elder sister. Uretsiti and Naotsiti stood up before dawn and waited for the first rays of the sun. Naotsiti said, "Whoever the sun strikes first, her children shall be valuable; whoever the sun strikes last, her children shall be worthless." She was boasting. Then the sun rose. Its first rays fell on the hair of Uretsiti. They spread to her eyebrows, and when they had rested there, the first light of the sun fell on the top of the hair of Naotsiti. They spread down to her cheeks, and when they rested there they touched the eyebrows of Naotsiti. They spread to her chin, and when they rested there they touched the cheeks of Naotsiti. They spread to her chest, and when they rested there they touched the chin of Naotsiti. The light of the sun completely covered Uretsiti, and still the shadow had not gone from Naotsiti. When Naotsiti saw her sister already standing in the full sunlight, she was angry and said, "Why is it that you are standing covered with sun and I am still in shadow?" Uretsiti answered, "It is not I who have done this. It is our great mother.² This was your challenge, but

* From *Tales of the Cochiti Indians* by Ruth Benedict. Smithsonian Institution, Bureau of American Ethnology, Bulletin 98. Washington, D.C., U.S. Government Printing Office, 1931.

232   A FOLKLORE READER

she has given me power to overcome." Then Naotsiti said,
"Do with me as you please. If you kill me, do not put it off."[3]
Uretsiti took up her rabbit stick and threw it at Naotsiti. She
turned into a large woodrat and ran in among the rocks.
Uretsiti could not follow her in the crevices. So she was saved.
Just as the mother of the pueblos was safe and won in this
contest, so whenever there is fighting between the Navahos and
the pueblos, the people of the pueblos are safe and win. Only
once in a very long time one man is lost from the pueblos in
fighting with the Navahos. And as the Mother of the Navahos
saved herself by running in among the rocks, so the Navahos
still save themselves in war by hiding among the rocks.[4]

Variant[5]

Naotsiti (mother of the Navahos) challenged Uretsiti
(mother of the Cochiti[6]) to a contest. She was taller than her
elder sister and she chose what the contest should be. She said,
"Whoever the sun sees first shall be the winner." They called
together all their people, and before sunrise they stood together
on a line, facing toward the east. But when the sun rose, it was
Uretsiti first. Then Naotsiti said, "You have won. In four days
we shall contest again." In four days they rose early and scattered cornmeal to the Kopishtaya. All the people came together, and Masewi and Oyoyewi were in charge of the contest.
When all the people were ready they brought the Mothers into
the center of the people. Uretsiti had her hair cut in old Cochiti
fashion,[7] and Naotsiti in Navaho fashion. They each of them
carried a grinding muller. The first turn was Naotsiti's. She
struck Uretsiti so that she fell to the ground. It was the turn
of our Mother. She rose and struck Naotsiti so that she fell to
the ground. They laid down their mullers and wrestled. Then
Uretsiti overcame Naotsiti and killed her. She turned into a

woodrat and ran off. That is why the Navahos avoid woodrats. They do not kill them because their mother is a woodrat. And this is why the men of Cochiti are strongest in war, and the Navahos call them "full of power." From all the pueblos, even from Zuni and Hopi, they come to our pueblo bringing belts and turquoises and mantas to offer to our Mother at her shrine at Koaske.[8]

Salt Woman is Refused Food

Old Salt Woman had a grandson. They were very poor. They came to Cochiti and went from house to house. People turned them away. The old woman said to her grandson, "We will go into this house," but again the people turned them away. The people were cooking for a feast. At that time they used no salt.

When Salt Woman and her grandson had been to all the houses, they came to a place outside the pueblo where lots of children were playing. Salt Woman had a magic crystal in her hand. All the children came to see. They came to a piñon tree. Salt Woman told them to have a good time playing under the tree. Then she told them each to take hold of a branch of the tree and swing themselves. She used her magic crystal, and they turned into chaparral jays (who live in piñon trees). Salt Woman said to the jays, "Now you are changed into birds because when we were in the pueblo nobody would invite us to stay. From now on you shall be chaparral jays."

They went south and came to Santo Domingo. They were well treated there and the people gave them food. After they had eaten Salt Woman said, "In Cochiti the people of the pueblo would not let us eat. My grandchild has suffered with hunger." When they were leaving she said, "I am very thankful for being given food to eat. I will leave my flesh for you."

She gave them her flesh. The people of the house ate it with their bread and meat. It tasted good—salty. This is how it happened. Salt Woman said to the people, "If I am in your food it will always taste better. When I left Cochiti I took all of the children outside the pueblo and we came to a piñon tree and there I changed them into chaparral jays. They treated me badly. I am thankful to you that you gave my grandson something to eat. I will go southeast and there I will stay, and if any of you want my flesh you will find it at that place. And when you come to gather, let there be no laughing, no singing, nothing of that kind—be quiet and clean." So she left Santo Domingo and went to Salt Lake, where we get salt today (a three days' journey in each direction).

Variant

The Indians were traveling south from White House. Before they all came out from Shipap, Masewa was told to tell all the Indians in White House where to live and what to call their pueblos. So they came to Cochiti, and afterwards they went out and settled the others.

Salt Woman and Salt Man came down to Cochiti. They were told, "If they do not receive you, you shall go on to the other villages." They started out. Salt Woman and Salt Man (her grandson) had been told to go into each of the houses and to greet the people there. But the people all said, "Do not shake hands with her. She has sores all over her hands and face." She was old, gray-haired, covered with scabby skin. As she left each house she said, "There are not sores on my hands and face. This is the way I was born." But nobody shook hands with her, or liked to have her in his house. She said, "I had better leave this place and cross the river with Salt Man." She went across and settled down in the meadow near Pena Blanca, but people came there and threw dirt over them. She said to Salt Man, "Let us move from here again." They moved farther off to Mosquito Place (a little farther up beyond Santo Domingo). Again they lived there a while, but cows and horses used to step on them, so Salt Woman said, "Let us go again." "All right," Salt Man said, "we'll start again and live far, far away from these people. Perhaps they do not want salt to flavor their food." So they went way down to Salt Lake (near Estancia). Since that time men have always had a difficult time to get salt. They have to remove all their clothes and even beads—naked as when they were born—and go in quiet as can be. They must not speak a word or laugh or make fun, and then they can take all they wish. If they speak or laugh or make fun, they will stand just where they are and die. It is always a great deal of trouble to bring the salt.

Notes

1.   Informant 1. See Dumarest, Father Noel, Notes on Cochiti, New Mexico, Mem. Amer. Anthrop. Assoc., vol. VI, p. 212. For discussion and abstract see Notes, p. 203.

2.   The narrator suggested that this referred to Thought Woman.

3.   Usually in this Keres story the life of the loser is staked upon the contest.

4.   Note on Dumarest, 215, n. 2.

5.   Informant 2.

6.   "Now even the mother of Santo Domingo."

7.   So that the line of the bang and the hair forms an uninterrupted half circle from ear to ear.

8.   A cave on the Rio Grande. Where the Bloody Hand katcina went in also.

FRANZ BOAS

Panther and Owl (Told 1891)*

There was the Owl and his chief. The Owl's chief was hunting elks every day. The people heard that he was always killing elks. Then Blue-jay told his chief's daughter: "Go to see the Owl's chief." In the morning she made herself ready and went. She went a long distance. She crossed five prairies. Then she saw a person. She approached him secretly. Now she reached him. He was dancing, and she hid herself. She looked at the person and thought: "Maybe that is the Owl's chief." The dancer had a flat head. She looked secretly. Now that person jumped, and she saw that he had caught a mouse. He had a mat on his back and put the mice into it. When he saw a tideland mouse he killed it and put it into his mat. That person was dancing all the time. Then a stick hit his nose, and blood came out of it. The person searched and found the woman. He said: "Oh, my wife. Let us go home." So the Owl found her first. She did not know him. Then he brought her to the house. The house was full of meat and grease. The grease on the one side of the house was all white. There at the end of the house the Owl was staying. The grease there was all green. It was the grease taken from the intestines. The Owl went to the end of the house and said: "I will take the grease of the man who is working for me,"and gave it to the woman. She ate it, and after she had finished he hid her. In the evening his chief came.The Owl had been there for a long time. The Panther carried one elk and said to the Owl: "Carry our elk in to the house." The Owl brought it and then they cut it. The Panther was going to give him grease, but he did not take it all. He only took some dung and a little

* From *Klathamet Texts* by Franz Boas in Bulletin 26, Bureau of American Ethnology, U.S. Government Printing Office, 1901.

fat. It became night. In the morning the Owl's chief made himself ready and went to hunt elks. Then the Owl went to steal at the end of the house from his chief. He stole the good grease and gave it to his wife. Then he went out and caught mice. He danced and sang all the time. He sang: "——" At noon the Owl went home˙ and stole some of his chief's grease and meat, and gave it to his wife. In the evening the Panther came home.

The woman made a hole in her mat and saw him. Oh, he was a pretty person. His hair was braided and reached below his buttocks. His face was painted with red stripes. Then the woman thought: "Oh, I made a mistake; I think he is the Owl's chief." Then the Panther said to the Owl: "Bring our elk and lick off its dung." Then the Owl scolded, "Qip, qip, qip," went his lips. The Panther spoke to him twice. Then the Owl rose and brought the elk into the house. They cut it, but the Owl was angry all the time. He received only the poor kind of grease. Then the chief said: "What do you think? Why are you angry all the time, you old Owl?" The Owl did not reply.

The next morning the Panther made himself ready again. Then the woman made a hole in her mat, and she saw him again. Then she was very much pleased with him. He always ate before he went hunting. Something was left over which he put up on the loft, and the woman saw it. In the morning the Owl arose and stole fat at the end of the house. He gave it to his wife. Then he hid her again. He went out. The Panther thought: "What is the matter with the Owl? He is always angry. He was not that way formerly." Thus thought the Panther. "I think I will go home when the sun is still up in the sky." He went home at that time and noticed that the Owl was there already. He said to the Owl: "Behold, you are here already!" "Yes; I am here already. Yes; I gave up hunting because I did not catch anything. Therefore I came home quickly." Then the Panther spoke to the Owl: "Oh, you old Owl; bring our elk into the house." "His ancestors called me that way." Then his lips went: "Qip, qip, qip." "Don't scold, old Owl." A long time he was angry; then he arose and brought in the elk. They cut it. The Panther gave him only the poor kind of fat, and the Owl took it.

Now the Panther really took notice. The two went to bed, but the Panther remained awake. He listened, and he heard the Owl talking in a low voice. All the time he was laughing in a low voice. Now he really took notice.

Early the Panther arose. He ate before he left. Now the woman again made a hole in her mat, and she looked at him when he had finished eating. He put on the loft what he had left. Then the Panther went, and the Owl arose. He said: "I am going to steal from my workman." He stole fat and meat, and gave it to his wife. Then he went. A little while he danced, and he came home again. He had caught only a little. About noon the Panther came back. The Owl was there already. He said: "Why do you always come home first?" Thus spoke the Panther. The Owl replied: "I caught all the mice; therefore I came back." "What do you always whisper in the evening? You keep me awake." The Owl replied: "I was dreaming." The Panther said: "Bring our elk, old Owl." The Owl scolded for a long time. He did not want to go. Then he went out and carried the elk into the house. The Owl took only the poor kind of grease. "Why do you always scold?" said the Panther to the Owl. The Owl replied: "You always give me all kinds of names." The Panther replied: "For a long time we two have been living all alone; don't scold. You have changed altogether; you are scolding all the time."

It grew dark. Then the Panther lay down at the end of the house and the Owl at the other end. The Panther was awake. The Owl asked that woman: "What is that?" "My hair."

"Oh, our hair, my wife." "What is that?" he said to her. "My ears." "Oh, our ears, my wife." "What is that?" he said. "My face." "Oh, our face, my wife." "What is that?" "Oh, my eyebrows." "Oh, our eyebrows, my wife." "What is that?" "My forehead." "Oh, our forehead, my wife." "What is that?" "My mouth." "Oh, our mouth, my wife." "What is that?" "My throat." "Oh, our throat, my wife." "What is that?" "My arm." "Oh, our arm, my wife." "What is that?" "My hand." "Oh, our hand, my wife." "What is that?" "My belly." "Oh, our belly, my wife." "What is that?" She was silent. Twice he said: "What is that?" He became angry. "What is that, woman?" She said: "My navel." "Oh, our navel, my wife." "What is that?" She did not speak to him. He said to her: "What is that? I shall scratch you." She was silent for a long time. Then she said to him: "My private parts." "Oh, our private parts, my wife." The Panther heard it.

Early he arose, and ate before going. He went. Then the Owl arose. He stole some grease and gave it to his wife. Then he went out for the fifth time. He danced a short time and came home. They left the woman alone. Then she arose and went to the end of the house. She looked at the food which the Panther had put aside. It was elk-marrow. Now she pulled out two of her hairs and tied one around one piece of marrow. She took the other hair and tied it around another piece of marrow. Then she put the food back there and hid in the Owl's bed. The Owl danced for a short while and came home. He stole some grease at the end of the house. At noon the Panther came back, but the Owl was there already. He did not say anything. Now he really took notice. The Panther stayed there some time. Then he took that marrow. He wanted to eat it. He broke it and the hair became loose. He stretched it out. He saw it was one fathom long. Then the Panther thought: "Oh, the Owl is hiding a woman." He broke another piece of marrow, and found another hair. After he had eaten, they cut the elk. He did not say anything. The night came on and they lay down. Then he heard the Owl laughing.

The Panther arose early and said: "Why did you laugh, Owl?" The Owl replied: "I dreamt the mice were climbing over me." The Panther went out. He stayed in the woods a little inland from the house. Then the Owl looked secretly and rose. He went out and went around. The Panther saw him. Then the Owl entered again. He spoke much in the house. The Panther heard the two speaking together. After some time the Owl went out again and went to catch mice. The Panther saw the Owl going. When he had gone a little while the Panther entered and searched in the Owl's bed. There he found a woman. He said to her: "Rise!" and he carried her to his bed, he said to her: "Did you hear about the famous Owl? You went to him." Now the Owl was dancing. A stick struck his nose and it began to bleed. Then he went home. The woman was already at the end of the house. She was lying down with the Panther. Then the Owl was angry. "I bought that woman for him and I went out in the canoe singing to buy the woman for him there at the end of the house." The Owl scolded for a long time.

Then the Panther said to that woman: "Look out! We shall fight. When we fly up higher and higher fighting, we shall kill each other. When green flesh falls down, you must burn it; when red flesh falls down, keep it, and do the same with the bones. When green bones fall down, burn them; when white bones fall down, keep them." The Owl scolded for a long time. Then the Panther said: "You are talking all the time. Come! we will rise to the sky and fight." The Owl made himself ready. He put on five raccoon blankets. The

Panther made himself ready. He put on five elkskin blankets. Now they began to fight. First they tore their blankets. When they had torn the blankets, they tore their bodies, and they began to rise upward. They flew to the sky, and the flesh began to fall down. Sometimes green flesh fell down. This the woman burned. When red flesh fell down, she kept it. Now they had torn all the flesh. Finally they tore their bones. When green bones fell down, the woman burned them. When white bones fell down, she kept them and put them into the basket. Then the intestines fell down. They looked just alike; some she burned, some she kept. Now she heard a noise of something falling down. The heads came down biting each other. Then she put a stick between them and tore them apart. She burned the Owl's head. Now she went down to the water and threw the flesh and that head into the water. She went up again. She waited a little while, then she saw her husband, the Panther. He came up to her and said: "Behold, you burned my intestines! These are the Owl's intestines. Go to your brother-in-law, the Bear, and tell him to give you one-half of his intestines." He gave them to her and she carried them home. He tried them, but they were not good. They made him feel sick. She carried them back and returned them to the Bear. She said to the Raccoon: "Oh, your elder brother sends word to you to give him your intestines." He gave her one-half. She took them and he tried them, but they were not good. They made him feel sick. He told her: "Carry them back. Tell the Wolf to give you one-half of his intestines." The Wolf gave them to her. She took them home and he tried them, but they were not good. They made him feel sick. He told her: "Go to the Beaver; he shall give me one-half of his intestines, but they were not good. They made him feel sick. He said to her: "Go to the Otter, your brother-in-law. He shall give you his intestines." She told him: "Your elder brother tells you to give him your intestines." He gave her one-half, and she took them home. He tried them, but they were not good. They made him feel sick. He tried all the quadrupeds and asked for their intestines. Last of all he asked the Lynx. She went to take his intestines. She got them and took them home. They were right. They did not make him feel sick.

They stayed there a long time. Then the woman was about to give birth to a child. She became sick, and she gave birth to two children. First she gave birth to an Owl, then to a Panther. The Panther said : "I will kill your owl-child." But the woman said : "No; the poor one. Let them grow up together!" They played together, and the Panther washed his son. The woman washed her son, the Owl. They grew up. The Owl's child killed shrews; the Panther's son killed chipmunks. Now they were really grown up. The Owl's son killed young mice and the Panther's son killed fawns. They did what their fathers had done. That is the story. To-morrow we shall have fine weather.

ARCHER TAYLOR

Introduction*

We can recognize several kinds of proverbial comparisons and similes : similes having the form *As black as pitch;* comparisons having the form *Like a bull in a china shop;* of which some may be used with a certain degree of independence and others are characteristically associated with a particular noun *(Eyes like saucers)* or a particular verb *(To swim like a fish);* and formulas that have been called proverbial exaggerations. There are rather few illustrations of the last variety in the present collection. *As much chance as a snowball in Hell* may serve as an example.

Two minor varieties of proverbial similes I suppose to be of recent origin because I have not found many examples antedating the mid-nineteenth century. The first of these varieties is a comparison naming a creature in a special situation, usually one peculiarly appropriate or entirely inappropriate to its nature. Examples are *As happy as baby beavers in a toothpick factory, As miserable as a horsefly at a dog show,* and *As unhappy as a tea sipper in a coffeehouse.* These do not seem to be securely established in tradition and may be casual inventions that will perhaps disappear, only to be replaced by other equally ingenious and temporary phrases. *Like a bull in a china shop* has, however, made a place for itself, and no doubt other phrases will become part of our folklore. The second minor variety of proverbial simile that seems to be of recent origin involves a pun. Examples are *As broke as the Ten Commandments,*[1] *As corny as Kansas in August, As lit* (drunk) *as a lamp, As nutty as a fruitcake,* and *As seedy as a*

* From "Introduction" of *Proverbial Comparisons and Similes from California,* by Archer Taylor, University of California Press, Berkeley and Los Angeles, 1954.

watermelon. To these we may add such comparisons as *Off like a pot leg, To lie like a rug,* and *Always behind* (tardy) *like a dog's tail*. Although many of these phrases are extremely popular, as may be seen from the figures below, they do not seem securely established in tradition. Even a simile so often reported as *As nutty as a fruitcake* may not prove a permanent addition to our traditional phrases and will probably disappear if *nutty* ceases to be a frequently used word.

Ironical similes and comparisons like *Crazy like a fox, As graceful as a cow* or *As quiet as an Irish wake* have been used for a long time. Apperson cites such examples as *As straight as my leg and that's crooked at the knee, As welcome as water in one's shoes,* and *As wise as Waltham's calf*. Many more can be gleaned from the collections. I cannot cite an old parallel to *As clear as mud,* but *As clear as ink* has been current in Dutch and German for several centuries.

The present collection offers a good but not exhaustive survey of proverbial similes *(As black as pitch)*, an inadequate survey of adverbial and adjectival comparisons *(To sing like a bird, Eyes like a cat)*, and an altogether inadequate account of proverbial exaggerations.[2] Perhaps the instructions to the collectors did not make clear the desirability of including the two latter varieties of proverbial phrases. Proverbs that employ comparisons *(Like master, like man; Example is better than precept)* will be included in a forthcoming collection of California proverbs.

The question "Who made these proverbial phrases?" is as badly formulated as the old and tiresome question "Who made the ballads?" No doubt some person first put into words the idea found in the traditional simile *As bitter as gall*. What precise Greek words he used, if Greek was the language he spoke, we can never know. The process of oral transmission determined the original manner of expression or shaped the form that his words later assumed. Both the speaker and oral transmission have "made" these phrases, and both the speaker and oral transmission are proper subjects of study. Only rarely can we put our finger on the person whom we can name with some show of probability as the inventor of a phrase that has become proverbial. Walter.Winchell or Irvin S. Cobb has been said, although incorrectly, to have invented *As much privacy as a goldfish,* a simile that borders on the proverbial.[3] We can now and again identify the circumstances or the age in which a proverbial phrase was invented, without being able to discover the inventor's name. For example, B. J. Whiting describes the circumstances in which *Thought like Jack Robinson* (i.e., thought wrong) arose.[4] We should not desist from efforts to find the inventors of proverbial materials, but we dare not often hope for success in them.

Proverbs, proverbial phrases, and proverbial comparisons and similes are clearly separated in folk speech. A few proverbial comparisons have been made from proverbs : *Like calling the kettle black* is based on *The pot calls the kettle black.* The idea in *Like bringing coals to Newcastle* may also be expressed in the proverbial phrase *To bring coals to Newcastle.* In general, however, the three categories are kept apart. A proverb can often be turned into a simile, but when it is so used it is felt to be an adaptation of the original proverb.

Details characteristic of oral transmission are easily discernible in any collection of proverbial materials. Proverbial similes are, for example, prone to add unnecessary or inappropriate embellishments. *As hungry as a wolf* appears in this collection in the form *As hungry as a she-wolf with pups. As homely as a mud fence* has the variant *As homely as a mud fence staked and redered* (daubed?) *with tadpoles.* Elaborations are, in general, few in number, often recent in origin, and uncertain of traditional permanence. We are poorly in-

formed about the nature of these elaborations and the circumstances in which they arise. Very old and widely disseminated
similes rarely admit them. For example, *As bitter as gall* has
been in use for more than two thousand years and occurs in
all the languages about which I can get information. I can
cite no elaborated version of it. *As busy as a bee* is also old
and widely known, but exhibits only a few casual and unimportant elaborations.

Associational thinking or the process of oral transmission is
seen in the creation of new comparisons out of old materials.
As honest as the day is long is, I suppose, the original comparison. From it one California speaker has formed *As straight
as the day is long* by substituting the synonym *straight* for
honest. He could do so all the more easily because he remembered *As happy as the day is long*. Inventions of this sort are
likely to sacrifice appropriateness and vigor. *As ugly as sin* was
once conceived in a very real physical sense. A weakened
sense of sin has brought with it the possibility of using *as sin*
in other contexts. *As mean as sin* may still preserve some recol-
lection of the wickedness of sin, but the pictorial conception
is not present. *As clever as sin* seems to have degenerated to
a stage in which *as sin* is merely an intensification. The degeneration is not complete, because *as sin* is still used only in
contexts having an association, however remote, with wickedness. *As hell* has, on the other hand, become virtually colorless. One can say both *As ugly as hell* and *As thirsty as hell*,
but one cannot say *As thirsty as sin*.

New words replace old ones. *As crazy as a bedbug* becomes
As batty as a bedbug, and *As crazy as a loon* becomes (mis-
takenly, because it is not the loon, but its laughter, that is
insane) *As screwy as a loon*. The adjective *thin* suffers in com-
petition with *skinny*, and *sharp* supersedes *clever*, *smart*, and
bright. We see currents in folk speech but can only occasion-

ally guess what their effect may be. They will not sweep every-thing before them. *Fleet* has, I dare say, disappeared almost completely from folk speech, but it survives in *As fleet as a deer* and *As fleet as the wind* (NC$_{197}$). Assonance has probably helped preserve the first of these. The present collection shows, as any collection would do, the invention of new versions and phrases and the preservation of old materials. If we had at our disposal texts representing a longer period of time and a wider geographical range, we could see more clearly than this col-lection permits us to do the operation of forces that create and preserve folklore.

The use of comparisons and similes in tales, ballads, and riddles exhibits peculiarities that deserve notice. I confine my remarks to references to colors because only such references occur with any frequency in all three genres. Although Ger-hard Kahlo has written briefly on colors in tales, he does not make special mention of similes.[5] B. J. Whiting has collected and put in convenient order the comparisons and similes used in ballads.[6] I have grouped together the English riddles con-taining similes.[7] This material is abundant enough to permit us to draw inferences from it. Narrators of tales use freely *As black as a raven, As red as blood,* and *As white as snow.*[8] These old similes do not exchange with such other old and well-established formulas as *As black as pitch, As red as a rose (cherry, ruby),* and *As white as milk.* In countries where snow is unfamiliar, we may have *As white as marble.* The reasons for this limited choice of similes are not obvious. Ballad singers have a much greater freedom in the use of similes and comparisons. This freedom arises, at least in part, from the fact that ballads often use descriptive adjectives and tales rarely do. The three similes characteristic of Little Snow White that I have just mentioned occur frequently in ballads, and others occur equally or even more frequently. *As white as milk,* which is (as far as I know) almost never found in tales, is the most popular of all color similes in ballads. The heroine has *milk-white* hands, and the hero rides on a *milk-white* steed. *As white as a lily* appears perhaps half as often as *As white as milk* and is a similarly characteristic detail of ballad style. *Nut-brown,* which never occurs in the form *As brown as a nut,* is a ballad cliché[9] Ballad singers show a remarkable preference, which does not seem explainable by metrical needs, for the para-synthetic compounds, *raven-black, blood-red, lily-white, milk-white,* and *snow-white.* In riddles, *As black as a raven* almost never occurs, and *As black as pitch,* which Whiting found only once in more than two thousand ballads, is very popular. *As red as blood* and *As white as snow* are acceptable in riddles, tales, and ballads. *As white as milk* is also found in riddles, but not *As white as a lily.* Ballad singers and riddlers use freely *As green as grass,* which could not be easily introduced into a tale. Riddlers virtually never use *As red as a rose (cherry, ruby).* They have kept some old similes like *As round as an apple, As round as the moon,* that have otherwise largely passed out of use. We lack a sufficiency of material that would permit us to interpret fully these stylistic variations and cannot extend these comments to German or Romance folklore, where the similes in ballads, riddles, and tales have not been conveniently tabulated.

Rare or obsolete words and allusions to forgotten customs or objects are surprisingly few. Their rarity is all the more surprising in view of the tenacity with which traditon often retains ideas that are no longer understood. A cursory reading of the two hundred and fifty similes printed by John Ray in 1670 shows that tradition was more vigorous and varied than it is now. Much of the material in our collection is hackneyed. It may not give an altogether correct picture of the actual state of traditional comparisons and similes, but I am not certain of my ability to remedy its deficiencies.

There are, to be sure, curious references to old ideas in this collection. I am not altogether sure that I have fully explained the allusion which underlies *To write like an angel. As cross as a bear* presumably refers to the old sport of bearbaiting and does not suggest the annoying friendliness of bears in zoos and national parks. A captive bear's disposition depends on circumstances. Twenty years or so ago, as B. J. Whiting tells me, gasoline-station proprietors in Maine kept bears caged to lure in customers. The bears were neglected and ill used and two at least retaliated by killing their careless keepers. The legislature then passed a law against the commercial display of bears. *To work like a charm* was readily intelligible in a day when magical practices were more general or at least more acceptable than they are now. Alliteration probably explains the retention of the word *doornail,* an old name for a nail or bar on a door, in *As dead (deaf) as a doornail,* but the explanation is not altogether convincing and is still an occasion for dispute. The allusion involved in *Like the Devil hates holy water* has survived in a Protestant population. *To run around like a dog on a spit* concerns a turnspit, but I am not sure that the California speaker was fully aware of the allusion. The museum piece *mumchat*—a word first reported in the seventeenth century—is a strange survival. In this California collection it does not seem to be a bit of book learning borrowed from a dictionary or collection of proverbs. *As strong as an ox* probably refers to the use of an ox as a draft animal. Although oxen are still occasionally used for hauling, the simile was more obvious and more generally intelligible in a former day. *As uncomfortable as a cat on a grindstone* looks like a rationalization of the seventeenth-century references to a cat on a hot bakestone. In *As welcome as the pox* the word *pox* has the old meaning 'syphilis.'

With a few exceptions Biblical religious allusions have become colorless and restricted in variety. There are references to Adam's off ox (which is scarcely Biblical), Balaam's ass, Bashan's bull (which is a misunderstanding of the original), Beelzebub, Gabriel's trump, Job's turkey (which is also a creature not found in the Bible), Joseph's coat, Lucifer, Methuselah, Moses, Pharoah's heart, Solomon, the Ten Commandments, Tophet, and the writing on the wall in Belshazzar's palace. Except the obscure allusion to Job's turkey, these similes are not often reported in this California collection. There are a few quotations of Biblical passages like *As harmless as a dove,* but I am not sure that the speaker was always aware of the source. The references to the Devil are almost meaningless. The references to Hell and its synonyms (blazes, blue blazes, Hades, the hot place, the place you read about) are curious. They include allusions to the gates of Hell, the hinges of Hell, and the hubs of Hades. No one has offered an explanation of the last of these. Svartengren (424–25) collects more Biblical allusions and points out the almost complete lack of similes suggested by the New Testament. He explains it as something "to be expected from a puritan people." This may be a correct explanation, but two casual readings of Rodriguez Marin's collection shows that similes suggested by the New Testament are equally rare in Spanish.

Allusions to literature and history are not numerous. There are reminiscences of Croesus and the Gordian knot and, from modern literature, of the Babes in the Wood, Foxy Grandpa, Old Dog Tray, Old Mother Hubbard, the last rose of summer, and the wreck of the Hesperus. An obvious historical allusion concerns the Black Hole of Calcutta. Perhaps the references to Dick's hatband can be explained by the low esteem in which Richard Cromwell was held, but they are more probably allusions to some unidentified local character of more recent date. Such allusions to obscure historical figures and events are extremely difficult to run down. It seems probable that the diligence of the contributors to *Notes and Queries* has brought to light the allusions underlying *Like a bull in a china shop* and *The mad hatter.*

A proverbial comparison owes its effectiveness to its obvious pertinence to a situation, but it may survive traditionally until the allusion becomes obscure. Most of the foregoing Biblical, literary, and historical allusions are readily intelligible, but we have noted some exceptions to the rule. One can imagine that *To act like Foxy Grandpa, Like Grand Central Station, To have more money than Carter has pills, To grow like Topsy,* and *To look like the wreck of the Hesperus* may become obscure. *As bare as Old Mother Hubbard's cupboard* will not soon lose its pertinence, because nursery rhymes are very nearly indestructible. The use of topical allusions in proverbial comparisons and similes has probably decreased somewhat. A casual reading of Morris P. Tilley, *A Dictionary of Proverbs in England in the Sixteenth and Seventeenth Centuries,* reveals many proverbial comparisons with little meaning today.[10] In a few of them we can discover what the speaker meant, but this is often a desperate enterprise with small chance of success. Klein points out (pp. 20–24) that topical allusions are rather numerous in the Romance languages and especially in Spanish, but I am not sure that there is any significant difference between Romance and English usage in this regard.

The investigation of the syntactical and stylistic peculiarities would force us to go beyond the limits of this collection, but the nature of the problems may be briefly indicated here. Many old comparisons occur in two forms, a simile *(As black as pitch)* and a parasynthetic compound *(pitch black).* The circumstances in which the compound can be formed are obscure. Some compounds like *Sky blue, stone dead,* and *stone deaf* are freely used today, while the corresponding similes like *As dead as a stone* are of infrequent occurrence. *Pea green* is, for example, heard often enough, but *As green as a pea* is rare. Some compounds like *honey sweet* and *brasse bold* have become unusual or have disappeared entirely. Still others seem never to have been formed, although the simile, like *As bitter as gall,* may be very old. Recognition and discussion of these compounds have been made more difficult by the invention of modern descriptive color adjectives like *Nile green,* which does not (I believe) imply the existence of a simile *As green as the Nile.* Likewise, *Orinoco green* is more likely the product of a paint company's advertising department than a traditional development in folk speech or a traveler's observation of the river. Svartengren maintains (p. 461) that a synthetic language like Old English no doubt preferred the compound similes of the type *stane-still.* His opinion calls for further investigation. The discussion of another syntactical peculiarity goes far beyond the scope of this collection and my comments. In their earliest occurrences certain English comparisons are reported in the form *As black as any coal.* It is not clear how long the use of *any* in comparisons persisted and whether it shows any peculiarities. Examples could be cited from the early nineteenth century. Svartengren (463) comments briefly on the use of *any.* A modern stylistic cliché is the use of proverbial as in *It's green like the proverbial grass.* I cannot venture a guess about the age or history of this cliché.

Notes

1. The speaker thinks of a low state of morality or finances, but probably does not remember Exod. 32: 19.

2. See Herbert Halpert, "A Pattern of Proverbial Exaggeration from West Kentucky," *Midwest Folklore,* I (1951), 41–47; Martha Bell Sanders, "Proverbial Exaggerations from East Kentucky," *ibid.,* II (1952), 163–166.

3. See Whiting, NC 416 (his reference to "Some Current Meanings of 'Proverbial'" should be to p. 233). Stevenson 1948 reports an example from 1904 (it is not in the form of a simile) that long antedates any use by Winchell or Cobb.

4. See Whiting, NC 430.

5. "Farben," *Handwörterbuch des deutschen Märchens,* II (Berlin, 1934–1940), 51–56.

6. "Proverbial Material in the Popular Ballads," *Journal of American Folklore,* XLVII (1934), 22–44.

7. *English Riddles from Oral Tradition* (Berkeley, 1951), pp. 533–570, Nos. 1260–1408.

8. These comparisons are especially characteristic of Little Snow-White (Brothers Grimm, *Household Tales,* No. 53). For references see Stith Thompson, *Motif-Index* (Bloomington, Ind. 1932–1936), V, 429, Z 65.1.

9. See Marcel Francon, *Notes sur l'esthétique de la femme au XVI siècle* (Cambridge, Mass., 1939); Doris Massny, *Die Formel "Das braune Mägdlein" im alten deutchen Volkslied* (Breslau dissertation; Breslau, 1937), reprinted in *Niederdeutsche Zeitschrift für Volkskunde,* XV (1937), 25–65; V. Russo, "La razza e due epigrammi pompeiani: ancora della bianca e della bruna," *Archivio per la raccolta e lo studio delle tradizioni popolari italiane,* XV (1940), 96–97.

10. From Tilley's collection I select the following examples in the letters A and B. A 95: As mad as Ajax, who killed sheep; A 410: He looks like a Lochaber ax; B 96: To be dressed like Bartholomew babies; B 112: As bold as blind Bayard; B 162: As bold as Beauchamp; B 721: As mad as the baiting bull of Stamford. Some of them have been explained, but others are entirely obscure.

VANCE RANDOLPH

Miscellaneous Items*

The folk beliefs lumped together under this chapter's heading have little in common, beyond the fact that they do not
easily fit into any of the previous chapters. How should one
classify, for example, the hillman's strange notions about the
physical characteristics correlated with honesty and depend-
ability? There are still old-timers who will have no business
dealing with a man whose beard is of a noticeably different
color than his hair; I have talked with men and women, as
recently as 1936, who refused to support a candidate for public office because his hair was gray and his mustache red.

Colonel A. S. Prather, who lived near Kirbyville, Missouri,
in the eighties, always said "Never trust a man with ears too
close to the top of his head." And Mrs. C. P. Mahnkey,
daughter of the Colonel, told me that she thought there must
be some truth in it. Mrs. Mahnkey also quoted Uncle Jim
Parnell, who placed small confidence in "a feller who rattled
money in his pocket whilst he was a-tradin'." A person with
very small ears is generally supposed to be stingy or "close." If
a man's fingers are straight and held together in repose, so that
one cannot see the light between one finger and another, it
is also a sign of stinginess or at least frugality. When a man
begins to speak, and then forgets what he was about to say,
many hillfolk believe that the statement he intended to make
was a lie.

The common expression "never trust a feller that wears a
suit" does not really represent a superstitious belief, but merely
the universal prejudice against men from the cities. The backwoods boys seldom wear suits. They buy expensive trousers

* From *Ozark Superstitions* by Vance Randolph, copyright 1947 by
Columbia University Press.

sometimes but prefer leather jackets or windbreakers to matching coats. A woman in Bransom, Missouri, once said to me : "Them Bull Creek boys is hell on big-legged pants. Don't keer much about coats, but *pants is their pride*." Many a prosperous young countryman, in possession of a farm, a car, some cattle and other livestock, has never owned a suit of clothes in his life.

It is natural perhaps, in a fox-huntin' country, that a man who doesn't make friends with dogs should be regarded as a suspicious character. Related to this, no doubt, is the old idea that a beekeeper can always be relied upon, while a fellow who doesn't get along with bees is likely to be untrustworthy in financial matters. But what can we make of the old saying that "an honest man never rides a sorrel horse"? I have heard references to this sorrel-horse business in many parts of the Ozark country, over a long term of years, but even today I'm not sure just what is meant by it.

There is a very old sayin' to the effect that a thief always looks into his cup before he drinks. This is quoted in a joking way, but I once met a deputy sheriff in Eureka Springs, Arkansas, who said that he had studied the matter for many years and was almost convinced that there was something in it. "Them old fellers that figgered out such notions," he told me, "was hunters an' Indian fighters. They had sharp eyes, an' they watched ever' thing mighty close."

In a poverty-ridden region such as the Ozarks, one would expect to find a number of superstitions relating to wealth. If a gray moth called the money miller hovers over you, or a little red money spider crawls on your clothes, you are sure to become rich some day. When a honeybee buzzes about your head, it is a sign that you will get a letter with money in it, or at least good news about financial matters. Mr. Clarence Marshbanks, of Galena, Missouri, says that the children used to cry "Money 'fore the week's out!" whenever they saw a redbird; the idea is that if you could get it all said before the bird was out of sight, there would be money coming your way by the end of the week.

A person whose initials spell a word is certain to be rich, sooner or later. A man with a wart or mole on the neck is supposed to be fortunate in money matters, according to the old rhyme :

> Mole on the neck,
> Money by the peck.

A woman with conspicuous hairs on her breasts will attain riches, if we are to believe the old-timers.

Ozark children are often told that if the lucky-bones taken from crawfish are buried in the earth, they'll turn into nickels in a fortnight. Many a credulous mountain boy has tried this, and one youngster said disgustedly : "God, what a lie old Granny Durgen told me!"

The man who has an eye tooth extracted should hasten to bury it in a cemetery, on an infidel's grave, because this is sure to bring money within six months. When you see a lot of bubbles on the surface of your coffee, try to drink them all before they disappear, for if you succeed it means that you are about to make a large sum of money.

On seeing a shooting star, always cry out "money-money-money" before it disappears, and you will inherit wealth. When you first glimpse the new moon, turn over a coin in your pocket without looking at the moon again, and you will be fortunate in money matters. It is always a good idea to be touching a silver coin whenever you see the moon, and it may be for this reason that rings hammered from silver coins are so popular in some sections. A girl who happens to see the new moon "cl'ar o' brush" hastens to kiss her hand three times and expects to find something worth a lot of money before the moon changes.

Like most primitive folk, the Ozark natives attach considerable importance to dreams, but their dream interpretations don't seem to differ greatly from those current among unlettered people in other parts of the country.

To dream of muddy water means trouble, to dream of snakes presages a battle with one's enemies, to dream of money means that the dreamer will be poorer than ever before. A dream of white horses is unlucky and may mean sickness or death in the family. A dream of death is good luck if the dream comes at night and usually signifies a wedding, but to fall asleep in the daytime and dream of death is very unfortunate. A dream of childbirth is always welcome, a sign of a happy and prosperous marriage. The man who dreams repeatedly of fishes will attain great wealth. To dream of chickens is bad luck, and the vision of a black boat means an early death. A lady at Fort Smith, Arkansas, told me that she had discarded nearly all the superstitions of her childhood, but still felt that it is bad luck to dream about cattle. To dream of a hoe or a rake signifies a happy marriage. The girl who dreams always of storms and floods will marry a rich man. It is good luck to dream of pigeons or doves, and usually means that a fortunate love affair is just around the corner.

The first dream that one has in a new house, or when sleeping under a new quilt, will nearly always come true— many mountain girls are anxious to "dream out" a new quilt or coverlet. The same may be said of a dream related before breakfast, or of one dreamed on Friday and told on Saturday :

> Friday night's dream, on Saturday told,
> Will always come true, no matter how old.

An old woman at Pineville, Missouri, told me that as a

little girl she dreamed of a gigantic snake coiled around her father's log house. She says this was a sign of the Civil War which broke out a few months later, in which her father and two brothers were killed. In 1865 she dreamed that the big snake was dead, upon which she knew that the War would soon be ended.

Mrs. May Kennedy McCord, of Springfield, Missouri, says that the best way to stop unpleasant dreams is to stuff cloth into the key hole. But I'm not sure that she means this to be taken literally.

Some people are accustomed to place a knife under the dreamer's pillow, to prevent nightmares. I once noticed a small girl, not more than ten years old, sleeping with the handle of an enormous homemade bowie knife sticking out from under her pillow. "Maizie used to wake up a-hollerin'," the mother told me, "but since I put that there knife under the piller, we aint had no more trouble." Somnambulism is related to nightmares in the hillman's mind, and there is a widespread belief that one should never awaken a sleepwalker, as this may cause instant death. The Ozarker who sees a friend walking in his sleep just strides along beside him and tries to keep him from getting into danger, but makes no effort to wake him up.

At several places in Missouri and Arkansas one hears of "electric springs." I never saw one of these, but persons in Lanagan and Anderson, Missouri, told me that if you dip your knife in the waters of a certain spring branch north of Anderson, the steel blade becomes a magnet. A boy assured me that the blade of his clasp knife retained its magnetic properties for several months, after being immersed in the "electric water" about five minutes.

Most hillfolk believe that all water which is clear and cold is good to drink—they cannot understand that such water may carry deadly organisms. Many persons contend that any spring water, no matter how contaminated, is purified by running over a hundred feet of gravel.

It is said that a man who takes three drinks in three minutes from any Ozark spring is bound to return for another drink before he dies. In one form or another, that story is heard all over the Ozark country. But whether it is really old-time stuff, or was cooked up by the Chamber of Commerce propagandists, I have been unable to find out.

There is an odd belief that stalactites or stalagmites are somehow deadlier than other stones, and that even a slight blow from a piece of "drip rock" is generally fatal. Carl Hovey, of Springfield, Missouri, was killed years ago by bumping his head on a stalactite and is still remembered and talked about whenever this superstition is mentioned.

The "git-your-wish" class of superstitions is rather large, but I don't think it is taken very seriously by many adults nowadays. Grown people still go through the motions, but it is only the children who really believe that their wishes will come true.

When a little girl sees a redbird she "throws a kiss an' makes a wish." If she can throw *three* kisses before the bird disappears, she is certain that her wish will be granted unless she sees the same bird again, in which case all bets are off. Some say that if one spies a cardinal in a tree he should always make a wish and then throw a stone; if the bird flies upward the wish will be granted, but if it flies downward the desire will never be satisfied.

The hillman who sees a snake trail across a dusty road often spits in the track and makes a wish; such wishes are supposed to come true, particularly if nobody is within sight of the spitter at the time.

When a plowman hears the first turtle dove in the spring, he makes a wish and turns round three times on his left heel.

Then he takes off his left shoe, and if he finds a hair in the shoe which is the color of his wife's or sweetheart's hair, he feels that his wish will be realized. Several sober and generally truthful farmers have told me that they have tried this and actually found the hair; one man said it was a very long hair, coiled up as if it had been placed in the shoe deliberately.

Some hillfolk "stick a wish" on a soaring buzzard high up and far away; if the bird passes out of sight without flapping its wings, they think that the wish will be granted. "When you see a little new colt," said one of my neighbors, "always spit in your hand an' make a wish; your wish is bound to come true, 'cordin' to the old folks."

Many Ozark children believe in "stamping mules," especially gray or white mules. On seeing one of these animals the child wets his thumb, presses a little saliva into the palm of the left hand, and "stamps" it with a blow of his fist. When he has stamped twenty mules he makes a wish—it's sure to be granted. In some parts of the Ozarks, where Negroes are rare but not entirely lacking, I am told that the children "stamp niggers" the same as mules. I met children near Mena, Arkansas, who were stamping white horses too, but without much enthusiasm; they said it was necessary to stamp a hundred horses before making a wish.

An old woman near Noel, Missouri, always makes a wish when she sees a spotted horse, believing that if she refrains from looking at the animal again and tells someone about the occurrence as soon as possible, her wish will come true. "But it won't work in Oklahomy," she said with a toothless grin, "there's too many paint ponies over there."

If a hillman happens to see a star before dark he shuts his eyes for a moment, spits over his left shoulder, and makes a wish. Many an Ozarker "sticks a wish" on a falling star; if he succeeds in pronouncing the words under his breath before the

star is out of sight and refrains from telling anybody the
nature of the wish, he believes that it will come true. When
the first star of the evening appears backwoods children make
a wish, then cross their fingers and chant:

> Star light, star bright,
> First star I seen tonight,
> I wish I may, I wish I might,
> Git the wish I wish tonight!

Children at Reeds Spring, Missouri, when they see a yellow
boxcar standing still, stamp their feet and make a wish. If the
yellow car is moving, the charm doesn't work.

Some hillfolk say that if you make a wish at the bottom of
a long steep hill and don't speak or look back until you have
reached the top, your wish is sure to be granted. It is well
to make a wish, also, when one walks on strange ground for
the first time. Some people make a wish whenever they see a
woman wearing a man's hat.

In Taney county, Missouri, they say that the first time a
woman sews on a button for a man, she should make a wish
about that man's future, and such a wish invariably comes
true.

It is bad luck to drop a comb, but when an Ozark woman
does so she invariably puts her foot on it and makes a wish.
When a girl's dress turns up accidentally, she knows that her
lover is thinking of her and hastens to kiss the hem and make
a wish, confident that it will be granted. If her shoestring
comes untied she asks a friend to tie it, and while this is being
done she makes a wish. When a child's tooth is extracted he
doesn't throw it away but puts it under his pillow and sleeps
on it, confident that this will cause his chief desire to be
granted within a few days.

When a young girl in Springfield, Missouri, finds one of

her eyelashes has fallen out, she puts it on her thumb and makes a wish; then she blows the eyelash away and believes that her wish will come true.

If two Ozark children happen to pronounce the same word or phrase at the same time, they must not speak again until they have hooked their little fingers together, made wishes, and chanted the following:

First voice:	"Needles,"
Second voice:	"Pins,"
First voice:	"Triplets,"
Second voice:	"Twins."
First voice:	"When a man marries,"
Second voice:	"His troubles begin,"
First voice:	"When a man dies,"
Second voice:	"His troubles end."
First voice:	"What goes up the chimney?"
Second voice:	"Smoke!"

This done, the youngsters unhook their little fingers and go on about their business, each satisfied that his or her desire will be fulfilled. A girl in Stone county, Missouri, told me that all her schoolmates were familiar with this ceremony, and that many practiced it even after they were old enough to attend the village high schools.

A woman at West Plains, Missouri, places her right hand on the closed Bible, makes a wish, and opens the book at random. She does this three times, muttering the same wish under her breath. If the opened Bible shows the words "it came to pass" three times in succession, she is sure to get her wish. This woman tells me that she has been doing this for many years, and that perhaps 90 percent of her prayers have been granted. "Of course," she told me smiling, "a body shouldn't wish for somethin' that aint *reasonable*."

Another semi-serious ceremony occurs when the first louse

is found on a boy baby's head. This is quite an occasion in some families, and the other children all gather round while the mother kills the louse by "popping" it on the family Bible. While doing this she intones a wish about the children's future profession and salutes him as lawyer, doctor, merchant, farmer, preacher or what-not. This ritual is not exactly a joke—children are not allowed to laugh at anything in which the Bible is concerned—but I do not think that many adults really believe that the child's future is determined by "louse poppin'."

One sometimes hears cryptic references to one hillman "drivin' a stake" or "plantin' a bush" in another's dooryard. My first impression was that these phrases referred to what the hillfolk call "family matters," but I learned later that sometimes they are to be taken quite literally. A lawyer in McDonald county, Missouri, told me that our local rich man, in a towering rage had exhibited a "green stake" which an enemy had driven into his front lawn at midnight. He wanted the lawyer to see that the stake driver was arrested and flung into jail. "He thought the fellow had made a *wish* on the stake, or something," the attorney chuckled. "A kind of spooky business. No sense to it at all. I just threw the stake in the fire, an' advised my client to go back home an' forget it."

In the *Taney County Republican*, a weekly newspaper published at Forsyth, Missouri, February 20, 1941, appeared the following bit of gossip: "Rita Reynolds and Arnold Davis are planning on planting a tree in Alvin Huff's yard." The neighbors told me that Rita had been "goin' with" Alvin, but the two had quarreled, and now she was "goin' with" Arnold Davis instead. Some members of the Huff family were said to be considerably displeased about this item in the *Republican*. But nobody seemed willing to tell me just what was meant by it.

Some hillfolk believe that if the cicadas or "locusts" have a black *W* on their wings it is a sure sign of war. Mrs. May Kennedy McCord insists that there is something in this notion and recalls that she saw the fatal *W* on locusts' wings the year of the Spanish-American War.[1]

An old man near Bentonville, Arkansas, told me that it was no trouble to predict the result of any national election. If the Democrats are going to win, every garden is full of dog fennel; if a Republican victory is in the cards, dog fennel will be scarce, and plantain will choke every fence corner in Arkansas,—which God forbid! Asked about the best method of doping out the democratic primaries, the old chap just grinned and shook his head.

During the presidential campaign of 1928, many Ozarkers saw a strange light in the sky, doubtless the aurora borealis. Some people in Christian county, Missouri, were very much frightened; they thought the end of the world was at hand, so they held a big prayer-meeting. Clay Fulks, a professor at Commonwealth College, near Mena, Arkansas, told me that his neighbors believed that the light was a sign from God Almighty, warning the people not to vote for Al Smith.

In the early days of the New Deal, many Holy Roller preachers wandered through the backwoods of Missouri and Arkansas denouncing the "Blue Eagle" of the NRA, claiming that it was the evil sign described in the Apocalypse. The Joplin (Missouri) *Globe* (Aug. 29, 1933) discussed this matter seriously at some length, estimating that "between 20 and 25 percent of the population of the foothill region" identified the NRA symbol with the seven-headed beast of doom mentioned by St. John. In 1942 I heard one of these fellows in the courtyard at Galena, Missouri, preaching against the government sugar rationing; he placed great emphasis upon the "mark" or "stamp" which he said was predicted in the Bible. "Right over thar at Troy Stone's store," he cried, "you caint even git a little poke o' sugar without that stamp!"

Many Ozarkers feel that there is some religious or political significance connected with any unusual mark on an egg shell, and such marks are carefully studied. Old-timers in southern Missouri and northern Arkansas still talk of the "hen-egg revivals" which swept over this region in pioneer days. The story goes that some old woman found an egg with the words "Judgment is at Hand" plainly marked on the shell. Ministers of various sects came long distances to examine this egg and preached about it. The general impression prevailed that it was a "token" or omen and meant that the end of the world was soon to come. People became very religious for awhile, but after a year or so had passed and nothing happened, the excitement gradually died down, and the "hen-egg revival" was regarded as a sort of joke.

As recently as 1935 a similar excitement arose in the village of Couch, Missouri, when Mrs. Henry Bennett found an egg imprinted with the phrase "Here my Word 35." Viewing this as a religious portent, Mrs. Bennett told her neighbors about it. "A wave of excited piety overtook Couch," reports *Time,* February 4, 1935. "To Mrs. Bennett's home went visitor after visitor, to emit fervent prayers. When, in a fit of devout jitters, a female preacher dropped the egg and broke it, Mrs. Bennett succeeded in gluing enough pieces on another egg so that the words were still visible." Mrs. Bennett said that she did not know what the egg meant, but "it was sent to us for some good reason, and there is no need for the children of God to be afraid."

A woman once showed me a strange scar, something like a Chinese ideograph, on an egg shell. Later she told me privately that her husband, who was a Pentecostal preacher, had fallen into a trance at sight of the "inscription" and translated it. The message stated, he said, that Jesus Christ was going to visit the United States, run for President on the Democratic ticket, and "stump the whole State of Arkansas!"

Well, so much for superstition in the Ozark country. When I began to collect material for this book, more than twenty-five years ago, it seemed to me that these old folk beliefs were disappearing very rapidly and would soon be rejected and forgotten. I intimated as much in my first paper on the subject, published in 1927.[2] We all talked at length about scientific progress, and enlightenment, and the obvious effect of popular education. But now, I am not so sure. I am not so sure about anything, nowadays.

Notes

1. Springfield (Missouri) *News & Leader*, Jan. 4, 1933.
2. *Journal of American Folklore*, Vol. 40 (1927), pp. 78–93.

ARTHUR H. FAUSET

Riddles*

Was a body met a body
In a patch of beans.
Kin a body tell a body
What a body means?

> A man had a field of beans. Two rabbits met
> together in the field.

I was sitting in my chair,
I spied the dead carrying the living,
And oh, wasn't that a dreadful wonder!

> A vessel.

One thing it bites like fury but it never stings. It crawls slow
in its movement.

> Bedbug.

If he comes, he no comes,
If he come, he no comes,

> Corn (and crow). If the crow comes, the corn doesn't.
> If the crow doesn't come, the corn does.

When is a door not a door?

> When it's ajar.

When is a cat not a cat?

> When it's a kitten.

Variant: Acts like a cat,
Looks like a cat,
Yet it isn't a cat,
What is it?

> A kitten.

* From *Folklore from Nova Scotia* by Arthur H. Fauset. Published as
Vol. XXIV, Memoirs of the American Folklore Society, New York:
1931.

267

What is the difference between a colored baby and a white baby?

A colored baby is crow-shade (crocheted), and the white baby is knitted.

What wears a shoe like a horse?

A mare.

What makes more noise under a gate than a pig?

Two pigs.

Why does a rooster cross the street in the mud?

To get on the other side.

Why does a hen go across the road?

Cause she can't walk round.

What stops a hen from going across the road?

None of the rooster's business.

Why is a rooster's feathers always smooth?

Cause he always carries a comb.

Why is the house of a bald-headed man easier to break into?

Because he has no locks.

What's the difference betweeen a postage stamp and a mule?

One you stick with a lick, and the other you lick with a stick.

Why is a black hen wiser than a white one?

Because a black hen can lay a white egg, but a white hen can't lay a black egg.

What two things grow downward?

An icicle and a cow's tail.

Why did the Titanic sink?

'Cause John Jacob Astor.

If you woke up at night and scratched your head, what time would it be?

> Five after one.

Can you put your left shoe on first?

> No, because one is on the floor, and that's left.

What block aboard a vessel don't need to shieve?

> The cook's chopping block.

What was the bravest battalion went over seas?

> Fast colors guaranteed not to run.

What there are the easy thing to catch?

> Yer breath.

Spell hard water in three letters.

> I c e.

What is it got a head and can't think? It stands on the ground, sits on the grounds, all at the same time. It leaves, but yet it's there.

> Cabbage.

Why does a barrel roll?

> 'Cause it can't walk.

What goes all round the house and makes a thousand tracks?

> Green grass growing.

Bull, bull, ox, ox,
Stood in the woods,
And a carpenter made it.

> Yoke.

Big as a barn,
Light as a feather,
And sixty horses can't pull it.

> Shadow of the barn.

Why does a chimney smoke?
'Cause it can't chew.

When is a ship not a ship?
When she's a-float.

Why does a dead dog's tail stop wagging in the road?
He was dead, his tail couldn't wag.

What's the difference between the clothes line and the molasses keg?
The clothes line flies the drawers and the molasses keg draws the flies.

Why do they always call a ship in the feminine gender?
Because she goes creaking and cracking under taut stays.

What goes across the bridge and cuts the hay and you can't see it?
Bullet out of a gun.[1]

What is it that's spelt with five letters, by taking away two, you have five (!ten) left?
Often.

Why is the letter K like a pig's tail?
Because it is the end of pork.

Riddle, riddle, come rest.
What does a boy take first in his hand when he goes to school?
The door latch.

On my belly I am fixt,
Two holes and a bridge betwixt.
A fiddle.

As I went across London Bridge,
I met a boy and he was cryin'.
I asked him what he was crying for?
He said his father had dyed (died)
Seven years before he was born.
Dyer.

Variant: There was once a boy who wore a red cap which his mother dyed before he was born.

> She dyed the cap.

Up the chimney down,
Down the chimney up,
Won't go up the chimney up.
Or down the chimney up.

> An umbrella.

Variant: What goes up the chimney down, and can't go up the chimney up?

A riddle, a riddle as I suppose,
A thousand eyes and never a nose.

> Flour sifter.

It takes ten men to haul a lilly bag up a flat hill.

> Man puttin' on a pair of pants.

What has two heads and one body?

> Barrel.

Variant: Wriggledy, wriggledy,
Two heads and one body.

Four legs and doesn't move around the floor.[2]

> A table.

Got two eyes and can't see.

> Potato.

What has a tongue and can't talk?

> Shoe.

Goes upstairs and downstairs and always on its head?

> Nail in a shoe.

Variant: What is it that always walks with its head on the ground?

What's got an eye and never closes its eye?

A needle.

What runs all round the house[3] and makes but one track?

Wheelbarrow.

Snake.

Notes

1. Heard in Gaelic.
2. Variant: Can't walk.
3. Variant: What goes round the house and round the house?

CHARLTON LAIRD

Folk Etymology, or Every Man a Lexicographer*

Folk, or popular, etymology does not usually create words, but it provides lore about words which is as pleasant as it is unreliable, and it frequently changes the form of the words which are its subject. Consider, for instance, the sleepy little limestone village, formerly known as Tete de Mort, which rests in a valley between bluffs on the west side of the Mississippi River. In the early days some Indians killed a French fur trader and thrust his head upon a pole. It was one of the sights on the Upper Mississippi River, and the place was known by the French word for death's-head, *tête de mort*. Many of the early visitors in the area were French, and few wondered at the name. Later came Irish, Germans, and various sorts of Yankees to turn the bluffs into a farming country. What did French mean to these people? Nothing, but here was a name that had to be accounted for. They called the place *Teddymore*, doubtless assuming that some mythical Teddy Moore had lived there "a long time ago." Similarly, *Mary-la-Bonne* (Mary the Good) becomes *Marylebone* (pronounced as though it were spelled *Marly Bone*), *St. Anne* becomes *Sent Ten*, and *Mean's Well* becomes *Means Well*—after all, to get to the place you take a desert road, which becomes a desert track, which becomes a desert trail, which practically disappears. That the place means well is the most charitable remark one can make.

People like to make up, and repeat, stories to account for these fantastic forms, unaware that the forms *are* fantastic, and to account for all sorts of words which seem strange. Take the word *gandy*, which in some areas means any railway track

* From *The Miracle of Language* by Charlton Laird, copyright 1953 by Charlton Laird.

worker. A "long time ago" a Hindu beggar was put off a
train out in the West (usually near the home of the storyteller)
because he lacked the price of the ticket. He had with him a
bear, named for Mohandas Gandhi. Down the track he saw a
section crew working, and went with his bear to collect a few
pennies. The bear did his act, standing on his hind feet,
lumbering in a crude dance, and holding out a cup for coins
while the Hindu played a tune. The section crew was replacing
some ties, tamping the gravel back around the ties with
tamps which they worked up and down with both hands. They
looked so much like the clumsy bear that the section boss burst
out laughing and called them *Gandhi-dancers*. And that is the
way the word got started.

This story is implausible on the face of it, but implausibility
never deterred a lover of folk etymologies. There are few
Hindu beggars in this country, and they do not transport bears
over transcontinental lines—particularly not in passenger
coaches, where they find themselves without a ticket for the
bear. If the peddler had been a Hindu he would not have
pronounced *Gandhi* in any way which to a Western section
boss would have sounded like *gandy*. Furthermore, the word
gandy long antedates the career of the Mahatma. Actually, the
explanation is obvious. The tamps used in setting railroad ties
were long made by the Gandy Manufacturing Company of
Chicago; they had *Gandy* stamped on them. The man who
waltzed one of these things about was called a *gandy dancer*,
and eventually just a *gandy*. The story about the dancing bear
never became very popular; if it had, no doubt the spelling of
the word would have tended to become *gandhi*. After all, one
must be correct.

People are uncommonly credulous of these tales. Well-
educated people, who should know better, will tell you that the
Latin-American insult for a *norteamericano, gringo,* comes

from the following supposed incident. An American sailor in a
Latin-American port, joyful at having shore-leave, walked
down the gangplank singing "Green Grow the Lilacs." A
native, making nothing of the words, thought the song began
with the sailor's name for his countrymen, and consequently
North Americans were called *gringos*. I have heard educated
people defend this etymology with the argument that it seemed
very plausible. When I suggested that it was not plausible,
they suggested it was similar to other etymologies—which
were, of course, also folk etymologies.

The "gringo" story is anything but convincing. Sailors do
traditionally sing songs, but not songs concerning botanical
phenomena of the culture of lilacs. Furthermore, South
America is a very diverse continent. Is it likely that a random
word picked up casually by some wharf rat spread through the
jungles of the Amazon and over the Andes to become the
common epithet for a Yankee? And is it likely that this word
would then spread north and become so common among
Latin-American sections of dwellers in the United States that
Audubon's party was "hooted and shouted at . . . and called
Gringoes" even before we have evidence that the song had
become popular?

There is no secret about the etymology of the word *gringo,*
although it is one of those words about which the public has
the vague feeling that nothing is known. It is in all good
modern dictionaries. But folk etymologists prefer pleasant
fancies to good modern dictionaries. The word is a specialization of Mexican Spanish *gringo,* meaning "gibberish," and of
course to uneducated Mexicans the speech of their nearest
neighbors, the *norteamericanos,* is gibberish. Supposedly the
word comes from an old form of the Spanish *griego* (a Greek).
For very much the reasons that a speaker of English may say,

"It's all Greek to me," the Latin Americans must have linked *griego* to *gringo*.

These tales of the *gandy* and the *gringo* represent folk etymology only in a limited sense; the word has presumably given rise to the story, but the story has not in turn influenced the word. Often, folk etymologies do so, as with the barnacle goose. The growth of the word *barnacle* is not quite clear, but it stems from a common word for a rather small wild goose, and seems to be the equivalent of "little bare neck," an obvious epithet. The word apparently got into the zoological books in Latin as the name for the goose, where it acquired Latin endings and developed derivative forms in Italian, Portuguese, German, and Danish. Supposedly the word had become attached meanwhile by comparison and specialization to another goose-necked creature which clung to rocks and the bottoms of ships. This marine crustacean was also called a *barnacle*. By this time the name for the goose was no longer recognized, and consequently the *barnacle* which was a goose became a *barnacle goose*. Perhaps because of this reversal from the marine to the ornithological barnacle, folklore began to spring up about the barnacle goose. It came from the barnacle tree which grew on the shores of Ireland. Shellfish clung to this tree as barnacles, and then grew up to be geese. Or the fruits of the tree fell into the water and became shellfish, and then geese. Or the fruits of the tree just flew away as geese after they had sprouted wings. Thus poor little bare-neck acquired a new name, and became the *tree goose*.

Usually the process is not so elaborate. An archaic or foreign word seems forbidding, and is accordingly changed enough to look and sound familiar. Thus we make the Dutch *pappekak* into *poppycock,* which seems to be composed of English words, and which carries an appropriate air of impertinent banter or patronizing insult. Meanwhile, we are unaware that the Dutch word implied an analogy suggested by its literal meaning, "soft manure."

Such are the linguistic skeletons in the closet of the human race. Many of them can be traced to strange ancestors; others are just there in the closet.

4

Folksong

FOLKSONG, AS THE NAME IMPLIES, IS THE UNTUTORED SONG of the people. Untutored song is learned by imitation, and since both words and music are involved, many changes may occur in transmission. In the culture of the English-speaking peoples, the ballad, or narrative song, has received more scholarly attention than has any other form. This is apparently the natural result of the fact that the popular ballad has persisted so well in tradition over several centuries that it may be studied in its historical depth and transoceanic dispersion.

Because intellectual scrutiny results in comment, and comment results in debate and more comment, the scholarly literature pertaining to ballads, especially the English and Scottish popular ballads makes up an imposing portion of the whole of folklore literature in English.

Popular revival movements and their commercial exploitation have greatly increased public awareness of, and interest in, folksong. These movements have also created some academic problems in definition and identification. Does a folksong cease to be a creation and possession of the folk once it has been widely published? Does wide distribution of a recording of a folksong professionally arranged and performed affect its traditional life? If so, to what degree? If a professional singer composes a "folksong" and it becomes popular enough to persist in tradition and undergoes changes in transmission, can the song properly be called a folksong? Is learning a song from a recording merely adding a mechanical convenience to the ancient process of learning directly from the singer in person?

The selections in this chapter have been assembled to reflect the questions above and to suggest many others.

LOUISE POUND

Introduction*

The oral versions of folk-song are practically innumerable.
A book of the size of the present volume could be filled by the
variant versions of half a dozen of the pieces included in it.
But it should be borne in mind that the variations of the folk
are instinctive and unconscious, not deliberate. There are
countless shiftings and omissions or additions in the mouths
of varying singers, but they are unintentional. Alteration arises
through slips of memory, local adaptations (as the substitution
of names), and through the omissions and the insertions of the
individual singers. Many are due to confusion with other
ballads or to personal tastes or prejudices. Nor is it always the
fortunate changes which persist, though some scholars seem to
think this. Stupid or garrulous changes persist also. Crossings
with other ballads may disorder a song until it remains merely
a heap of confused materials. Another song may glide onward
from generation to generation keeping the situation—generally
a tragic situation—which is its soul; but transforming its
phrases and stanzas. Sometimes very old narratives, despite
their multiform transformations, have in most variants not yet
lost their thread of story or become transformed beyond
recognition. This is the case in the well-known ballads *Lord
Randal* and *The Two Sisters*.

On the whole, the influence of folk-transmission is a levelling
influence. It conventionalizes according to its traditions. The
total effect of its alterations, contributions, and curtailments is
to bring homogeneity in style and manner of narration.
Imported songs, once of totally different character, accom-
modate themselves to the regional modes and characteristics of

* From *American Ballads and Songs,* collected and edited by Louise
Pound. Copyright, 1922, by Charles Scribner's Sons.

281

their new home. Some effective incident or story, presented in a simple memorable way, commends itself to the folk-consciousness. Gradually it transforms itself in agreement with the tastes and traditions of the localities where it becomes domesticated, and sometimes it ends as something quite different from what it was when it began.

It is usual to look upon ballads with some degree of indulgence as verse of a singularly "artless" kind. For that reason those who are in reaction from book verse find in it peculiar pleasure. The truth is, however, that the antithesis should be drawn between poetry of the folk and poetry of culture, not poetry of "art." Art is not the same thing as culture and is not dependent upon it. The most primitive people may have its own kind of art. Ballads are often themselves relics of culture poetry, and they have their own art, traditions, and etiquette. These may be naive, but it would never occur to the singers to wish for innovations, or for something more elaborate. From the art, traditions, and etiquette that it knows, the folk never wavers. Departure from them, within the limits of a period or place, is out of the question. It is always surprising that such variety may appear in the handling of stock material, yet so little inventiveness be exhibited, or novelty in technique.

ENGLISH AND SCOTTISH POPULAR BALLADS

Introduction*

We have touched upon most of the problems that confront the investigator of the popular ballad. Certain others, like that of the transmission of ballads from country to country, which includes the special question of kinship between the English and Scottish ballads and those of Scandinavia, do not come within the scope of this introduction. The same is true of the history of ballad collections, which would take much space, and in lieu of which the reader is referred once more to the List of Sources on pp. 677–684.

Of the merit of the English and Scottish ballads nothing need be said. It is unhesitatingly admitted by all persons who care for ballads at all. There is no occasion to make comparisons as to excellence between these pieces and the poetry of art. Such comparisons are misleading; they tend only to confound the distinctions between two very different categories of literature. The ballads must stand or fall by themselves, not by reason of their likeness or unlikeness to Dante or Shakespeare or Milton or Browning. Above all things, they should not be judged indiscriminately or in the lump. There are good ballads and poor ballads, as there are good dramas and poor dramas, and this volume contains an abundance of both sorts. On the whole, however, the average of excellence is probably as high in most volumes of verse of equal dimensions. Finally, the popular ballad, though it may be despised, cannot be ignored by the student of literature. Whatever may be thought of the importance of such verse in its bearing on the origin of poetry in general, or of epic poetry in particular, the ballad, like other forms of popular material, has in the last two cen-

* From *English and Scottish Popular Ballads,* ed. by Helen Child Sargent and George Lyman Kittredge, copyright 1904 and 1932 by George Lyman Kittredge (Boston: Houghton Mifflin Company, 1932).

turies exercised a powerful influence on artistic literature, and it will always have to be reckoned with by the literary historian.

G.L.K.

The Maid Freed from the Gallows

All the English versions are defective and distorted. In many others, both from northern and southern Europe, a young woman has fallen into the hands of corsairs; father, mother, brother, sister, refuse to pay ransom, but her lover, in one case husband, stickles at no price which may be necessary to retrieve her. The best ballad of the cycle is the Sicilian 'Scibilia Nobili' (Salomone-Marino, Leggende pop. siciliane in Poesia, No. 29). There are very numerous versions in Finnish and Esthonian, and numerous variations on the theme occur in Russia and elsewhere.

A

Percy Papers, communicated to Percy, April 7, 1770, by the Rev. P. Parsons, of Wye, from oral tradition.

*   *   *   *   *   *

1 'O good Lord Judge, and sweet Lord
      Judge,
    Peace for a little while!
    Methinks I see my own father,
      Come riding by the stile.
2 'Oh father, oh father, a little of your
      gold,
    And likewise of your fee!
    To keep my body from yonder grave,
      And my neck from the gallows-tree.'

3   'None of my gold now you shall have,
     Nor likewise of my fee :
     For I am come to see you hangd,
     And hanged you shall be.'

4   'Oh good Lord Judge, and sweet Lord
     Judge,
     Peace for a little while!
     Methinks I see my own mother,
     Come riding by the stile.

5   'Oh mother, oh mother, a little of your
     gold,
     And likewise of your fee,
     To keep my body from yonder grave,
     And my neck from the gallows-tree!'

6   'None of my gold now shall you
     have,
     Nor likewise of my fee;
     For I am come to see you hangd,
     And hanged you shall be!'

7   'Oh good Lord Judge, and sweet Lord
     Judge,
     Peace for a little while!
     Methinks I see my own brother,
     Come riding by the stile.

8   'Oh brother, oh brother, a little of your
     gold,
     And likewise of your fee,
     To keep my body from yonder grave,
     And my neck from the gallows-tree!'

9   'None of my gold now shall you have,
     Nor likewise of my fee;
     For I am come to see you hangd,
     And hanged you shall be.'

10 'Oh good Lord Judge, and sweet Lord
     Judge,
     Peace for a little while!
     Methinks I see my own sister,
     Come riding by the stile.

11 'Oh sister, oh sister, a little of your
  gold,
  And likewise of your fee,
  To keep my body from yonder grave,
  And my neck from the gallows-tree!'
12 'None of my gold now shall you have,
  Nor likewise of my fee;
  For I am come to see you hangd,
  And hanged you shall be.'
13 'Oh good Lord Judge, and sweet Lord
  Judge,
  Peace for a little while
  Methinks I see my own true-love,
  Come riding by the stile.
14 'Oh true-love, oh true-love, a little of
  your gold,
  And likewise of your fee,
  To save my body from yonder grave,
  And my neck from the gallows-tree.'
15 'Some of my gold now you shall have,
  And likewise of my fee,
  For I am come to see you saved.
  And saved you shall be.'

I

Scotch Ballads, Materials for Border Minstrelsy, No. 127,
Abbotsford. Sent to John Leyden, by whom and when does
not appear.

1 'Hold your hand, Lord Judge,' she
  says,
  'Yet hold it a little while;
  Methinks I see my ain dear father
  Coming wandering many a mile.
2 'O have you brought me gold, father?
  Or have you brought me fee?
  Or are you come to save my life
  From off this gallows-tree?'

3 'I have not brought gold, daughter,
  Nor have I brought you fee,
  But I am come to see you hangd,
  As you this day shall be.'

("The verses run thus until she has seen her mother, her
brother, and her sister likewise arrive, and then
        Methinks I see my ain dear lover, etc.")

4 'I have not brought you gold, true-love,
  Nor yet have I brought fee,
  But I am come to save thy life
  From off this gallows-tree.'
5 'Gae hame, gae hame, father,' she says,
  'Gae hame and saw yer seed;
  And I wish not a pickle of it may grow
      up,
  But the thistle and the weed.
6 'Gae hame, gae hame, gae hame, mother,
  Gae hame and brew yer yill;
  And I wish the girds may a' loup off,
  And the Deil spill a' yer yill.
7 'Gae hame, gae hame, gae hame, brother,
  Gae hame and lie with yer wife;
  And I wish that the first news I may hear
  That she has tane your life.
8 'Gae hame, gae hame, sister,' she says,
  'Gae hame and sew yer seam;
  I wish that the needle-point may break,
  And the craws pyke out yer een.'

Lamkin

The versions are very numerous,—Professor Child prints
twenty-six, including fragments,—but the story does not vary
essentially. Only three are given here. One of these (K) is
defective, but it is the oldest version, except perhaps P, which

is greatly inferior. The tale has been localized in various places in Scotland. The name Lamkin is probably an ironical designation for the bloody mason, the terror of countless nurseries.

A

'Lamkin,' Jamieson's Popular Ballads, I, 176; communicated by Mrs. Brown.

1   It's Lamkin was a mason good
     as ever built wi stane;
   He built Lord Wearie's castle,
     but payment got he nane.

2   'O pay me, Lord Wearie,
     come, pay me my fee :'
   'I canna pay you, Lamkin,
     for I maun gang oer the sea.'

3   'O pay me now, Lord Wearie,
     come, pay me out o hand :'
   'I canna pay you, Lamkin,
     unless I sell my land.'

4   'O gin ye winna pay me,
     I here sall mak a vow,
   Before that ye come hame again,
     ye sall hae cause to rue.'

5   Lord Wearie got a bonny ship,
     to sail the saut sea faem;
   Bade his lady weel the castle keep,
     ay till he should come hame.

6   But the nourice was a fause limmer
     as eer hung on a tree;
   She laid a plot wi Lamkin,
     whan her lord was oer the sea.

7   She laid a plot wi Lamkin,
       when the servants were awa,
    Loot him in at a little shot-window,
       and brought him to the ha.

8   'O whare's a' the men o this house,
       that ca me Lamkin?'
    'They're at the barn-well thrashing;
       't will be lang ere they come in.'

9   'And whare's the women o this house,
       that ca me Lamkin?'
    'They're at the far well washing;
       't will be lang ere they come in.'

10 'And whare's the bairns o this house,
       that ca me Lamkin?'
    'They're at the school reading;
       't will be night or they come hame.'

11 'O whare's the lady of this house,
       that ca's me Lamkin?'
    She's up in her bower sewing,
       but we soon can bring her down.'

12 Then Lamkin's tane a sharp knife,
       that hang down by his gaire,
    And he has gien the bonny babe
       a deep wound and a sair.

13 Then Lamkin he rocked,
       and the fause nourice sang,
    Till frae ilkae bore o the cradle
       the red blood out sprang.

14 Then out it spak the lady,
       as she stood on the stair :
    'What ails my bairn, nourice,
       that he's greeting sae sair?

15 'O still my bairn, nourice,
        O still him wi the pap!'
    'He winna still, lady,
        for this nor for that.'

16 'O still my bairn, nourice,
        O still him wi the wand!'
    'He winna still, lady,
        for a' his father's land.'

17 'O still my bairn, nourice,
        O still him wi the bell!'
    'He winna still, lady,
        till ye come down yoursel.'

18 O the firsten step she steppit,
        she steppit on a stane;
    But the neisten step she steppit,
        she met him Lamkin.

19 'O mercy, mercy, Lamkin,
        hae mercy upon me!
    Though you've taen my young son's
            life,
        ye may let mysel be.'

20 'O sall I kill her, nourice,
        or sall I lat her be?'
    'O kill her, kill her, Lamkin,
        for she neer was good to me.'

21 'O scour the bason, nourice,
        and mak it fair and clean,
    For to keep this lady's heart's blood,
        for she's come o noble kin.'

22 'There need nae bason, Lamkin,
        lat it run through the floor;
    What better is the heart's blood
        o the rich than o the poor?'

23 But ere three months were at an end,
    Lord Wearie came again;
    But dowie, dowie was his heart
    when first he came hame.

24 'O wha's blood is this,' he says,
    'that lies in this chamer?'
    'It is your lady's heart's blood:
    't is as clear as the lamer.'

25 'And wha's blood is this,' he says,
    'that lies in my ha?'
    'It is your young son's heart's blood;
    't is the clearest ava.'

26 O sweetly sang the black-bird
    that sat upon the tree;
    But sairer grat Lamkin,
    when he was condemnd to die.

27 And bonny sang the mavis,
    out o the thorny brake;
    But sairer grat the nourice,
    when she was tied to the stake.

B

'Lambert Linkin,' Motherwell's MS., p. 15; from the recitation of Mrs. Thomson, Kilbarchan, February 25, 1825.

1 Balankin was a gude a mason
    as eer picked a stane;
    He built up Prime Castle,
    but payment gat nane.

2 The lord said to his lady,
    when he was going abroad,
    O beware of Balankin,
    for he lyes in the wood.

3   The gates they were bolted,
      baith outside and in;
      At the sma peep of a window
      Balankin crap in.

4   'Good morrow, good morrow,'
      said Lambert Linkin :
      'Good morrow to yoursell, sir,'
      said the false nurse to him.

5   'O where is your good lord?
      said Lambert Linkin :
      'He's awa to New England,
      to meet with his king.'

6   'O where is his auld son?'
      said Lambert Linkin :
      'He 's awa to buy pearlings,
      gin our lady lye in.'

7   'Then she 'll never wear them,'
      said Lambert Linkin :
      'And that is nae pity,'
      said the false nurse to him.

8   'O where is your lady?'
      said Lambert Linkin :
      'She 's in her bower sleeping,'
      said the false nurse to him.

9   'How can we get at her?'
      said Lambert Linkin :
      'Stab the babe to the heart,
      wi a silver bokin.'

10   'That would be a pity,'
      said Lambert Linkin :
      'No pity, no pity,'
      said the false nurse to him.

11 Balankin he rocked,
 and the false nurse she sang,
Till all the tores of the cradle
 wi the red blood down ran.

12 'O still my babe, nurice,
 O still him wi the knife!'
'He 'll no be still, lady,
 tho I lay doun my life.'

13 'O still my babe, nurice,
 O still him wi the kame!'
'He 'll no be still, lady,
 till his daddy come hame.'

14 'O still my babe, nurice,
 O still him wi the bell!'
'He 'll no be still, lady,
 till ye come doun yoursell.'

15 'It 's how can I come down,
 this cauld winter nicht,
Without eer a coal,
 or a clear candle-licht?'

16 'There 's two smocks in your coffer,
 as white as a swan;
Put one of them about you,
 it will shew you licht down.'

17 She took ane o them about her,
 and came tripping doun;
But as soon as she viewed,
 Balankin was in.

18 'Good morrow, good morrow,'
 said Lambert Linkin:
'Good morrow to yoursell, sir'
 said the lady to him.

19 'O save my life, Balankin,
   till my husband come back,
And I 'll gie you as much red gold
   as you 'll hold in your hat.'

20 'I'll not save your life, lady,
   till your husband come back,
Tho you would give me as much red
      gold
   as I could hold in a sack.

21 'Will I kill her?' quo Balankin,
   'will I kill her, or let her be?'
'You may kill her,' said the false nurse
   'she was neer good to me;
And ye 'll be laird of the castle,
   and I 'll be ladie.'

22 Then he cut aff her head
   fram her lily breast-bane,
And he hung 't up in the kitchen,
   it made a' the ha shine.

23 The lord sat in England,
   a drinking the wine :
'I wish a' may be weel
   with my lady at hame;
For the rings of my fingers
   the 're now burst in twain!'

24 He saddled his horse,
   and he came riding doun,
But as soon as he viewed,
   Balankin was in.

25 He had na weel stepped
   twa steps up the stair,
Till he saw his pretty young son
   lying dead on the floor.

26 He had not weel stepped
   other twa up the stair,
Till he saw his pretty lady
   lying dead in despair.

27 He hanged Balankin
   out over the gate,
And he burnt the fause nurice,
   being under the grate.

FRANCIS B. GUMMERE

The Epic*

Everyone knows that two of the most important factors in human affairs are Church and State. Again, every student of history is aware that the further back we go, the more intimate are the relations between these two great powers. Looking towards the beginnings of civilization, we see the lines of state-craft and priestcraft steadily converging. Where a Gladstone stands to-day, stood, some three centuries ago, a Cardinal Wolsey. In the remote past, in the dawn of history (a relative term, differing with different nations), we find law and religion to be convertible terms. Even in highly-civilized Greece, the Laws—*cf*. Sophocles, *Oed. Tyr.* 864 *sqq*.—were sacred. So it was with our own ancestors, the Germanic tribes, whose nature and customs fell under the keen eyes of Tacitus, and are noted down in his *Germania*. Let us take his description of the Germanic custom of casting lots,—a ceremony at once legal and religious. He says (c. 10) that "a branch is cut from a fruit-bearing tree and divided into little blocks, which are disinguished by certain marks, and scattered at random over a white cloth. Then the state-priest if it is a public occasion, the father of the family if it is domestic, after a prayer to the gods, looking toward heaven, thrice picks up a block. These he now interprets according to the marks previously made."

What renders the ceremony of importance to us is the fact that the "interpretation" Tacitus mentions was *poetical,* and that the "marks" were *runes, i.e.,* the rude alphabet employed by the Germanic tribes. According as these mystic symbols fell, the priest made *alliterating verses* declaring the result of the ceremony. The letters gave the key to the rimes. Since the

* From *Handbook of Poetics* by Francis B. Gummere. Copyright 1885 by Francis B. Gummere. Boston: Ginn and Company, 1885.
296

beech-tree (Anglo-Sax. *boc*, "book," but also "beech," like German Buch and Buche) was a favorite wood for the purpose, and the signs were cut in (A.–S. *writan*, "cut into," then "write"), we win a new meaning for the phrase "to write a book." Further, *to read*, really means to *interpret*,—as in the common "rede the riddle." So in the original, literal sense, the prie*st read the writing of the book*. Since he read it poetically, and as a decree of the gods, and as something legally binding on the people, we may assume (bearing in mind the antiquity of priestcraft) that *poetry, the earliest form of literature, begins among the priesthood in the service of law and religion.*

But this unit of sacred law had two sides. On the one hand were such ceremonies as the above,—a practical use, which concerned the people. Late "survivals" of these rites may still be found in the peasant's hut and in the modern nursery, *e.g.*, the time-honored custom of saying a rime to see who shall be *"it"* for a game. But on the other hand was formal worship,—the purely religious side. The tribe boasted its origin from a god, and at stated seasons joined in solemn worship of its divine ruler and progenitor. To this god the assembled multitude sang a hymn,—at first merely chorus, exclamation and incoherent chant, full of repetitions. As they sang, they kept time with the foot in a solemn dance, which was inseparable from the chant itself and governed the words. As order and matter penetrated this wild ceremony, there resulted a rude *hymn*, with intelligible words and a connecting idea. Naturally this connecting idea would concern the *deeds* of the god,—his birth and bringing up and his mighty acts. Thus a thread of *legend* would be woven into the hymn,—a thread fastened at one end to the human associations of the tribe, but losing itself in the uncertainty of a miraculous and superhuman past.

But a third element comes in. Besides the legendary thread, we have the *mythological*. In order to explain the natural processes about him, early man peopled the universe with a multitude of gods. Or, to speak more clearly, he attributed will and passion to the acts of nature. Something dimly personal stood behind the flash of lightning, the roaring of the wind. The ways and doings of these nature-gods were set in order, and, of course, were in many cases brought in direct connection with the tribal or legendary god. Hence a second sort of thread woven into the hymn,—*mythology*. But both legend and mythology are *narrative*. The hymn thus treated ceased to be a mere hymn. The chorus and the strophe were dropped; instead of sets of verses (strophe) the verses ran on in unbroken row. Single persons (minstrels) took the place of the dancing multitude, and chanted in a sort of "recitative," some song full of myth and legend, but centered in the person of the tribal god. Now what is such a song? It is *The Epic*. (Epic, from Greek *Epos*, a "word," then a "narration": cf. Saga= something *said*.)

It is important to remember that the Epic was not the result of that individual effort to which we now give the name of poetical composition.

To use Mr. Tylor's words (*Primitive Culture*, I. 273), epic poetry goes back "to that actual experience of nature and life which is the ultimate source of human fancy." Perhaps "source" is not quite accurate; we should prefer to say that it is experience of nature and experience of life (*i.e.*, mythology and legend), which awaken and stimulate the inborn human fancy, that is, the creative power of poetry. This creative power, in early times, when the great epics were forming, when their materials were gradually drawing together, lay rather in the national life itself than in any individual. There were no poets, only singers. The race or nation was the poet. For the *final shape* in which these epics come down to us, we must assume the genius of a singer-poet.

We note further that the personages of the Epic must be humanized,—*i.e.*, partake of our passions and other characteristics. Otherwise they could not awaken human interest. But the background across which these huge beings move must be the twilight of legend and myth,—Instead of taking the Homeric poems as illustration, we prefer to give a brief outline of our own national epic—*Beowulf*. . . .

The northwest coast of Europe, where our epic had its origin, is exposed to the ravages of ocean storms. Over the low lands, along the borders of the Cimbrian peninsula, swept in fury the tempests of spring and fall. The sea broke its bounds and raged over the flat country, sweeping away houses and men. Against these wild storms came the gentle spring-god of warmth and calm. This god men called *Beowa*. The god conquers the monsters of the stormy sea, follows them even into their ocean home and puts them to death. Grendel and his mother may fairly be taken as types of these storms. In autumn they burst forth afresh. The waning power of summer closes with them in fiercest struggle. After long combat both the year and the storms sink into the frost-bound sleep of winter.

So much for "the experience of nature,"—*i.e.*, mythology. Now for the "experience of life,"—legend. History tells us that early in the Sixth Century, one Hygelac, king of the Getae, came down from the north and went plundering along the Rhine. The Frankish king, Theudebert, met and fought Hygelac, and the latter fell. His follower and nephew, however, Beowulf, son of Ecgtheow, did great deeds. Fighting until all others had fallen, he escaped by a masterful piece of swimming, and went back to his island home. His fame spread far and wide. He grew to be a national hero. Songs were sung about him. Wandering minstrels chanted his praise from tribe to tribe. What these wandering minstrels were, and how important was their profession, may be gathered from an Anglo-Saxon poem, which is probably "the oldest monument of English poetry,"—*Widsith*, "the far-wanderer." In the one hundred and forty-three verses preserved to us, the minstrel tells of his travels, of the costly gifts he has received, of maxims of government he has heard, of famous heroes, kings and queens whom he has visited (a wild confusion of half historical, half mythical names from different lands and times), and of the countries he has seen. He refers to some evidently well-known legends. Widsith is the ideal minstrel; and this strange poem gives us ample hints as to the spread of legends by men of his craft. Then, too, Tacitus tells us of this custom (*Ann.* 2, 88); Arminius, liberator of Germany, "caniturque adhuc barbaras apud gentes."' In all this singing, there was small risk that Beowulf's deeds would lose any of their greatness. In fact, they acquired at length certain touches of the supernatural.

Thus, then, we have hymns in honor of Beowa, the liberating and national god; songs in honor of Beowulf, the national hero. Little by little, the two became one person; and myth and legend, hymns and songs, crystallized about the common centre, until some gifted minstrel gave them form and unity in the epic of Beowulf. Unfortunately the form halts behind the matter : owing to the rapid christianizing of England, the epic, says Ten Brink, was "frozen in the midst of its development." Such as it is, however, it is a noble herald of the long line of English poetry.—We now abandon the historic method, and look at the epic as it lies before us as well in the *Iliad* and the *Odyssey*, as in Beowulf. . . .

Legends Accepted as True

The tendency to sing about national heroes, and the battles which they fight, continues in force. Thus in the Anglo-Saxon

Chronicle, scattered songs flash out from the monotony of prose, *e.g.*, *The Battle of Brunnanburh* (937). Another such battle-ballad (not in the Chronicle) is *Byrhtnoth's Fall* (sometimes called *The Battle of Maldon*, a spirited song, composed, says Rieger, so soon after the fight that the poet is ignorant of the hostile leader's name. All the fire and the impetuosity of the old epic style live again in this 'ballad' (993). Under the Norman yoke, our forefathers still sung their favorite heroes; though not preserved to us, these songs were used by the later prose chroniclers of England. Then there were legendary characters of a less definite kind : *cf.* the Lay of *Horn* and of *Havelok*. In another similar story, Ten Brink sees a late form of the Beowulf myth.

The most important of these legendary poems is the famous *Brut* of Layamon (about the beginning of the Thirteenth Century). It is simply the mythical history of Britain. In tone and manner the *Brut* approaches the old national epic; it is partly based on tradition by word of mouth, though Wace's *Geste des Bretons* was Layamon's chief authority. Compared, however, the modern ventures in the same field—say, with Tennyson's *Idylls of the King*—the *Brut* has much of the real epic flavor. From Layamon down, these national legends have been extensively drawn upon by our poets. A catalogue of such poems belongs to the history of our literature.—The above concerns *(a) National* legends. We now glance at *(b) Legends of the Church*.

In the first place, many paraphrases were made of the Bible. The Old Testament was partly done into English verse. Thus, that Ms. which Franciscus Junius took to be the work of Beda's hero, Caedmon, but which is really a collection of poems by several authors and from different times, contains, among other poetical versions of the books of the Bible, a splendid paraphrase of *Exodus*. Later, there were other versions of

Genesis and Exodus. There is also preserved the conclusion of a noble Anglo-Saxon epic poem,—*Judith*. Cynewulf turned for material to the numerous sacred legends : cf. his *Elene, or the Finding of the Cross*. Later poets treated the lives of the saints. Hovering between national and sacred legend are such cycles of poetry as that which treats the legend of the Holy Grail,— *e.g.*, the story of "Joseph of Arimathie." These all have a strongly marked moral purpose,—something foreign to early epic. But in the way of pure narrative for the narrative's sake, nothing can be better than those of Chaucer's *Canterbury Tales* which treat sacred legend : *e.g.*, the exquisite *Prioresses Tale*.

We have, further, international literature as source for poetry,—*Legends based on General History (c)*. Latin once made possible the ideal for which Goethe sighed,—a world literature. In the medieval Latin there was already collected a rude history of the world. In distorted shape, the heroes of old time passed through the Latin into the various literatures of Europe, which all began with and in the Latin itself. Each great hero formed a centre for certain 'cycles' of stories and legends : prominent were the Alexander Legends, the Aeneas Legends;—later, the Legends of Charlemagne, though these are more *national*. A branch of the Aeneas or Troy legend was that of *Troilus,* which afterwards busied the pens of Chaucer and Shakespeare, and was immensely popular in the middle ages. A great aid to these legends was the mass of stories which had their origin in the East,—in India and elsewhere,—and came in the wake of the returning crusades, gradually drifting into every literature in Europe. Such is the famous story of the *three caskets,* brought in with so much effect in *The Merchant of Venice*. (Cf. the story itself in the E. E. T. Soc.'s ed. of the *Gesta Romanorum*.) Stimulated by these stories, and fed by them in great measure, arose a vast array of *Romances,* all of a historical coloring. Their name is derived from the Romance or corrupted and popular Latin, in which many of these tales appeared. Romances were greatly beloved in the middle ages, and made an important part of the first books printed by Caxton,—"joyous and pleasant histories of chivalry." Finally, they were killed by their folly and extravagance. *Cf.* Chaucer's *Tale of Sir Thopas;* for the prose romances, *Don Quixote* was at once judge and executioner.—More serious work—not strictly romances—may be seen in Chaucer's *Legende of Goode Women,* and above all in the great *Canterbury Tales.* As writer of tales, as "narrative poet," Chaucer is without a peer in English Literature. His reticence, in that garrulous age, is sublime. He omits trifling details, not caring "who bloweth in a trump or in a horn."—We must here note a strange use of the word "tragedy." It meant for Chaucer's time the story of those who had fallen from high to low estate. It had nothing dramatic :—

> "Tregedis is to sayn a certeyn storie,
> As olde bokes maken us memorie,
> Of hem that stood in greet prosperité
> And is y-fallen out of heigh degré
> Into miserie and endith wrecchedly."

A "comedy" was a narrative that did not end tragically : *cf.* Dante's great work.

With far wider sweep of history, modern poets have greatly increased the variety of romances and legendary poems. Think of *Evangeline* or *Hiawatha* on one hand, and on the other, of the Norse legends or the classic stories of William Morris. No classic themes have ever been revived with such power as in Marlowe's (and Chapman's) *Hero and Leander,* and in Keats' *Hyperion.* The field is practically boundless. There is great license of treatment. The poet can adhere closely to his original, or he can invent and change at will. Such cases may be cited as the romances of Scott and Byron.

Under this head belong the *Riming Chronicle* and the *Narrative Didactic* poem. The first is a history in rime. In the Thirteenth Century Robert of Gloucester wrote such a chronicle of England; later (end of Fifteenth Century) we have Harding's Chronicle. As poetry they are of no value whatever. —The second class we may illustrate best by describing its best example. In 1559 appeared a book called "*A Myrroure for Magistrates,* wherein may be seen by example of other, with how grevous plages vices are punished, and howe frayle, unstable worldly prosperitie is founde, even of those whom fortune seemeth most highly to favour. *Felix quem faciunt aliena pericula cautum,* Londini, &c." This work, begun by Sackville on the model of Boccaccio's *De casibus virorum illustrium,* resembles in plan the "*Tregedis,*" described above, which make up the *Monk's Tale* in Chaucer's *Canterbury Tales,* except that in the former the characters are all English.

(*d*) Lastly, we note *the revival of the supernatural* in modern tales. This sort assumes a belief on the part of its readers that the supernatural is possible. The greatest example is Coleridge's *Christabel: cf.* the same poet's *Ancient Mariner,* and Scott's less successful *Lay of the Last Minstrel.*

The Ballad or Folk-Song

We see that from the original epic sprang many kinds of poetry that all had the common trait of telling something known, or supposed, or feigned to have happened. Other characteristics were simplicity, absence of personal property (authorship), truthful mirroring of nature, lack of a moral or reflective element. These qualities vanished in later epic poetry. But as in the natural world, when we have ploughed under some old wheat-field and planted a new crop of other grain, there will be crevices and corners where odd patches of wheat will spring up and flourish by the side of the regular crop, so it is in the world of literature. The old wheat-field of epic poetry, long after it was ploughed under, kept sending up scattered blades, which we call *ballads* or *folk-songs*. Except in authority, national importance, and kindred qualities, we may use the same definition for the (narrative) folk-song that we use for the early epic. Both names, ballad and folk-song, are suggestive : *ballad* means a song to which one may dance; *folk-song* is something made by the whole people, not by individual poets. Wright, in speaking of certain songs of the Fifteenth Century (Percy Soc., vol. XXIII.), says : "The great variation in the different copies of the same song shews that they were taken down from oral recitation, and had been often preserved by memory among minstrels who were not unskilful at composing, and who were . . . in the habit . . . of making up new songs by stringing together phrases and lines, and even whole stanzas, from the different compositions that were imprinted on their memories." The importance and influence and, we may add, the worth, of the folk-song are in inverse ratio to the spread of printed books. As the minstrel's welcome vanished from the baron's hall, and his audience degenerated to peasants and serving-people, we note a corresponding degeneration from the highest poetical merit to the level of modern street-songs.[2] It easily follows that much of the best folk-poetry must be lost,—not because, like the heroes before Agamemnon, it lacked the pious poet to sing it, but rather the 'chiel' to take notes and 'print it.'

The folk-song is a complete satisfaction of the demand for "more matter and less art." It is very artless and full of matter. The passions jostle each other terribly, as they escape from the singer's lips :—

"I hacked him in pieces sma',
For her sake that died for me."

The historical or narrative ballad is what we now consider.
Like the early epic, it refers often to subjects made up partly
of legend and partly of myth,—such as the Robin Hood ballads. But unlike the epic, the folk-song is often made immediately after a great battle or similar event. In the *Battle of
Maldon,* or *Byrhtnoth's Death,* a stirring ballad of the later
Anglo-Saxon period, the song follows the event so closely that
the singer has not had time even to find out the name of the
enemy's leaders. It is full of epic phrases and figures, and is
thoroughly in the objective manner. The event seems to sing
itself. . . .

Antique spelling and archaic phrases do not make a ballad.
Many ballads, too, are not of native origin, but blown from
the East over Europe, dropped seed in many countries. Hence
a number of similar ballads (*cf.* the extraordinary spread of a
ballad known in English as *Lady Isabel and the Elf-Knight*)
in the different literatures of Europe. Again, like fairy and
nursery tales, like superstitions and folk-lore of every sort,
many strikingly similar European ballads point to a common
mythical source. But amid the diversity of subject and origin,
the general spirit of the ballad or folk-song remains one and
the same. The genuine ballad is one thing, and the imitated
ballad—even such an imitation as Chatterton could make—
is quite another. To understand this clearly, read a good specimen of each kind; compare, say, *Thomas of Ercildoune* with
Keats' *La Belle Dame Sans Merci, a Ballad.* The latter is
wrought by the fancy of a poet under certain influences of the
past; the other, written in the Fifteenth Century, but older in
composition than that, is the work of a single poet or minstrel
only in the sense that this minstrel combined materials which
had been handed down from remotest times. The study of

these materials leads in all directions,—to the prophecies of Merlin, the story of the Tannhäuser, and so forth; the floating waifs of myth and superstition had gathered about the legendary (or historical) form of Thomas the Rhymer, and under one minstrel's hands take this definite shape as ballad. It is the old epic process in miniature. Even in the *style* we may distinguish the two. "I am glad as grasse wold be of raine" is the ballad style *(Marriage of Sir Gawayne);* "With kisses glad as birds are that get sweet rain at noon" is the imitated ballad style (Swinburne, *A Match*).

The ballad, with the spread of letters, degenerates into the streetsong or broadside. It bewails abuses in government, the wrongs of the poor, satirizes the follies of the day, and the like. For a collection of such, see (among others) the *Roxburghe Ballads*.

Notes

1. Jornandes, writing about 552 A.D., mentions the legendary songs of the Goths. Thus, in regard to their migration toward the Black Sea: "Quemadmodum in priscis eorum carminibus, paene historico ritu, in commune recolitur." *Cf.* W. Grimm, *Heldensage,* I.

2. . . . "the usual marks of degeneracy (of ballads), a dropping or obscuring of marvellous and romantic incidents, and a declension in the rank and style of the characters." Child, Ballads, 2d Ed., vol. I., p. 48.

GORDON HALL GEROULD

Ballads and Broadsides*

Though the use has been consecrated by time, the ballad of tradition has, one must admit, only the cuckoo's right to that name. A great deal of confusion would have been avoided if, in the sixteenth century, this way of designating narrative songs in popular circulation had not been adopted. And not until the end of the eighteenth century, indeed, did the traditional ballad come to be so termed at all frequently. In other languages a similar vagueness of nomenclature is found, but none that is quite so unfortunate. The French, the German, the Scandinavians have been content to call their ballads 'soﬃgs,' with or without some modifying element to indicate a connexion with the folk; only the Anglo-Saxons have chosen to adopt a foreign term for a sophisticated product and apply it without discrimination to at least five or six different sorts of verse.

The name originally meant a dance song, as is suggested by its ultimate derivation from the verb *ballare*. After it reached France from Italy and Provence, it became the designation of a conventialized lyric of a form fixed within narrow limits. Chaucer wrote ballads of this sort, as every one knows, with great success; and it has been practised both in French and English down to our own day. In modern English we have come to distinguish this use of the word by the variant spelling 'ballade.' In the fourteenth century, as is clear from a reference by Chaucer,[1] such ballads were associated with both dancing and singing, although it is equally obvious that Chaucer did not write most of his own for musical accompaniment of any kind. Lydgate used the strict form as the

* From *The Ballad of Tradition* by Gordon Hall Gerould, copyright, 1932, republished as a Galaxy Book, 1957.
[1] See *The Legend of Good Women*, Prologue A, vv. 199–202.

verbal substance of a masque at Eltham in 1427 or 1428.[2] In this case the verses must certainly have been recited, as must also have been the *balades* in stanzas lacking the final recurrent lines, which he prepared a little later for mummings at Windsor and London.[3]

As the fifteenth century went on, the meaning of the word 'ballad' seems to have been extended to include lyrics in various metrical forms, though always of a sophisticated sort. Apparently the notion of dancing continued to be associated with them, as we can be sure it did on the Continent from the fact that the madrigalists of the late sixteenth century, who borrowed their 'ballet' from the Italian *ballata,* recognized that it was based on a dance song.[4] The ballet is, however, to be distinguished from the ballade of the fifteenth and sixteenth centuries, since it was explicitly a song with a dance rhythm and an elaborate musical refrain to which the syllables *Fa la la* were customarily set.[5] Some of the most notable of the Elizabethan madrigalists, like Morley, used this form.

Until some time in the sixteenth century, clearly enough, the word 'ballad' was not applied to narratives of any kind, but only to various lyrics that were sometimes closely and sometimes only remotely connected with song and dance. By the middle of the sixteenth century, however, 'ballad' had come to mean—among other things—a story told in song. In the words of Professor Baskervill,[6] 'the Stationers' register leaves no reasonable room for doubt. Almost from the beginning, narratives were freely entered for broadside publication as ballads. While the name at first designated also songs of merely lyric nature, these became increasingly subordinate. The develop-

---

[2] See R. Brotanek, *Die englischen Maskenspiele,* 1902, pp. 305–8.
[3] *Op. cit.,* pp. 317–25.
[4] See E. H. Fellowes, *The English Madrigal Composers,* 1921, p. 58.
[5] *Op. cit.,* p. 57.
[6] C. R. Baskervill, *The Elizabethan Jig,* 1929, p. 30.

ment by the end of the century of a number of compounds
like "balladry," "balladize," and "balladmonger," applicable
chiefly to the field of the broadside ballad, shows the change
in meaning as practically complete.' Why this extension in the
use of the term should have taken place is not so easy to explain. Possibly it came in through the dialogues, set to music,
which became popular about this time. Since such dialogues
were often danced—and acquired the name jigs thereby[7]—
and since the word 'ballad' had never lost its original
connotation of dancing, there may well have sprung up the
fashion of calling any song and dance of the popular kind a
ballad. Dialogues almost inevitably present a situation, even
if only in a rudimentary way, which would make the application of the term to pure narrative quite natural.

We can be certain, I think, that the kind of narrative song
either composed for broadside production, or very suitable
for printing in that way, was influenced in its development by
what we are calling the ballad of tradition—not then known
as a ballad, of course. Professor Baskervill has recently shown[8]
that the literary folk of London took a warm interest in popular forms between 1550 and 1580. The movement seems to
have died out because it was taken over by the unworshipful
lot of poetasters who provided copy for the printers of broadsides, thus developing the journalistic ballad but bringing all
such forms into disrepute. By Shakespeare's day 'ballad' was
a term of reproach among the literate, as we know from the
dramatist's numerous and always contemptuous references.
'An I have not ballads made on you all and sung to filthy
tunes,' says Falstaff;[9] 'I love a ballad in print, o' life,' says
Mopsa,[10] 'for then we are sure they are true;' and Autolycus

[7] *Op. cit.,* p. 6.
[8] *Op. cit.,* pp. 30–1.
[9] *I Henry IV,* II, ii. 48–9.
[10] *Winter's Tale,* IV, iv. 262–70.

responds: 'Here's one to a very doleful tune, how a usurer's wife was brought to bed of twenty money-bags at a burden.' 'But a month old' was this choice morsel. The narrative ballad was well established, but only for the delight of the baser sort. We must remember, however, that at the same time exquisite 'ballets' were being composed by such men as Thomas Morley, who published a set in 1595. A fine confusion in nomenclature had been achieved, which needed only one further step to become the chaos that has remained to this day to trouble us.

The ballad of popular tradition meanwhile went on its course, unaffected, as far as one can see, by changing fashions in lyrical poetry and in the music and dancing that accompanied it, unaffected also for the time being by the insidious assault that was to be made on its integrity by the chapmen, who from London were scattering their sheets of 'odious ballads' through the countryside. Journalism had come to birth, and in its lusty infancy had many of the worst features commonly supposed to be the product of American enterprise in the later nineteenth century. The ballad of tradition had no name as yet : Sidney referred to the 'old song of Percy and Douglas,' and Thomas Deloney to *The Fair Flower of Northumberland* by the same term. It had no name because it was the product of an art that had nothing whatever to do with fashions at court or in the city. People went on singing their old songs, sometimes dancing to them while they sang, or listening to the humbler sort of minstrel like Sidney's 'blind crowder,' who lacked the sophistication of Autolycus, though for anything we know he may have been equally weak in ethics. New songs came into being after the old model, and were to do so for some time yet, by which good tales were added to the repertory of the singers. The ageless and anonymous art of narrative song, which nobody thought of recognizing as an art at all, continued to flourish.

There would be no excuse, indeed, for including even a brief discussion of broadside ballads in a study of the ballad of tradition if nothing more than names were concerned. The broadside, difficult to define because so various in substance and form, being almost anything in verse that a printer chose to circulate, acquired the name in the sixteenth century and kept it by right of possession as long as publication went on. But something more than a name involves our traditional ballads with those printed sheets. The connexion is threefold, which makes it imperative for us to look carefully at what happened as a result of the circulation of broadsides.

In the first place, the ballad-mongers often set their words to old tunes. Frequently, to be sure, there stood at the top of the page, 'To a pleasant new tune,' or the like, which might mean that a melody had been composed for the occasion, although one suspects that the notoriously unscrupulous publishers of such wares would have been capable of setting a ballad adrift with that caption when no tune had been provided. If the words could be sung at all, they would find a musical accompaniment easily enough among people to whom singing was still a universal accomplishment. More commonly, however, the maker had some tune in mind when he wrote, and sent out the ballad with the proper instructions at its head. There thus came about immediately what one might call an engraftment of new words on traditional tunes. An old song might serve as the accompaniment for half a dozen sets of words, all of them without merit as poetry and many of them vulgarly smart in the journalistic fashion. It should be borne in mind, in this connexion, that the Elizabethans distinguished what they called 'tunes'—simple melodies of popular origin—from 'airs,' which were the highly sophisticated products of schooled musicians. Naturally the stall ballads were intended for singing to melodies of the former kind.

These tunes were common property, no matter how they originated.

Although we have no record of what happened when the new songs set to old tunes got into circulation, we can very well see what must have occurred. Sometimes the ballad-monger's fabrication would have a brief life and leave the melody to run its course with the older set of words. Sometimes, however, one or another of the various new ballads written to a single old tune must have sunk deep into popular memory and quite ousted the traditional narrative. There can be little doubt that this was the genesis of many a ballad which continued to be in favour with folk-singers down to the time of our modern collectors. *The George Aloe and the Sweepstake* (285) with its successor *The Coasts of Barbary*[11] is an example in point; and another may be the very far from attractive *Queen Eleanor's Confession* (156), which had a long history despite its theme. Quite possibly, it seems to me—though it be blasphemy to make the suggestion—some of the tales of Robin Hood may have a source of this kind. *Robin Hood and the Tanner* (126), for example, might have begun its course in some such way.[12] It would be most interesting to determine, if we could, how frequently such adoptions took place; but it is impossible to do so, because of the processes of variation that we have studied in an earlier chapter. As soon as a broadside ballad became the property of folk-singers, it would inevitably be subjected to changes such as all songs were constantly undergoing, and would take on in course of time the characteristics of far older productions made in quite

[11] See C. J. Sharp, *J.F.-S.S.* v. 262 (1916); F. J. Harvey-Darton, *The Soul of Dorset*, 1922, p. 250; and Barry, Eckstorm, and Smyth, *British Ballads from Maine*, 1929, pp. 413–18.

[12] In addition to Child's version from four stall copies see Sharp, *English Folk-Songs*, i. 8–12; and Davis, *Traditional Ballads of Virginia*, 1929, pp. 333–6.

other ways by quite other poets. The reason why such ballads lack the dramatic intensity of the best ballads, why they seldom contain a moment of breath-taking emotion or a phrase of magical power, is that they have not been submitted to the full operation of those processes by which traditional songs have at times become great poetry. Or so the case looks to me, though it cannot be satisfactorily proved.

A second connexion between the stall ballad and the ballad of tradition was formed by the habit, into which printers fell, of occasionally printing a song gleaned from oral circulation. Some of the Robin Hood stories, for instance, have been preserved only by this means. We should not know *Robin Hood and Little John* (125) except for broadsides,[13] or *Robin Hood and Allan a Dale* (138). Similarly the admirable *Adam Bell* (116), *Rookhope Ryde* (179), and *Bewick and Graham* (211) have come down to us only in this way. In other cases, our versions of earliest record are from prints, though we also have variants collected from singers of recent times. *Little Musgrave and Lady Barnard* (81), for instance, was licensed for printing three times before the end of the seventeenth century,[14] from 1630 on, and a text represented by an apparently unlicensed broadside in the Pepys collection seems to be quite as old at least; yet nearly fifty variants of the ballad have been garnered from oral tradition.

The circulation of songs in printed texts necessarily dislocated the normal curve of things, since it spread them widely in a fixed form and indicated the melodies by which they should be accompanied. In place of the slow processes of dissemination that had been customary, from singer to singer,

[13] Fragments, to be sure, have been found by Williams, *Folk-Songs of the Upper Thames,* 1923, pp. 237, 296, and Cox, *Folk-Songs of the South,* 1925, p. 174.
[14] See H. E. Rollins, *Analytical Index to Ballad Entries,* 1924, nos. 1506–8.

from older folk to younger, there came in at a single stroke a totally alien process, swift in operation, which could bring the words of a ballad into districts where it had been unknown before, and probably confuse the memories of singers in other districts where a tradition had long been established. Thus in a third way broadsides had a marked influence on balladry. Too little has been made of this, I believe, by students of the traditional ballad, though the effect on individual specimens has been admirably investigated.[15]

Since variants that derive ultimately from printed texts are found in the most isolated parts of the United States and Canada, it is clear that broadsides affected an exceedingly widespread area; and since the oral tradition of some of the texts so derived is in itself a long one, it is evident that the influence began a great while ago. There can be no doubt whatever that a pure tradition of oral descent became an impossibility as soon as the purveyors of broadsides had established their trade in the sixteenth century. Contamination, if one choose to regard it as such, became possible in the case of any ballad whatsoever. Since the printing of traditional ballads was sporadic rather than general, the majority of them have never been subject to this artificial interruption of their proper course; but so many have been affected as to cast suspicion on any specimen that is being studied. The possibility of contamination should always be kept in mind.

As we have noted earlier, the tenacity of popular memory is as extraordinary as its fallibility. Variation appears to be incessant, yet sometimes a text survives almost unaltered the chances of oral repetition for a century and more. The evidence for this rests chiefly upon versions of songs that have in

[15] See, for example, the illuminating notes of Mr. Barry in *British Ballads from Maine*.

one way or another got into print.[16] It seems to me clear that the effect of circulating them has been to retard variation quite markedly, as if verses one learned directly or indirectly from broadsides and the like made a deeper impression on memory than those learned wholly by ear. One can only wonder whether there has been a feeling for the sanctity of the written words, or whether in some obscure way minds have registered differently verses fixed in print. At all events, it appears that the normal fluidity of alteration has been disturbed whenever publication has taken place.

Apart from the effect on individual ballads of the traditional sort, the circulation of broadsides inevitably produced changes in the art of folk-song as a whole. The rapid adoption of a great number of pieces both lyrical and narrative, some set to old tunes and some to new, and for the most part completely devoid of beauty in form and substance, could not have failed to lower the standards of taste that had been developed. The wonder is that the power of musical and poetical expression among common folk was not altogether destroyed by this, the first assault of many in modern times on the integrity of the traditional art. That it was weakened, there can be no doubt, I believe. There are numerous good ballads from the north that cannot have originated before the seventeenth century, but almost none traceable to districts nearer London. One thinks of *The Fire of Frendraught* (196), *The Bonnie House o Airlie* (199), *The Gypsy Laddie* (200), and *The Baron of Brackley* (203), to name only a few. In a very thoughtful book, published posthumously in 1913, Bryant called attention to this state of things,[17] though he under-estimated the extent to which older ballads survived in the south. It is not a ques-

[16] See the history of *Lord Lovel* (75) or *Barbara Allan* (84). Menendez Pidal has shown traditional versions may sometimes remain unaffected by printed ones. (See *ante,* p. 170.)

[17] *A History of English Balladry,* p. 192.

tion of a finer development in Scotland than in England, but
of an earlier decay in regions nearer London as a result of the
infiltration of songs from Grub Street. What appears to have
occurred was a serious, though not mortal, injury to the traditional art, affecting verse much more profoundly than music
and operating less disastrously in regions that were relatively
free from the influence of printed texts.

There could be no better evidence of the vitality of folk-song
than the fact that it survived the cheapening and deadening
effect of broadsides, which for more than two centuries were
hawked about the countryside. We have to remember, in this
connexion, how very few specimens of traditional ballads are
extant that antedate this period. Our studies must largely be
confined to specimens as they have been remembered and sung
in this later time, and our judgements are formed upon
material so gathered. The verse and music that have furnished
inspiration and technical guidance to our modern poets and
composers were collected, for the most part, after the ballad-
monger had done his worst. We should not minimize the evil
that he accomplished—certainly not ignore it, as many students
of ballads have done. We should not forget that a collection
like that made by Child necessarily includes a great number
of pieces either originated by hirelings of the printers or deeply
marked by the influence of their work. At the same time,
having taken these factors into account, we are justified in saying that folk-song was neither destroyed nor irretrievably
harmed by the flood of new ballads that poured over the
country during the sixteenth, seventeenth, and eighteenth
centuries. One may fairly put it that the art suffered from a
severe case of indigestion, that the glut of mediocre songs could
not be properly absorbed and adapted to the gracious ways of
tradition; but further than that one cannot go. Not until the
spread of primary education and the conversion of the general

public from oral to visual habits, which took place in the nineteenth century, was folk-song marked for destruction. And even now it remains, not altogether dead, in certain remoter parts of the English-speaking world.

It is probable, though I do not see how it can be definitely proved, that balladry of the traditional sort suffered a decline in social esteem with the advent of the broadside. Later collectors have gathered their material for the most part from quite humble folk, or else from persons of higher station who have had the good taste to store their minds with songs learned from more simple people. This cannot be denied. On the other hand, such earlier references to popular songs as we have do not seem to imply that they were the property of the lowest social orders. Sidney, with his 'blind crowder', belonged of course to the higher aristocracy and could have had little intimate knowledge of how things went on in the villages of England. It was inevitable that he should condescend, though he felt his heart moved. The argument of Olrik[18] that the aristocracy of Denmark made the ballad what it was, as well as collected specimens of it, may hold for a country with a simple social organisation such as he describes; but in England there can hardly have been so complete a community of interests. Yet the manors and villages of England had a stable and homogeneous population, among whom those higher in station may well have participated as a matter of course in the pleasures of their dependents, and indeed have contributed very notably to the arts of song and dance that were their common property. It is probably safe to assume, therefore, that folk-song did not become a peasant art until the broadside gave balladry a bad name.

No stall ballad is extant that can be dated before the third decade of the sixteenth century. Professor Rollins, who in our

[18] A. Olrik, *Danske Folkeviser i Udvalg,* 3rd ed. (1913), pp. 5, 16–24.

time has acquired a greater mastery of such literature than any one else who has worked in the field, sets 1559 and the work of one William Elderton at the beginning of such balladry,[19] unless we count John Skelton's topical poems as belonging to the *genre,* which is scarcely permissible. About 1535, however, there was printed *Luther, the Pope, a Cardinal, and a Husbandman,* which 'may have been sung',[20] and unquestionably is 'one of the earliest extant broadside ballads'. Later in the century the numbers increased enormously, and throughout the seventeenth century the business of making and selling them flourished beyond all computation. Not until the newsletter in the eighteenth century did the trade begin to decline. The registers of the Company of Stationers, kept from 1557 to 1709, contain the entries of more than 3,000 ballads, according to the invaluable index compiled by Professor Rollins;[21] and the efforts of the company to make their record complete were by no means successful. Broadsides were also sometimes collected in volumes, after the fashion of miscellanies, which may be illustrated by *A Handful of Pleasant Delights,* first issued in 1566.[22]

The interest of stall ballads lies almost wholly in the picture they give of the way ordinary men looked at life and the events taking place about them. As John Selden wrote, 'Though some make slight of libels, yet you may see by them how the wind sits. As take a straw and throw it up into the air, you shall see by that which way the wind is, which you shall not do by casting up a stone. More solid things do not

[19] H. E. Rollins, *A Pepysian Garland,* 1922, p. ix. See also Rollins, *Studies in Philology,* xvii. 199–245 (1920).

[20] See Rollins, *The Pepys Ballads,* i. 3–7 (1929).

[21] 'An Analytical Index to the Ballad Entries in the Registers of the Company of Stationers of London', *Studies in Philology,* xxi, 1–324 (1924).

[22] See Rollins, *A Handful of Pleasant Delights,* 1924.

show the complexion of the times so well as ballads and libels."[23] They reveal how political occurrences appeared to the observer in the street or on the backstairs, with what interested disapproval the solid citizen regarded criminals, how excited the populace became at the news of something monstrous in nature. In the words of Professor Rollins, 'journalistic ballads outnumbered all other types. Others were sermons, or romances, or ditties of love and jealousy, of tricks and "jests," comparable to the ragtime, or music-hall, songs of the present time."[24] Very seldom do they rise above the level of capable verse-making, though the tunes that were in the minds of the scribblers when they wrote gave their work a lively rhythm.

In considering these ballads as a valuable record of the time when they appeared, as it is fair to do, there is only one exception to be taken. The views they express, the pictures they present, are those of the townsman rather than that of the countryman. They were written in the cities—chiefly in London; and, though intended for distribution throughout the kingdom, they reflect the interests of the moment in the larger centres. I believe that this aspect of the matter has never been sufficiently stressed. Its implications are far-reaching. On the one hand, they give a partial picture of things : we cannot be sure that they represent at all correctly the sentiments of villagers, even though we can be reasonably certain that they interpret with complete accuracy what town-dwellers felt. On the other hand, the dissemination of the sheets must have influenced very strongly the opinions and the tastes of the rural communities to which they were brought. In other words, they began that musical hegemony of town over country which has been increasingly—and unfortunately—apparent ever since.

Before the middle of the seventeenth century men of dis-

[23] *Table Talk*, lxxx, ed. S. H. Reynolds, 1892, p. 102.
[24] *A Pepysian Garland*, p. xi.

cernment had come to see the value of broadside ballads as a record of events and popular notions. I have quoted John Selden, who was the first great example of a line of collectors, some of them scholarly like Selden, some inveterately curious like Pepys, and some merely acquisitive like Bagford, to whom we owe much for their preservation of this fugitive material— and incidentally of many good things like stories of Robin Hood. Selden died in 1654, but was followed by Samuel Pepys, whose magnificent collection was based on that of his predecessor. Pepys—characteristically—arranged his plunder in five volumes, which he bequeathed to Magdalene College, Cambridge, together with the rest of his library, thus securing for them a permanent abode.[25] Pepys had finished making his collection before 1703. It remains one of the greatest ever brought together, containing 1671 ballads, exclusive of duplicates, nearly a thousand of which are unique.

The only rival of Pepys as a collector in his own time was the Oxford antiquary, Anthony Wood, who died in 1695. Wood was less happy than Pepys, however, in the fate of what he garnered, for only 279 items remain in his collection. The evidence is fairly clear that one John Bagford, in the service of Robert Harley, first Earl of Oxford, stole on a grand scale from the Ashmolean Museum, to which Wood had bequeathed his ballads. Harley's acquisitions, before his death in 1724, filled two volumes,[26] while Bagford had three volumes of his own.[27] Towards the end of the eighteenth century, the third Duke of Roxburghe, who at that time owned Harley's collection, added another great volume, largely made up of material likewise abstracted from Wood's papers. Who served

[25] Ed. H. E. Rollins, *A Pepysian Garland*, 1922, and *The Pepys Ballads*, 1929–31, 6 vols., with others to follow.
[26] See *The Roxburghe Ballads*, ed. W. Chappell and J. W. Ebsworth, 1871–97 (Ballad Society).
[27] See *The Bagford Ballads*, ed. J. W. Ebsworth, 1878 (Ballad Society).

the duke in this somewhat ignoble business has not been discovered. Presumably he did not soil his hands by stealing the broadsides for himself any more than did Harley, though the Duchess of Marlborough—had she known—would have been glad to believe the worst of the latter gentleman. It is amusing to note—to complete this tale of ancient perfidies—that the contents of still another volume are suspect, the Rawlinson collection, which was made at about the same time as the Roxburghe and may well contain things taken from Wood's papers, and that it in turn has been rifled by a later thief.[28] The only other collection rivalling in scope those mentioned above is that formed by Francis Douce (1757–1834), but there are several minor ones of considerable importance.[29] We ought to note, too, that a large number of ballads were copied from broadsides, and exist in manuscript. There is one group of eighty, for example, in the library of Shirburn Castle, Oxfordshire, which some one took the pains to put together during the reigns of Elizabeth and James I.[30]

The activities of copyists and collectors during the seventeenth and eighteenth centuries furnish the best possible evidence for the genuine, if perhaps condescending, interest taken in stall ballads by men of education at the time. No one, indeed, whatever his station, could well have escaped some knowledge of the ubiquitous sheets. In Shakespeare's extraordinary memory dozens must have stuck, along with the country songs he had learned as a boy. The two kinds were not distinguished by any one, as we see from the account of Captain Cox in Laneham's letter from Kenilworth in 1575.[31]

[28] See A. Clark, *The Shirburn Ballads,* 1907, p. 5, for an account of these misdemeanors.
[29] For example, the Luttrell and the Osterley Park, the latter edited by F. B. Fawcett, *Broadside Ballads of the Restoration,* 1930.
[30] See A. Clark, *op. cit.*
[31] Ed. F. J. Furnivall, *Captain Cox,* 1871 (Ballad Society).

That amateur of popular literature, who loved everything in print that came to hand, is said to have had 'oversight' of 'stories' like *Robin Hood* and *Adam Bell,* as well as of 'a bunch of ballets and songs, all auncient . . . fair wrapt up in parchment.' How impossible it must have been to avoid acquaintance with broadsides is shown by Walton in *The Complete Angler*[32] when he makes Piscator say : 'I'll now lead you to an honest ale-house, where we shall find a cleanly room, lavendar in the windows, and twenty ballads stuck about the wall.' Two generations later Addison was bearing testimony to the same use of ballads.[33]

With Addison, we begin to find the name 'ballad' applied not only to broadsides but to the traditional narratives with which the word was destined to be more closely associated as time went on. Although he called *Chevy Chase* a song, in his enthusiastic and somewhat laboured defence of the 'Gothic manner,' he referred to it as 'the favourite ballad of the common people of England.' [34] To him ballads had a certain importance, it is evident, and he gave them his serious attention. In contrast to his attitude was that of the editor—probably Ambrose Philips—of *A Collection of Ballads,* published in 1723-5, which was altogether condescending and feebly jocose. For the most part he printed stall ballads, though he included a few traditional ones, and he gave no hint that he saw any difference between the two sorts. The importance of his three volumes, as has been well observed, lies in this : 'What Addison was in the history of literary criticism of the ballad, this editor was in the history of publication. The one

[32] Chapter ii.

[33] *Spectator,* no. 85.

[34] *Spectator,* nos. 70, 74. See S. B. Hustvedt, *Ballad Criticism in Scandinavia and Great Britain,* 1916, pp. 65–78, for an account of Addison's criticism and the controversy aroused by it.

said that the ballads were worth reading; the other offered them to the curious to read.'[35]

To Joseph Ritson, near the end of the century, has often been attributed the credit—if there be credit—of reserving the name 'ballad' for narratives, but improperly, as Professor Hustvedt showed in his able volume on *Ballad Criticism*. William Shenstone, the poet, made the point clearly in two letters to Percy in 1761. In the second of these he said: 'It is become habitual to me, to call that a *Ballad,* which describes or implies some action; on the other hand, I term that a *Song,* which contains only an expression of sentiment.'[36] Doubtless Percy had this distinction in mind when he used, as the running title of the *Reliques,* the heading 'Ancient Songs and Ballads.' In his prefatory essay he distinguished between romances and ballads, but either he had not fully grasped or he did not see fit to accept Shenstone's categories of ballad and song, which were, after all, perfectly arbitrary in view of accepted nomenclature. He was content to employ both terms for narratives like *Chevy Chase,* and in his preface he made an apology 'for having bestowed any attention on a parcel of old ballads'[37]—quite in the pre-Addisonian manner. He did, however, mark a difference in style between 'the more ancient ballads of this collection' and productions by 'the latter composers of heroical: I mean by such as professedly wrote for the press.'[38]

Ritson went much further, and adopted Shenstone's categories outright, however he came by a knowledge of them. According to his own statement, they appear to have come into general use by this time, which may well have been the case in view of the interest aroused by the *Reliques.* In *A*

[35] Hustvedt, *op. cit.,* p. 105.
[36] See Hustvedt, *op. cit.,* pp. 160–1.
[37] 2nd. ed., 1767, i. XVI.
[38] *Op. cit.,* i. XXXVII.

Select Collection of English Songs, which he published in
1783, he said : 'It may not be impertinent to premise, that,
as the collection, under the general title of *Songs,* consists, not
only of pieces strictly and properly so called, but likewise,
though in great disproportion as to number, of *Ballads* or mere
narrative compositions, the word *Song* will, in the course of
this preface, be almost everywhere used in its confined sense;
inclusive, however, of a few modern and sentimental ballads,
which no reader of taste, it is believed, will be inclined to
think out of place.'[39] He was more explicit and less confusing
in a note subjoined to the 'Historical Essay on the Origin and
Progress of National Song' that follows his preface : 'With us,
songs of sentiment, expression, or even description, are properly termed *Songs,* in contradistinction to mere narrative compositions, which we now denominate *Ballads.*'[40] It is evident
that Ritson had no more intention than Percy of reserving the
name ballad for traditional narratives in verse, but that he did
wish to use it for what he surprisingly calls 'mere narrative
compositions' of the popular sort, whatever their origin.

Thomas Gray appears to have been quite alone, throughout the eighteenth century, in comprehending the true value
of strictly traditional poetry; and indeed few commentators
have ever understood so well as he the structural merits of
such pieces. In saying of *Child Maurice* (83), 'It begins in the
fifth act of the play,' he showed a critical acumen that was
amazingly far ahead of his age.[41] Not until the nineteenth
century, and then only very gradually, did ballads gathered
from oral sources, whether recitation or singing, come to be
generally regarded as more interesting and valuable than the
dubious products of the London hacks. More than forty years
after Gray wrote the remarkable words I have quoted, Words-

[39] Preface, p. ii.
[40] 'A Historical Essay', p. i, n.I.
[41] Letter to Mason, June 1757, ed. Tovey, *Letters,* i. 336.

worth cited a stanza from *The Babes in the Wood,* in his famous Preface to the *Lyrical Ballads,* to illustrate his theory of poetry; and in his remarks on *Goody Blake and Harry Gill* he showed that he took broadsides as his models.[42] It is not at all strange that differences of opinion have continued ever since as to the beauty of some of the verse included in the *Lyrical Ballads.* Nothing could show Wordsworth's genius in a clearer light than the fact that other pieces in the same volume and in the same strain have the hall-mark of great poetry. But the *Lyrical Ballads* included also, we must remember, Coleridge's *Rime of the Ancient Mariner,* which 'was professedly written in imitation of the style, as well as the spirit of the elder poets,' as the preface to the volume informed the public. Although *The Ancient Mariner* owes a good deal to medieval romance, it is even more plainly an adaptation in its rhythmical form and rhetoric of the traditional ballad. All the suggestions Coleridge needed he could have got from Percy's volumes. He and Wordsworth thus differed in what they took from balladry, as they did in so much else. It does not appear that either of them distinguished between kinds, but each simply followed his own bent.

With Scott the case was still different. Saturated in ancient lore of all sorts, he imitated the ballad style as easily as that of medieval romance, and so closely that no one can be quite sure to what extent *Kinmont Willie* is the child of his imagination. The collection of ballads from oral tradition had gone on meanwhile at an ever-increasing pace. Ritson's sour comments on the editorial alterations of Percy, though they did not keep Scott from tampering with the texts he printed in the *Minstrelsy of the Scottish Border,*[43] doubtless helped spread the notion that a song found in oral circulation had peculiar virtues and was worth recovering, however much it might be

[43] 1802-3.

the duty of an editor to 'improve' its form. Scott was an ardent collector, as every one knows. His boundless enthusiasm, which led him to expand his first scheme for the *Minstrelsy*, did much, and the quiet persistence of Jamieson[44] in gleaning waifs and strays, helped a little, to popularize the traditional ballad as distinguished from the product of the stalls. When Keats, who was of the next literary generation, came to write *La Belle Dame sans Merci*, he had absorbed the essential qualities of the type so completely as to the structure as well as style that he was able to put them to his own uses with complete freedom. He did not even find it necessary to label his poem a ballad. Only a few years later Motherwell[45] showed by precept and example that editorial tampering with texts was wrong in principle and useless in practice. The ballad of tradition had by this time acquired the sanction of poets and scholars.

Yet the name has never come to mean one thing only. The poets of the so-called Romantic Period and their successors have often imitated the traditional ballad, frequently with great advantage to their work; they have used technical devices learned from such ballads to the enrichment of lyrics that are only to be called ballads because the term has always been ambiguous; and they have made other excellent ballads that may be said to derive from the broadsides, though so far superior in literary merit that their origin is not too obvious. There is no point in trying to rule out of court any of these kinds. At one time or another so many sorts of verse have borne the name that it is impossible to restrict its use in any way. The lover of folk-song may be glad that increasingly the unmodified word has come to suggest verse narratives moulded by the tradition of singers, but only because this furnishes an

[44] *Popular Ballads and Songs*, 1806.
[45] *Minstrelsy, Ancient and Modern*, 1827.

index to a deeper and wider appreciation of the qualities they possess. To claim more, or desire more, would be foolish.

EVELYN KENDRICK WELLS

Theories of Origin*

Early reference to ballads gives us no information as to the method of their composition : it proves only the existence, before 1300, the date of the "Judas" text, of the ballad form as we now know it. The vexed question of origin was launched in the eighteenth century by Percy's sweeping claim for minstrel authorship, and since then the matching of theories by scholars and collectors has drawn the literary world into increasingly fervid, if not heated debate. Stated over-simply, the varied sources of the ballad are held to be these :

(1) The dance, because of the rhythmic refrain, and because primitive races today make up songs as they dance. *Das Volk dichtet*—the "singing, dancing throng" is the poet. (2) Individual poets, also of the folk. (3) The courtly poets, often minstrels, since it is sometimes possible to trace the humble setting of today's ballad back to an aristocratic Medieval background. (4) The monks, because the ballad stanza shows a metrical similarity to the Latin hymn, thus bespeaking some learning and skill, and because the earliest text, "Judas" (23),† is religious in subject.

All these theories have their fallacies. It is difficult to see how "the singing, dancing throng" can give itself simultaneously to two different stimuli, that of rhythmic bodily movement in the dance, and that of intense interest in the story. A try at dancing a ballad soon shows the difficulties, though the Norwegians say it is possible. It is dangerous to argue for communal authorship from the analogy of primitive custom : although the South Sea Islanders of today compose songs as

* From *The Ballad Tree* by Evelyn Kendrick Wells, copyright 1950 by The Ronald Press Company.

† Numbers in parentheses refer to the order of appearance of ballads in *English and Scottish Popular Ballads* by Francis J. Child.

they dance, the resulting songs are lyrical and nonnarrative, not ballads. And although a ballad of humble background may be traced back to a Medieval courtly singer, this does not preclude all lowly authorship. Poetic skill has come from a Jonson, a Marlowe, a Burns, even a Shakespeare. The fact that our earliest copy of a ballad is on a religious subject is not enough to prove monastic authorship of all ballads. If the monks wrote the ballads, why are religious ones so scarce, and secular ones so plentiful? As for the minstrel authorship, ballads would seem to have been in the field long before the minstrels began to include them in their stock of trade.[1] The truth of ballad origin lies among the many theories. Verse so varied was born of varied strains—the clerical, with its Latin ancestry, the courtly, with its romance, the minstrel idiom, contact with the dance song and its refrain, and popular practice with its renewing pulse. The contributing elements were worked over by the sure canons of popular taste and polished in the process of tradition. Successive singers fused the many strains of ancestry, and obliterated all trace of individual composition. The ballad, if not communal in origin, was communal in development.

Some ballads, because of their simple structure, may indeed have evolved from the improvisation of the throng. "The Hangman," as sung in the Southern Appalachians, shows this possibility more clearly than its formally organized British cousin, "The Maid Freed from the Gallows" (95). More complicated, but still within the scope of communal composition by a group familiar with the method, is "Babylon" (14), in which the story grows by spontaneous imitation of the first incident. The incremental repetition which underlies its structure may have been developed by the improvising throng. Communal authorship, however, is inconceivable in ballads

[1] See page 208.

of more intricate structure. A poet of no mean ability must
have composed such a ballad as "The Wife of Usher's Well"
(79). Many ballads dealing with aristocratic life, sung today
by Scottish peasants or Southern Highlanders, were probably
born in court circles, becoming democratized as they were
appropriated by humble singers. Archer Taylor in his study of
"Edward" (13)[2] traces this ballad back from its present lowly
setting to a poet who knew courtly life : the old gray hound
that traced the fox in Tennessee is descended from a pedigreed
medieval grayhound. As for clerical authorship : the interplay
of learned and secular elements in Medieval poetry and music
has frequently been noted. If, as is claimed,[3] the meter of the
Latin hymns influenced both Latin and Anglo-Saxon secular
verse, it may well have helped to create the ballad stanza.
There is evidence that some monasteries supported minstrels,
and "Judas" (23) and its like may have been written by them
for the monks, or by the monks under minstrel influence.[4] For
the minstrels are indeed responsible for some of the ballads.
Thus clerks and minstrels, as well as courtly and lowly poets,
may all have taken a hand.

In the midst of all these commingled possibilities, it becomes
necessary to reconcile the two elements of narrative content
and rhythmic expression in the ballad, and to clarify the
connection between ballad and dance. It will therefore be
helpful, and not irrelevant to turn at this point to another
traditional survival, the carol, since its contribution to the
ballad form as we know it is fairly well substantiated.

The carol, like the religious ballad and the miracle play,
was another Medieval democratizing of religious themes for
the common people. As we know it today, it is lyrical, subjective, full of a merry piety; and it deals chiefly with the

[2] *Edward and Sven I Rosengard.*
[3] Discussed by Gerould, *The Ballad of Tradition*, pp. 218–23.
[4] Pound, *Poetic Origins and the Ballad*, p. 184.

Christmas story. But its scope was once greater, including New Year's, Easter, Whitsun, and Harvest songs, carols for any feast of the church year. Still older carols are secular, dealing with love, politics, hunting, or drinking. A refrain is inherent in the stanza; there may be also a burden, or a stanza at the beginning which is repeated at the end, somewhat disconnected from the song itself, such as a call for the music to strike up, or an invitation to sing. Both burden and refrain are popular in substance, and contribute to the mood rather than the content of the song. Their strong rhythm, and at times the indication of movement, like *"Come let us join hands,"* or *"Why stand we still? Why move we not?"* indicate a connection with dance and point to the word *carole,* Old French for a circular dance often accompanied by song. This in turn suggests the still current circle dances of the Balkans, the *horo* and the *kolo* (from Greek *choros*). Thus the evidence gathers for an earlier link between the carol and the dance.[5]

The origin of social dance in folk forms, and of folk dance in ritual forms, is practically established by the study of primitive art and customs. The earliest forms of folk dance are the circle, the double line, and the hey, or serpentine processional. Maypole dances are the remnant of ancient religious celebrations around some object of worship such as a well or a tree. The "Roger de Coverly" type of dance was earlier the primitive dramatization of the life principle symbolized by the contest and wooing of the sexes, of opposite forces in nature, such as light and darkness. The magic connotations of the key, or serpentine dance (still seen in the grand right-and-left of the

---

[5] *The Oxford Book of Carols* Preface gives a short history of the carol and quotes these derivations of the word. Sachs, in *A World History of the Dance* (p. 271), derives the word from *corolla,* Latin for "little crown." German *reigen* or ring-dances are also known as crown-dances. In 1943 a group of young Boston Greeks danced a horo at a folk festival in the Boston Garden.

country dance) are not well understood : some imitation of the movements of the serpent, often an object of fear and therefore veneration, may have been intended. Of all these forms, the circle dance was the most widely dispersed. As the carole, it became the social dance all over Europe, having completely lost any serious significance. When, after the Black Death, Europe was seized by a dance mania which was the expression of a hysterical gaiety in the face of doom, its medium was the carole, popular, hypnotic, and long familiarly practiced although people had forgotten why. The abuse of the dance offended decent and orderly folk, and Robert Mannyng in his homiletic poem, *Handlyng Synne* (1303), includes it with wrestling, May Games, interludes and the disorder inspired by the wanton pipe and tabor :

> Carolles, wrastlynges, or somour games,
> Whosoever haunteth any swyche shames
> In cherche other yn chercheyerd,
> Of sacrylage he may be aferd;
> . . . .
> All swych thyng forbodyn is
> While the prest stondeth at messe.[6]

By the fifteenth century there is graphic witness to the general performance of the carole. The peasant round in a Book of Hours is like that of the lords and ladies dancing in a formal garden, and even Botticelli conceived of his angels in heaven dancing in a ring.

There are traces of the secular medieval carole in the ring-games of the nursery and in play-party games of the South and Middle West. Most of us have left behind us "The Farmer in the Dell," but in some rural parts of our country grownups still sing and dance for hours at a time similar

[6] Robert Mannyng of Brunne, *Handlyng Synne*, II. 8987-94.

games, like "Old Bald Eagle" and "Jubilee." Here is the ancient ring dance, the lyric, local-allusion verse, the popular refrain, and the hypnotic rhythm, which help us understand the great vogue of the carole in the Middle Ages. From a comparison of early pictures and texts with present performance of ring-games, it seems probable that the leader of the carole not only directed the movement but sang the stanza, during which the dancers remained in position, swaying rhythmically; and that the whole group joined in the refrain as it moved around the circle. In "Captain Jinks" this distinction is made between the movement in place during the stanza, and the "rig-a-jig-jig and away we go" of the refrain.

The transference of this strongly entrenched song-dance from the secular to the sacred is one more instance of the use by religious reformers of a folk custom on which to build a better life for the people. The Franciscan friars were the chief agents of this change. "What are the servants of God, if not his minstrels, who ought to stir and incite the hearts of men to spiritual joy?"[7] In their sermons they emphasized the humility and poverty of Christ, and dwelt upon his birth in a manger; and they are said to have given great impetus to the use of the Christmas crêche. The existing caroles, often lewd but always rhythmic and popular, they turned from worldly uses to those of innocent piety, by writing new words for the popular refrain so that people might instantly join in. Like Wesley at a later date, they asked themselves why the devil should have all the good tunes. In their industry and sincerity they set up new associations for old tunes wherever they preached.[8] . . .

[7] Sabatier, *Life of St. Francis*, p. 307. Chambers, *Medieval Stage* I, quotes the Latin from *Speculum Perfectionis:* "Quid enim sunt servi Dei nisi quidam ioculatores eius qui corda hominum eriger debent et movere ad laetitiam spiritualem."

[8] Greene, *Early English Carols,* cxxi ff.

The carole's evidence of contributed refrain shows the influence of the dance. Social evidence as to the practice of song, in the carole and by minstrels of the lower orders, would account for the spread of the vogue. Three centuries, more or less, of indigenous cultivation would stabilize the form. Thus, by the fifteenth century, when we begin to find many ballad texts, the form has become fixed.

In Scandinavian countries, where almost all ballads have refrains, they are still danced. This is now a folk practice, but was formerly an occupation of the highborn. British observance of the custom, in comparison, does not seem to have been so widespread. British ballads are as often as not without refrain, and there is no indication of the danced ballad today, and little reference to it in the past. Early allusions are, moreover, not wholly clear. One, from Barbour's *Bruce* (1378), refers to the celebration of local events in song, but does not mention dance, unless we interpret "play" as "dance"—a somewhat fantastic claim.

> I will nocht reherss all the maner;
> For quha sa likis, thai may heir
> Young women quhen thai will play,
> Syng it emang thame ilke day.[9]

Another is from Fabyan's *Chronicles* (1516):

Than the Scottis enflamyd with pryde, in deryson of Englysshe men made this ryme :

> Maydens of Englonde, sore may ye morne,
> For your lemmans ye haue loste at Bannockisborne,
> With heue a lowe.
> What wenyth the Kynge of Englonde
> So soone to have woone Scotlande
> With rumbylowe.

[9] Barbour, *The Bruce*, xvi, 11 p. 399, 11, 519–22. In some remote parts of America "play" as a euphemism for "dance" is used to obviate religious prejudice.

This songe was after many days syngyn in daunces, in carolis of the maydens and mynstrelles of Scotland, to the reproofe and disdayne of Englysshemen.[10]

Some weight has been given to the listing as "dances" in *The Complaynt of Scotland* (1549) of three recognizable ballads, "yong tamlene," "Johny Ermistrangis daunce," and "Robene hude."[11]

It may be, however, that by this date ballad tunes, as we know from abundant evidence was true later, had already been separated from the songs and had been adapted to dancing. The ensuing centuries saw a continual borrowing of ballad tunes for dances, and of dance tunes for ballad settings. We assume that these later tunes were not sung as people danced, partly because there is no record of the fact, and partly because the tunes, in their dance versions, are not suited to singing. Deloney's *Jack of Newburie* (1597) gives a version of "The Fair Flower of Northumberland" (9). He is explicit as to the way of singing, but does not mention dance.

> The maidens in dulcet manner chanted this song, two of them singing the Ditty and the rest bearing the burden (refrain, in this case).[12]

Thus dance and song, whether ballad or carol, seem to have parted company in England before the sixteenth century. Whatever fragments of the custom of dancing to song are left today are found in the singing games and processional lyrics of some folk observances. The term "ballad," as has been pointed out in the Introduction, has been used through the ages for many forms of verse, both sophisticated and simple. We cannot, therefore, prove dance origin or dance association

[10] Fabyan, *Chronicles*, p. 420.
[11] *The Complaynt of Scotland*, pp. 65, 66.
[12] Deloney, *Jack of Newburie*, p. 33.

of the ballad from the derivation of the word itself, even though the word implies dance. We can at the most say that dance has been a contributing, but not dominant factor in the development of the ballad form.

ALBERT B. FRIEDMAN

Epilogue: The Ballad in Modern Verse*

By the end of the nineteenth century there had developed a vast repertoire of ways of translating the characteristics of folk ballads and the lesser genres of popular poetry into the terms of lettered art. The repertoire has grown steadily. If the novel refrains of Rossetti and Morris persist in the songs of Crazy Jane (and elsewhere in Yeats) and in the French burdens of Alfred Noyes's ballads, it is always with a difference. Yeats's "The Wild, Wicked Old Man" has a discordant refrain at the foot of each stanza which is intended by its "formally repetitive incongruity to disrupt the elevated arguments and recall the poet to a 'countertruth.'"[1] If so, Yeats has perpetrated an audacity his pre-Raphaelite masters had never conceived. Merely to mention that the ingenious choral refrain of "Sister Helen" inspired the dramatic strategy of Kipling's "Danny Deever" stanza is enough to suggest how radical the later adaptations could be. . . .

I

Perhaps John Davidson is the first modern poet in whom we can detect some of the attitudes toward the ballads later to become general. It was principally for the scope which the ballad gave to spontaneity that he valued it, and he therefore refused to hobble his directness with archaisms and artificial diction and phrasing, even when excerpting incidents from the legends of Tannhäuser and Lancelot. The bareness and simple structure of the ordinary ballad stanza abet the intensity of "A

* From *The Ballad Revival* by Albert B. Friedman, copyright 1961 by the University of Chicago.

[1] John Bayley, *The Romantic Survival* (London, 1957), p. 108.

Ballad of Hell" by concentrating attention on the daring story; conversely, the same qualities, by hindering the creation of a morbid *ambiance,* check the extravagant sentiment of Davidson's more melodramatic pieces. His finest poems, "A Ballad of a Nun" and "A Runnable Stag," are distinguished from other verse of the period by a language wholly contemporary and colloquial. Historically they occupy the same position with regard to modern notions of poetic diction as Henley's *London Voluntaries* do in the establishment of cadence as a principle of poetic structure.

Indeed, Davidson's ballads and naturalistic vignettes of life among the London desperate belong to a reaction against richness and rhetoric which was one of the healthiest currents of *fin de siècle* verse. Verlaine's injunction to "wring the neck of rhetoric" had been heard in Britain, and because folksong is "never declamatory or eloquent," it came, in Yeats's words to "fill the scene."[2] In "The Ballad of Reading Gaol," ballad discipline had shown itself capable of chastening even the lush allusiveness and verbal exoticism of Wilde. Obviously the pre-Raphaelite ballad, richly molded, effetely neomedieval, and incrusted with finery borrowed from romance, was of limited use in the new program of purification. Once again the ballads free of literary refinement, the simple folksong, the broadsides and their vulgar congeners, became the corrective models for a cult of simplicity. The devotees came to include, among others, Hardy and Housman, W. H. Davies and Yeats, Frost and De la Mare.

The new imitators of folksong were more successful than their Victorian predecessors, according to Yeats, because they knew folksong through living tradition. Actually most of the modern imitators came by their knowledge through books, just

[2] *The Oxford Book of Modern Verse,* ed. W. B. Yeats (London, 1936), p. xiii.

as the Victorians had. There are of course exceptions like Hardy, who makes informed references to folk-ballad performances and writes unself-consciously to the tune of folk lyrics, as in "The Vagrant's Song," which is "Waly, Waly" crossed with "an old Wessex refrain." But Yeats has in mind primarily his fellow poets in Ireland, "where still (1936) lives almost undisturbed the last folk tradition of western Europe." Modestly he instances Padraic Colum, who took his themes from tradition and had the honor of hearing them "sung to Irish airs" by persons "who had never heard the name of the author."[3] . . .

Yeats himself at various times during his career was intoxicated with folksong. In personal versions of folk rhythms he versified the tales told him by old peasant women, "The Host of the Air" being one such venture. Almost every one of his collections contains a set of experiments with folk refrains. "I am of Ireland" reconstructs a popular medieval lyric; "Down by the Salley Gardens" is based on a wisp of folksong; "The Three Bushes," the rewriting of a ballad of Dorothy Wellesley, is very nearly a parody of the rose and briar ballad ending. One can also find in Yeats patriotic broadside ranting like "Come Gather Round Me, Parnellites," village tragedies in the Wordsworthian vein ("Moll Magee"), and in "Colonel Martin" a tabloid crime detailed with such jaunty inconsequence that the fable tone supplied by the ballad conventions is barely able to keep the piece from lapsing into bathos. For Yeats folksong was more than a quarry for technique or an avenue to simplicity. It represented also the primeval emotions and symbols of universal experience, a world where myth and mystery were still operative, untouched by the blight of Victorion scientism. The danger for the folksong writer, and Yeats confesses to find it in "my own early work," was "a facile

[3] *Ibid.*

charm, a too soft simplicity." *A Shropshire Lad* barely eluded
the temptation—"a mile further and all had been marsh."
Thomas Hardy "made the necessary correction through his
mastery of the impersonal objective scene."[4]

It was not merely because the ballads and other kinds of
folksong provided easy tunes and encouraged a desired plain-
ness of language that poets risked the perils of balladic simplicity. The nostalgia of persons reared in an urban culture for
the simpler modes of rural life and for the countryman's
assumedly more direct and wholehearted responses to the
objects and dynamics of nature explains the appeal of a large
segment of twentieth-century poetry. Simply by naming
Hardy's Wessex, Frost's North of Boston, Yeats's Sligo, and
Housman's Shropshire, one enforces the correlative point that
the preferred imaginative terrain for the cult of simplicity is
the countryside, made more glamorous usually by being
pushed a generation or two into the past or set in a temporal
limbo. Since folksinging and ballad recitation are an expected
part of country life, it was peculiarly appropriate that rustic
events and poetic meditations in a rural setting should
regularly be cast in an approximation of the rural poetic
idiom—that, for example, Nell in Hardy's "Harvest Supper,"
who sings the venerable ballad of "False Sir John" (a version
of Child No. 4), should have her own unfaithfulness chronicled
in ballad language and meter. . . .

In his monologues, and in other respects as well, Hardy's
ballad poetry links the cult of simplicity with the early
Romantics. The pastoral atmosphere of Wessex seems lately
blown from the Lake District, and Hardy frequently prefers
the Napoleonic scene to the contemporary. Like the Romantics, Hardy elects the ballad as the proper form for local
legends—for example, "At Stag's Heath," the remorseful wail

[4] *Ibid.*, pp. xiii–xvi.

of the woman who betrayed Monmouth in 1685. In "Retty's Phases," the focus of interest is the poignancy of the narrator's reaction, as in the Lucy poems. "The Carrier" who keeps an empty seat beside him for his dead wife is a Wordsworthian eccentric, his foible being described with something like Wordsworth's wry understatement. But the differences between Hardy and the Romantics are profound. Unlike Wordsworth, he is as much interested in the story as in his people, and again unlike Wordsworth, he does not guide his reader's sympathies overtly. There is a marked strain of irony in Hardy's ballads, although it is seldom developed at the expense of his characters. "The Turnip Hoer" in love with the duchess he once rescued is not ridiculous but merely the dupe of circumstances. . . .

Of modern poets Housman is decidedly the most thoroughly steeped in folk poetry. Those who have detected and tabulated his sources agree that "the influence of the Scottish border ballad is stronger and more pervasive than any other."[5] The debt to folksong in all its varieties is even greater than this statement suggests, for what Housman most admired in Shakespeare's songs, Scott's lyrics, and the shorter poems of Heine, his other principal tributaries, was their folksong qualities. And if a knowledge of street ballads were more general among Housman's source-mongers, much more would be made of the resemblances between many numbers of *A Shropshire Lad* and late Victorian recruiting ballads and soldier songs. For example, one of the *Last Poems* "The Culprit," is the literary apotheosis of the broadside "goodnight." . . .

In themes, setting, and lyrical intention, Housman very much resembles Frost. Both capitalize on the urban nostalgia for a lost paradise of rural simplicity, for though Shropshire is an unprosperous place for golden lads, it is a setting which

[5] Norman Marlow, *A. E. Housman* (London, 1958), p. 69.

lends a glamor even to doom. But the attitudes of the two
poets are widely divergent. Mixed with Frost's wise tenderness
is a certain complacency and authority which has no counterpart in Housman, and Housman's sad resignation is hardly to
be equated with the sanguine acquiescence in the claims of the
practical world that is general in Frost. Of the two, Housman
is the more genuinely "popular" poet, for the persona he
affects is more convincingly differentiated from the poet and
projects emotions in which the reader can more readily partici-
pate. Further, the melancholy cynicism with which Housman's
poetry is saturated represents to the unsophisticated reader the
poetic mood par excellence. It would be very wrong, however,
to see in Housman's melancholy desperation a latter-day version of the tragic view of life reflected in the folk ballads. The
ballad people mute their heroics and suffer horrors dry-eyed;
one rarely finds them luxuriating morbidly in suffering and
bleakness.

In that sense in which Housman can be considered a
"public" or "popular" poet, that is, a poet who performs something of the social function of folk and popular poetry, he is
far surpassed by Kipling. Kipling's "Johnny," a parody of
"Edward," and "The Last Rhyme of True Thomas," despite
the allegorical elements, are sufficient evidence that Kipling
was thoroughly grounded in the traditional ballad. But it is
not his formal imitations of the older ballads that prompt T. S.
Eliot to label Kipling a ballad-writer not a poet. He is a
ballad-writer, Eliot insists, because he writes with the same
intention as the naïve balladists : to create verses "immediately
apprehensible" that concentrate on the story or characters and
forgo "metrical complications corresponding to subtleties of
feeling that cannot be immediately responded to." . . .

A vulgar brand of patriotism permeates even Kipling's
historical ballads. Whether he writes of a centurion begging to

remain in Britain ("The Roman Centurion's Song") or of a Norman baron giving advice to his heir ("Norman and Saxon"), Kipling manages to make the poem a crude eulogy of the "passion and piety and prowess" of the native race. Because of its lingering communal connotations, the historical ballad continues a favorite vehicle for patriotic sentiment. The single episode ballad, however, no longer suffices; more ambitious designs and the emulation of the saga encourage ampler structures. Thus Chesterton's *Ballad of the White Horse* (1911), an account of Alfred's struggle with the Danes, assumes the proportions of a minor epic.

The American counterpart of Chesterton's epic, Stephen Vincent Benét's *John Brown's Body* (1927), is written in blank verse, but the poem includes insets in the form of sea chanteys, Negro spirituals, popular marching hymns, broadside doggerel, folk laments of unwed mothers of the type of "Careless Love" and "Waly, Waly" ("Love came by from the riversmoke"); and in John Brown's prayer are exhortatory stanzas strongly reminiscent of "Johnie Armstrong." Benét's "Ballad of William Sycamore" illustrates the American preoccupation with representative heroes, for Sycamore, one of whose sons died at the Alamo and another with Custer, lived a career which parallels the country's westward course. He is not a personality in his own right but the composite American of the period. . . .

II

The most subtle changes worked upon the ballad measure have been a result of its growing use for lyrical rather than narrative purposes, the emotional, personal tone of Housman, Yeats, and Frost tending to give the stanza a more aerated texture. Emily Dickinson's poetry had been largely of this strain. Her technical means for acquiring the deftness and airiness that suit her abbreviated gestures are deceptively simple : short run-on lines; catalectic lines; meaningful mixtures of what hymnologists call short and long meters; polysyllabic words in strategic positions, their secondary accents imparting a subtle buoyancy; and frequent suspended or imperfect rimes, which encourage diffuseness by relaxing the connection between rimed words and thus between the phrases and the ideas they couple. As with Blake, Dickinson's ballad measure has been filtered through the hymnbooks, but she has largely divested the ballad-hymn meter of the sonority it had acquired since Sternhold's jingling psalter had first introduced the ballad manner into hymnody in the reign of Edward VI.

The same lightness and airy music is found in the mystical visions of childhood conjured up by Walter De la Mare. The resemblance between his ballad-like song and the children's verses of Stevenson and Christina Rossetti is only superficial. He has a surer grasp of ballad language and is uncannily expert in finding modern correlatives for the traditional concrete ballad symbols; and though most of his ballad lyrics end, like "The Listeners," on a note of serene mystical emptiness, his narrative "Ballad for Christmas" contrives a shocking denouement as forceful as anything in ballad literature. Poets like Yeats, Colum, and Joseph Campbell had a tradition of folk lyrics at their disposal and quarried these lyrics industriously for new cadences.

The search for new cadences, indeed, accounts for much of the interest of modern poets in folksong. "A new cadence means a new idea," Richard Aldington proclaimed in the Imagist credo,[6] and Ezra Pound advised the Imagist poet to "fill his mind with the finest cadences he can discover," suggesting at the same time that "Saxon charms" and "Hebre-

[6] *Some Imagist Poets* (Boston, 1915).

dean Folk-Songs" were good places to look.[7] More recently, R. P. Blackmur has argued that "the music of words alone may lift common sentiment to great import . . . or at any rate we are faced with much great poetry which has only commonplace intellectual content and yet affects our fundamental convictions." In artistic maturity, he continues, "Waly, Waly," is on a level with *Antony and Cleopatra*.[8] The Imagist principle "to compose in the sequence of the musical phrase, not in sequence of the metronome,"[9] points to another way that folksong has been instructive to modern poets. For as prosodists have long recognized, it is partly the influence of balladry and folksong that has broken the tyranny of what Pound calls "the goddam iamb," and, through encouraging trisyllabic substitution and musical cadences, has liberalized English prosody. . . .[10]

For Randall Jarrell the ballad is a mode of detachment, allowing him to make melancholy events more poignant for being viewed obliquely ("When I Went Home Last Christmas," "In Camp There Was One Alive") or to reproduce the sentimental feelings of simple people without the intrusion of the poet's more sophisticated sensibility ("The Lost Love," "A Ward in the States"). In a set of eight ballads in *The Death Bell*, Vernon Watkins has produced perhaps the finest of recent literary ballads. Each is rich in stylized phrases patterned after traditional ballad expressions and passages of repetition that set up an incantatory rhythm in ballad fashion; and though the speakers (coins, darkness, a skeleton, a piece of driftwood) belong to allegory and animism and the poet assumes a vatic role, the concrete ballad imagery and the matter-of-factness of the medium make the experiences

---

[7] *Literary Essays*, ed. T. S. Eliot (London, 1954), p. 5.
[8] R. P. Blackmur, *The Double Agent* (New York, 1935), p. 156.
[9] *Literary Essays*, p. 3.
[10] See Paul Fussell, *Theory of Prosody in Eighteenth-Century England* (New London, Conn., 1954), pp. 127–145.

imaginatively palpable. Marianne Moore's poetry, a high development of the virtues of prose, intellectual, austerely concise, a tissue of recondite allusions, would seem the least likely partner of popular verse, yet her recent collection *O to be a Dragon* (1959) contains two ballads, one a song encouraging the Brooklyn Dodgers to the tune of "Mama goin' to buy you a mocking-bird," in which the ballad beat and discipline manage to make themselves felt despite the strange content.

The slender merits of the broadside ballads have perhaps best been appreciated in this century by Irish poets. Throughout the nineteenth century the Irish ballad-singers had lent their nasal drone to the nationalist movement; indeed, they were such valuable agents of subversion that when the sale of broadsides was forbidden by viceregal proclamation during the agitation for Catholic emancipation and repeal of the union, O'Connell thought up for the vendors the evasive tactic of selling straws and giving the ballads away free : "According to law,/I'll sell you a straw,/And make you a present of a ballad." The patriot Yeats was therefore following a venerable tradition in adopting the broadside style for "The Rose Tree" and "Sixteen Dead Men," poems written during the Irish rebellion.

When moved by patriotic fervor in later years, Yeats reverted to the turbulent anger of the seditious ballad-singers in "The Curse of Cromwell," "Come Gather round Me, Parnellites," a rally prompted by new light on the Kitty O'Shea scandal, and "Roger Casement," a ballad which Yeats hoped some fiery Irish undergraduate at Oxford would get by heart and sing under the window of the British diplomat he was reviling.[11] "The Rose Tree" was reprinted many years later among the numbered broadsheets published by Yeats through the Cuala Press (1935–37). The Cuala ballads, written expressly for broadside dissemination by Yeats, James

[11] *Letters*, ed. Allan Wade, (New York, 1955), pp. 868, 871.

Stephens, Dorothy Wellesley, and others, were ornamented by Jack Yeats's cut and set for the most part to folk tunes. Yeats separated his broadside activities from his other poetry, "the poems of civilisation,"[12] but his late letters are full of indulgent remarks on the special qualities of the street ballads[13]—although Yeats is never so audacious as Graves, who finds "The Night before Larry Was Stretched," an eighteenth-century Dublin hanging ballad, "good" in respects in which "Lycidas" is "bad"![14] . . .

In Britain broadside vendors vanished from the scene after the first World War, the broadside style lingering only in the Rabelaisian sexuality of military bawdry. This vein of sensual song has recently been raised to the literary level in Dylan Thomas' *Under Milk Wood*, notably in Polly Garter's obscene aria on the comparative sexual prowess of Tom, Dick, Harry, and Willy Wee and in Mr. Waldo's broadside parody "In Pembroke city when I was young" with its lascivious *double-entendre* in the manner of Victorian street ballads. The masterpiece of modern literary broadsides, however, is Betjeman's "Arrest of Oscar Wilde," a poem that brilliantly wrings a dramatic value from the very crudeness of street-ballad conventions, the coarse, unsympathetic description luridly lighting a scene in which elegance crumples under brutal blows.

The native American folk ballad, a species of balladry that first came to literary notice in the 1930's, has been more successfully cultivated, strangely enough, by British than by American poets, perhaps because the Americans find this stratum of popular poetry too near for aesthetic perspective. Louis MacNeice's "The Streets of Laredo," for example, is a surrealist parody of that famous cowboy lament; Auden has

[12] *Letters from W. B. Yeats to Dorothy Wellesley* (London, 1940), p. 148.
[13] *Ibid.*, pp. 87–88, 138–40, and *passim*.
[14] *The Crowning Privilege* (New York, 1956), pp. 101–2.

written a parody of "St. James Infirmary," which is the Negro blues version of the same ballad;[15] and the situation and phrasing of "The Streets of Laredo," though unacknowieged, are imbedded in the first of George Barker's "Song for Sailors." . . .

Ragtime and jazz, which in recent decades have become associated with balladry, first significantly entered the repertoire of modern poetic effects with Lindsay's frenetic "The Congo" (1914), with its choral notations and imperfect attempts at "a roaring, epic, rag-time tune." Jazz rhythms became thereafter almost a cliché of brash modernism. In "The Wasteland" the allusions to jazz and bawdy canteen "interminables" point up the bewildering chaos of contemporary experience and mock with seriocomic irony the raucous, vulgar sensuality which seems alone capable of affecting the sensibilities of jaded urban philistines. . . .

Of all Eliot's poems, the unfinished "Sweeney Agonistes" is most thoroughly permeated with jazz rhythms; indeed, it is more properly a jazz oratorio than an "Aristophanic melodrama." The title and two lines of the chorus of Wauchope and Horsfall's song "Under the Bamboo Tree" are taken from a popular song in diluted jazz style copyrighted by Bob Cole and J. Rosamund Johnson in 1905; the parody "My Little Island Girl" has a similar provenance; and of course the inane repetitions of the fragmentary prologue and the long lyrical dialogue in "Fragment of an Agon," in which Sweeney threatens to carry Doris off to a cannibal isle, are meant to suggest the negroid idiom which in the late 1920's dominated popular commercial music. Significantly, the original title of "Sweeney Agonistes" was "Wanna Go Home, Baby?"[16]

[15] *Song XII* ("Miss Edith Gee"), *Collected Poems* (New York, 1945), pp. 209–13.
[16] See Sears Jayne, "Mr. Eliot's Agon," *Philological Quarterly*, XXXIV (1955), 396–401.

The "dribbling moan of jazz" also plays over the "nifty argot" of many of E. E. Cummings' *calligrammes*. His typographical pointing gives the superficial impression that his effects are visual, but actually they are phonetic, for his readers are compelled to voice his 'lines or speak them internally in order to join or separate into sense what he has rudely fragmented or combined for emphasis or special symbolic value. . . .

As we come to the lower end of the spectrum of popular poetry, we realize that in moving from the imitations of traditional ballads towards the literary adaptations of less venerable varieties of popular song, we move from an attitude of emulation to one of condescension. The intellectual poets, the poets of irony, wit, and paradox—Eliot, Auden, Cummings, Betjeman, and others—exploit popular song but decline to entertain its spirit. Hostile to the dominant bourgeois culture, whose taste is reflected in the commercial songs of the motion pictures, television, and the musical comedies, and only casually in touch with proletarian and folk culture, these poets' forays into the substrata of song are marked by playfulness, dramatic dissonances, ironic juxtaposition, burlesque, and satire. The old traditional ballads resist such impertinences. Canonized in golden treasuries, endowed with glamorous mythic and magical import, and no longer current on the vulgar scene, the traditional ballad is accorded by high culture the deference owed to works of incontestable aesthetic superiority. If they are imitated, it must be in the respectful manner of the cult of simplicity. Yeats and Graves may employ the conventions of the folk ballad for ironical effect, but analysis will show that the irony is directed against the matter, not against the medium nor against the folk world of which the ballads are a reflex.

Quite apart from the imitations, the ballads have come to

have a new and special value for contemporary poets and critics. So often in their history an intrument of propaganda, the ballads have at last come to serve as propaganda for poetry itself, their easy and immediate appeal being used to awaken the uninitiated to the charms of poetry. Thus in the official anthology compiled by Auden and John Garrett for the British fighting services,[17] folk material, real or imitation, accounts for over three-quarters of the contents; and the textbook through which the New Critics have for over twenty years been teaching American college students to read poetry their way begins the initiation with a chapter of texts and explications composed almost entirely of old traditional ballads, American folk classics like "Jesse James" and "Frankie and Johnny," literary ballads by Housman, Kipling, Keats, and Scott.[18] In an age when "The Neglect of Poetry" is a standard symposium topic and poets find themselves speaking to a more and more restricted section of society and go so far as to entertain the notion that poetry is "superfluous and capable of elimination," it is inspiriting to have the ballads as visible proof of Vico's dictum, underlined by Croce, that poetry is "the primary activity of the human mind" and, even in primitive cultures, not an idle entertainment but a necessity.[19]

[17] *The Poet's Tongue*, (London, 1935).

[18] Cleanth Brooks and Robert Penn Warren, *Understanding Poetry* (New York, 1960; first published 1938), pp. 23 ff.

[19] Benedetto Croce, *Philosophy of Vico*, trans. R. G. Collingwood (London, 1913), p. 48.

D. K. WILGUS

Patterns of Inclusion*

Besides the perennial attack on the "mere accumulation" of texts and tunes, adverse criticism of American folksong collection has been directed at the sources of the material and the type of material itself. Most critics have found published collections too eclectic and lacking in academic and purist values; but one early critic found them too academic.

Writing in 1926, Edmund Wilson declared that "there are disadvantages in having ballad collecting become an established branch of academic study." Distressed because "folklore has become a science—running to the same narrow specialization and the same unintelligent amassment of data as the other sciences," he lamented the lack of esthetic values among the collectors, their exclusive concern with the illiterate, and their respect for "folk-etymological changes" and the "blurred or garbled" texts, which tends to make them "shy of such particularly witty or coherent versions of their ballads as can be found in print." He suggested that the collectors look in old college song books and cultivate "the uneducated people in every community who have a private local reputation for singing entertaining songs: these people, like the illiterate, transmit songs orally from generation to generation and they usually remember them better." To these sources he added the "professional ballad-singers of the bars and cabarets." Further, he pointedly approved the Percy-Scott method of emendation.[1] At first glance one might conclude that Wilson's ideal folklore journal would be *Captain Billy's Whizbang,* and his ideal collection, Charles O'Brien Kennedy's *American Ballads : Naughty, Ribald, and Classic* (1952). . . . In fact, though non-

---

* From *Anglo-American Folksong Scholarship Since 1898* by D. K. Wilgus, copyright 1959 by Rutgers University Press.

academic collections appeared to satisfy Wilson's demand for an esthetic anthology, the academic tradition managed to answer his valid criticisms without departing from its "scientific" aim.

More serious criticism, however, has attacked American collections from an almost opposite point of view, questioning their inclusiveness. One of the more recent critics states his conclusion pungently:

> The authors and editors seem to have no idea what "folk" literature or lore or song is, where its boundaries lie, or who belongs to the "folk" under what circumstances.[2]

Stanley Edgar Hyman was reviewing a number of what he termed "bankrupt treasuries," some of which deserve highly critical examination. . . .

Obviously, Hyman has little love for the noble sport of ballad hunting, preferring the ignoble sport of shooting fish in a barrel. He compares the great literary scholar who sorted and annotated written materials in the light of his immense but imperfect knowledge, with a great field collector who gathered the songs of a people and, whatever his errors in publication, saw to their preservation. Such a comparison can be made only by one who believes that proper scholarship is library scholarship and that one conjecture is worth a thousand facts. And so Hyman seems to believe, for he suggests that "a folk song is a song of anonymous collective folk origin, and a folk singer is a person who learns these songs through an unbroken line of oral transmission and sings them."[3] It is folly to demand that Hyman produce such a folksong. . . .

Most American collectors seem to have accepted at least tacitly Louise Pound's four tests of folksongs:

1. They are transmitted orally.
2. They have no fixed form, but are continually changing.

3. They "have retained their vitality through a fair period of time."
4. They have lost all sense of authorship and provenance.[4]

The collectors have not had the information to apply the third principle, and perhaps have not always taken account of the fourth. Although there have been protests that "songs sung by the folk . . . are not necessarily folksongs,"[5] the American collector has generally acted as if they are, with the distinction that while he has defined *folk* as "common people" or "the unsophisticated," he has collected on many levels of society, songs which meet Miss Pound's third and fourth tests. It is not fair to say exactly that the collectors accepted songs sung by the folk and folksongs sung by the nonfolk. Rather, they have followed a policy which approaches Barry's conclusion that whoever sings a song from memory is a folksinger.[6] . . .

Recent Trends in Anglo-American Collection

Discovery of industrial folksongs, as distinguished from occupational songs such as shanties and perhaps shearing and plowman's songs, can be largely credited to American collectors, though mining songs had been known from Northumbrian tradition, particularly in John Stokoe and Samuel Reay's *Songs and Ballads of Northern England* (1892?) and before that in John Bell's *Rhymes of the Northern Bards* (1812). But serious interest in British industrial and protest songs grew largely after World War II and with the emergence in the folksong field of what some writers might term *working-class intellectuals*—a term useful to describe their outlook—though in terms of collection they correspond to the American collector with a folk background. Men like A. L. Lloyd, Hamish Henderson, and Ewan MacColl have taken a somewhat

broader outlook than that maintained by the staid English
Folk Dance and Song Society.

The first collection of British industrial song was not
published until 1952, A. L. Lloyd's compilation, *Come All Ye
Bold Miners,* on which is based his singing book, *Coal Dust
Ballads* (1952). MacColl's *The Shuttle and the Cage* (1954)
includes some of the material previously printed by Lloyd but
adds songs from other industries, some from early collections
but mostly MacColl's own collection. MacColl, himself the
author of industrial and protest songs now in oral circulation,
is somewhat less orthodox than Lloyd, who not only apologizes
for the crudeness of the songs in *Come All Ye Bold Miners,*
but excludes "parlour ballads of the type of *Don't Go Down
in the Mine, Daddy*" as not "what we understood as folksongs" (p. 9). But the contents of the volume roughly parallel
Korson's American collections (some of the songs were first
published there), including songs from the late eighteenth century to 1934, the productions of local poets and songs circulated by broadsides and sheet music, and songs "barely kept
alive in the mouths of a solitary singer here and there." Such
inclusions and Lloyd's statement, "Aesthetics isn't everything,"
seem to indicate the British acceptance of an earlier American
trend. But the newer trend is shown not only by Lloyd's emphasis on the functional quality of the songs, but by his hope
for "the pit-songs of the future. If this humble collection can
encourage one miner to make up one ballad out of his working life, it will have achieved its aim" (p. 17).

Gummere's dictum that folksong is made by the people was
only a part of his theory of communal origin. His opponents
attacked both the communal and popular origin of ballads,
with the result that the criterion of folksong, in America at
least, became largely that of oral circulation, and folk authorship was judged to be after the fact. The concept of commu-

nal authorship died hard. Folk authorship slumbered, to awaken in an individual but still somewhat magical form.

If a goodly proportion of the American songbag is stuffed with *gesunkene Kulturgüter,* preserved or recomposed by the singers, a significant portion is the production of individuals on the same cultural level as the singers. The criterion of persistence, which ignores authorship, will not explain the presence of all the material, for investigations have shown that songs have been obtained at or near the source. Consequently it has been rediscovered that song is folk in composition as well as circulation. The resurrected principle has grown from the work of investigators who, searching for the background of songs or questioning singers, have found themselves in the presence of the bard himself. The first step has shown that traditional songs have been composed by folksingers. The next step is to shear the song of its traditional history : a folksong is a song composed by a member of the folk.

Emelyn Elizabeth Gardner approaches this position when, believing she is echoing Barry, she contends that such songs as "Floyd Collins," "Harry Bail," and "Little Mary Phagan" "were folk songs as soon as they were composed by someone close to the principals of the tragedies and accepted by those who sang them."' A crucial point involves the status of those who composed the songs (including their methods) and "those who sang them." *Those* has generally meant dwellers in an isolated region or persons engaged in a common occupation who, lacking the appurtenances of mass culture, have followed the traditional practice of composing their own material or recomposing traditional material : thus the lumberjack bards and the "minstrels of the mine patch." The problem could have been better understood and more reasonably dealt with had it not been for a recent extension of the magic word *folk.* The acceptance of the homemade song of the isolated community is one thing; the creation of an artificial folk is another.

The investigation of folk culture may convince the investigator that his role "is that of the advocate of the folk."[8] But it may also result in confusion between the value of the song and the song itself. Thus the discovery of democratic elements in folksong has led to the conclusion that American folksong itself is democratic.[9] The recognition that "singing has a direct and reciprocal relation to social, economic, and political issues"[10] has led to an equation of the "cry for justice" and folksong. The discovery of folksongs of social protest has led some to the conclusion that a protest song is *ipso facto* a folksong, and to the postulation of "a new folk community composed of progressives, anti-fascists, and union members."[11]

Such thinking lies behind *The People's Song Book* (1948), which contains tune-text units from oral tradition, new texts to traditional tunes, and fresh texts and tunes copyrighted. The use of folksong for political purposes is an old device; what is new is the use of the folk concept, the magic term *folk*. The misapplication of the term *folksong* to the copyrighted *"Investigator's Song"* has less justification than the application of the term by purveyors of commercial popular music to the new songs of country-western singers. But *The People's Song Book* is vouched for by two eminent folklorists, one of whom helped compose one of the texts. In part the group of "People's Artists" is merely a political aberrant of recent emphasis on performance and distribution of folk or folkish song, which includes the anticipation of the folk in composing and distributing "folksongs" of protest. . . .

In his *American Folksongs of Protest* (1953) John Greenway squarely faces the problem and, though illustrating the extension of the term *folksong* typical of American collectors, is unwilling to stretch the boundaries without considering the issues.

Greenway recognizes that American collectors have clung to the term *traditional* as the distinguishing mark of folksong; he recognizes just as clearly that his contemporary material "will have vanished by the time the next generation composes its songs of protest" (pp. 3–4). Faced with a conflict between restrictive definition and his collected material, he makes the choice typical of American collectors. . . . Therein lies the difference between the American collectors' expansiveness and Greenway's redefinition. Greenway is not simply garnering and publishing material for future study. He declares the requirement of persistence invalid because it fails to take into account the unconscious art of the folk composer. . . . "A folksong, therefore, is a song concerned with the interests of the folk and in the complete possession of the folk" (pp. 8–9).

In the first place, Greenway's *folk* is a highly restricted term, an economic term. Recognizing the disappearance of the agricultural folk, he finds a new folk in the industrial community (CIO, not AFL). But he seems to find them the only folk. . . .

Why are members of a college community necessarily any less a folk than members of the industrial community? Possibly because they don't sing about the right things, for one of Greenway's folk composers is a college graduate turned trade-union leader. Greenway is apparently willing that his folk composer "make an imitation ballad about kings and queens and lords and ladies," but thinks "he has much more business writing about" other things, such as "a mean mistreatin' railroad daddy."

But in writing that the "requirement of persistence" of a song "is a gauge of popularity, not of authenticity" (p. 7), Greenway has made an important point. Unfortunately, he chooses to remain on his opponents' ground, to retain the narrow sense of *traditional* and, though this might seem strange to his ears, a narrow concept of *folksong*. So his only recourse is the romantic concept of the unconscious art of the folk composer. The folk composer is not unconscious that he is an artist, only that he is a *folk artist*. His composition may be traditional without surviving for generations. There is tradition in space, or "horizontal tradition"—which Greenway may be referring to in the phrase "in complete possession of the folk." Then there are the tradition of form and even the tradition of composition itself. If "The Kentucky Miner's Dreadful Fight" became (as Greenway maintains) a folksong "the minute Aunt Molly Jackson scribbled it on a piece of paper" (p. 7), the explanation cannot be found in its "unconscious art": Gummere's dichotomy of art and nature which Belden so carefully destroyed. . . .

In addition to raising important theoretical questions, Greenway's anthology (for it is not completely a primary collection) is important in bringing together such an interesting group of protest songs, together with important comment. That many may be judged nontraditional is not a criticism. On any grounds, the broadside is a legitimate study of the folklorist, and Greenway is able to throw much light on the origin and history of traditional songs. Much adverse critical reception of the book may have been motivated by its very value, its bringing to light ephemeral material usually ignored by complacent academics.

Perhaps the most important recent trend in Anglo-American folksong collecting involves mechanical methods of collection and presentation. At the beginning of the twentieth century the field collector had the choice of noting by hand or using primitive cylinder recording machines. . . .

The disc belonged to the commercial recording industry which, however, began early—and at first unwittingly—to exploit folksong.[12] One method of this popular presentation developed from the "natural" appropriation by commercial entertainers of such folksongs as "Casey Jones" and "The Bully of the Town." . . . Of course a commercial—or commercialized—tradition was being established; and not all the recording artists were folksingers, nor was all the material from folk tradition. But in many instances the talent scout was actually a folksong collector, recording folk performers and performances which might otherwise have been completely lost—to name a few: Blind Lemon Jefferson, Jesse James, Buell Kazee, Doc Boggs, and Henry Whitter. And the parallel broadside traditions launched artists who affected the style and repertoire of the American folksinger.

By 1938 race and hillbilly records were a good deal farther removed from their folk roots. To be sure, country singers were still bringing new folksongs and fresh versions of old ones into the hillbilly field; and though the race record business was highly urbanized, it could still make temporary room for a folksinger like Leadbelly. But a market for folksong was developing among the general public, and radio broadcasts such as those by Alan Lomax on the "School of the Air" seem as much symptoms as causes. . . .

It would of course be a mistake to credit the trend solely to improved technical devices. Though the techniques were more crude, the approaches which seem to be innovations have been known and used for a long time. The release of folk performances began as early as 1920, though they were not then recognized as such. The collector who garners material that he can sing himself to another audience seems to be a new development. But Loraine Wyman was using that method in 1917, and it entered the recording field somewhat later in the work of such differing artists as Carl Sandburg and Bradley Kincaid. A broad public interest in folksongs is as much the cause as the result of presentation of songs in schools and night clubs, on radio, television, and recordings. One suspects that the great collections by the BBC, by Hamish Henderson for the School of Scottish Studies in Edinburgh, and by others would have proceeded without certain of the technical innovations which, however, improved and facilitated the work and its presentation.

Admittedly much of the material now labeled folksong on the commercial media is highly arranged, restyled, or even vulgarized. Yet these popularized presentations have aided in creating a market for and have made financially possible the more authentic releases. . . .

One conspicuous lack in collections of Anglo-American folksong has been pointed out on several occasions, most recently by G. Legman,[12] who excoriates Child and "all his progeny almost without exception" for their omission or expurgation of the bawdy ballad. Although Legman is not completely fair to the editors, the situation may be worse than he presents it —granting, of course, that the bawdy material is worthy of preservation and study. The general impression has been that folksong collectors, when they did not expurgate the songs as Legman charges, have retained quantities of unprintable material. The John A. Lomax papers do contain a number of bawdy songs of great importance, and Vance Randolph deposited a magnificent collection in the Library of Congress. But reports of vast holdings by many collectors seem exaggerated. A fact that makes the bawdy ballad even more important for study is that it tends to remain the oral possession of even the collector. . . .

Fortunately Legman promises a scholarly edition of the bawdy song in English, based on privately printed volumes and unpublished collections made available to him. Legman's rebuffs and difficulties in gaining access to the material and permission to print indicate the strength of forces still denying a full and honest picture of folksong and hampering the study of a tradition less affected by print than any in our time. Legman's collection will not make good all past losses, but it will be a great aid to the student of oral tradition and will indicate what might have been available if editors could have worked in Great Britain and the United States instead of waiting for one who of necessity works in France.

Notes

1. *New Republic,* XLVII (1926), 169.
2. *Kenyon Review,* X (1948), 491–492.
3. *Ibid.*
4. *American Ballads and Songs,* p. xiii.
5. W. Edson Richmond, *JAF,* LXVII (1954), 96.
6. *Bulletin of the Folk-Song Society of the Northeast,* No. 5 (1933), p. 4.
7. *Ballads and Songs of Southern Michigan,* p. 15.
8. Alan Lomax, in *Four Symposia on Folklore,* ed. Stith Thompson, p. 157.
9. Alan Lomax, *New York Times Sunday Magazine,* Jan, 26, 1947, pp. 16, 41–42.
10. B. A. Botkin, in *People's Song Book,* p. 6.
11. Alan Lomax, in *ibid.,* p. 3.
12. This discussion is based on the American recording industry, concerning which I have information. Until quite recently the only folk recordings available in Great Britain seem to have been an excellent Columbia issue of the singing of Philip Tanner and imported American recordings of the commercialized "folk music for the folk."
13. "The Bawdy Song . . . in Fact and in Print," *Explorations* 7 (March, 1957), pp. 139ff.

5

The Fringes of Folklore

THE ALERT STUDENT IS SOON MADE AWARE OF THE TENDENCY among folklorists and members of allied disciplines to disagree as to what is and what is not folklore. Enthusiasts seem prone to include too much, whereas members of other disciplines seem to be too restrictive in the boundaries they would set up. Some feel that folklore must be confined to the verbal arts, leaving out such considerations as dance, music, folk art, gesture, etc. For others practically anything learned by imitation seems acceptable—this to such a degree that a critical colleague is reputed to have remarked that folklore on X campus was anything told to Y folklorist.

Without splitting hairs, one can be on reasonably safe ground if he bears in mind some of the descriptive terms that have been in general use, such as *traditional, anonymous, orally transmitted,* and *changed* or *reshaped in transmission.* With these criteria in mind he can try to evaluate some of the controversial materials.

Those who study folklore inevitably discover that the study

is useful—not in the short-sighted and unworthy sense of useful to promote and exploit in the marketplace, but useful in obtaining understanding. Serious contemplation of folklore is useful in improving the understanding of literature, art, and music. The improved understanding of these permits one to perceive the processes which have created them, hence the vital processes of society itself. In short, the study of folklore is useful in the same way and to the same extent that most other studies are. It provides another link in the chain of understanding which permits us to know ourselves.

Because folklore is one of the links in the chain of understanding, and because some of the adjacent links, though similar, are different, the boundary dispute seems inevitable. For practical purposes this dispute is not particularly significant, for the bulk of the field is clearly apparent, and the hairsplitting around the edges is likely to be more theoretical than practical. Occasional difficulties have been experienced by immature students who have sucumbed to the temptation to exploit the sensational or attention-getting aspects of their material. Since most folklore has always been the entertainment of the folk (songs, tales, riddles, dance), the entertainment aspects of the study have been inescapable. This has been especially true of folk music and dance. The drift into imitation folk performance in the academic community can be instructive, but excesses and commercialization such as that which developed in the 1950's and finally the "hootenanny" craze of the 1960's undoubtedly brought some disrepute to folksong scholarship.

Similarly, the occasional student's lack of decorum in dealing with off-color or frankly obscene materials at his disposal can be damaging to the orderly process of constructive study. The oral expressions of the folk abound in elements rarely expressed in polite company. These expressions are quite properly collected, catalogued, and studied by some specialists, and, of course, are sometimes the proper content of articles in professional journals or papers read to learned societies. The immature student, however, can create unnecessary prejudice against himself, his colleagues, and his academic discipline by a sophomoric display of vulgarity when he mistakes academic freedom of speech for license to shock and annoy for no constructive reason.

Still another questionable approach to folklore is that which seeks to shape or reshape the materials for commercial or political propaganda. The tremendous appeal in stock figures and situations from familiar folk narratives or in group participation in familiar song has long been a tool for sharp operators in advertising, organizing, and promoting. The use or misuse of folklore for these purposes can range from a slogan to sell a can of beans to a corps of government experts dedicated to finding and exposing the creative genius of the folk to demonstrate its superiority to all others.

Of the various "fringe area" selections in this chapter, the short portion from *Russian Folklore* suggests the kind of propaganda that may attach to an otherwise sound and highly commended study. The selection from *The Story of Jazz* raises the question of how far the domain of the folklorist can extend into studies in allied fields. The selection from *American Folksongs of Protest* raises a question of the propriety of the use of the word "Folksong" in the title.

In any case, the selections in this chapter and many others like them inevitably attract the folklorist's attention. Even if they are not central to folklore studies, they are in some degree peripheral, and much accumulated human experience teaches that it is unwise to ignore either the peripheral or the ephemeral.

The selections in this chapter illustrate only a few of the frequently disputed boundaries and applications of folklore.

MARSHALL STEARNS

From Africa to the New World*

What are the roots of jazz and how did they take hold in the New World? We know quite a bit about the European music that contributed to jazz, but our knowledge of the African music that became an essential part of it is still scanty. Many African musical characteristics survived in the New World—adapted, blended, and changed to fit new conditions. The range and intensity of these survivals, however, is a subject that needs more study. Still and all, we do have enough information at present to indicate certain general patterns. Indeed, some day we may be able to identify the exact rhythms of the particular tribes that helped to create jazz.

It is becoming clear, for example, that the various stages in the development of the slave trade had a decisive influence on what part of Africa the slaves came from, as well as where they were taken in the New World. It was once thought that the slaves came from all over Africa and that only weak and 'inferior' Africans were captured and sold into slavery. Under such conditions, African customs would have a poor chance of survival. But the majority of slaves came from the West coast of Africa—especially Senegal, the Guinea coast, the Niger delta, and the Congo—as anthropologist Melville J. Herskovits has shown,[1] while inter-tribal raids and dynastic wars in West Africa led to the selling of kings and priests into slavery, people who were specialists in their own tribal music and rituals.

Thus, the fact that many West African customs, musical and otherwise, survived in the New World is not surprising.

* From *The Story of Jazz* by Marshall Stearns, copyright 1958 by Oxford University Press, Inc.

[1] See M. J. Herskovits, *The Myth of the Negro Past* (New York: Harper & Brothers, 1941), pp. 33–53.

Further, these customs were continually renewed by the arrival of more Africans for, although the slave trade was banned by the United States in 1808, contraband slaves directly from Africa were smuggled into the country as late as the Civil War days. At the same time, people from the West Indies with strong African traditions were immigrating to this country as, indeed, they still do to this day. Since West Africa had no literature, customs and rituals were always memorized and handed down by example and word of mouth. And elements of West African music, invisible and preserved in a state of mind that cannot be policed, are still very much with us.

Certain patterns evolved with the slave trade. As the search for slaves advanced down the West coast of Africa from around Dakar all the way to the Congo, first Portuguese traders, then Dutch, and then English—with the French a poor second—dominated the trade. Each European power supplied its own colonies in the New World with slaves from the tribes it had plundered, and the planters in each of the colonies naturally came to prefer the tribesmen supplied by the mother country. England, a partial exception, tended to sell slaves to anyone who would buy, and Spain tended to buy from anyone who would sell. Colonial preferences nevertheless became generally fixed.

Accordingly, Brazilian planters—supplied at an early date with Senegalese slaves by Portuguese traders—preferred Senegalese slaves thereafter. In the same way, Spanish planters came to prefer Yorubas, English planters Ashantis, and French planters Dahomeans. There were many exceptions, of course, but the over-all pattern survives to this day : the predominant African music in Cuba (originally Spanish) is Yoruban, in Jamaica (British) Ashanti, and in Haiti (formerly French) Dahomean. Now the Dahomeans were the original *vodun* worshippers—the snake god Damballa is one of their deities—and the fact that New Orleans was once a French colony helps to explain why this city is the 'hoodoo' capital of the United States today and may give us a clue as to why jazz was born in New Orleans.

At a later stage, after the Africans had arrived in the New World, the differing environments began to shape new patterns. The African fitted in as best he could and, since it was virtually the West African custom to adopt the deities and attitudes of one's conquerors, he soon began to assimilate the new culture. The colonies reflected the cultures of their mother countries and the slave met with a rather different music, religion, and attitude toward himself in the different colonies.

Much depended, for example, on whether the slave was sold to a British-Protestant or a Latin-Catholic colony. In the first place, the music of the Latin colonies, and especially the Spanish, had more rhythmic life. Perhaps because of the Moorish conquest of Spain in the Middle Ages—the Moors came from North Africa—Spanish music employed elements of improvisation and complex rhythms. An example that survives to this day is the *flamenco* (compare also the *fado* of Portugal). And the numerous church festivals in Latin colonies gave the slaves many opportunities to hear this music.

On the other hand, the Protestant hymns in British colonies were often 'droned out . . . like the braying of asses,' according to John Adams.[2] With the remote exception of the 'Scotch snap,' an elementary bit of syncopation that occurs only incidentally in jazz (hum the tune of 'Gin a Body Meet a Body Comin' thro' the Rye'), the slave heard little or no music with any rhythmic complexity in the African sense of the word. Perhaps the march came as close as any type of music to

[2] As quoted in G. P. Jackson, *White and Negro Spirituals* (New York: J. J. Augustin, 1943), p. 254n.

appealing to the African, simply because it lent itself to the addition of superimposed rhythms in the African manner.

In the second place, the general attitude and point of view of the Latin-Catholic planters, as contrasted to the attitude of the British-Protestant slave-owners, permitted the survival of more West African traditions. If a planter was Portuguese, Spanish, or French, he dominated the lives of his slaves outwardly—and often with cruelty—but he didn't seem to care about what a slave thought or did in his spare time so long as it didn't interfere with production. Perhaps the attitude of the planters was influenced by centuries of civilized interchange between the Mediterranean countries and North Africa. A kind of cultural *laissez faire* existed whereby the African retained his customs if only by default.

With a British owner, however, a slave was likely to change his ways more quickly, discarding his own traditions and adopting the new. For the British did not specialize in large plantations and each slave-owner possessed fewer slaves. Thus, a slave could come to know his master more easily. Sometimes he was employed as a house slave, and watching his master, became ashamed of his own customs which were thought savage and barbaric. Wanting to improve his condition, he frequently made a point of concealing his own traditions which, in many cases, were consequently forced underground.

Moreover, British-Protestant slave-owners appeared to be much more concerned about what a slave did or thought in his spare time and whether or not he was a Christian. One of the early justifications of slavery argued that it converted the heathen. But then, it followed logically that, once converted, a slave should be a free Christian. The State of Virginia solved this problem as early as 1667 by decreeing: 'Baptism doth not alter the condition of the person as to his bondage or freedom.' Thereafter slaves were permitted to become Christians and remain slaves. By contrast, this problem never bothered Latin colonies. Planters simply assumed, according to the *Code Noir,* that slaves remained slaves whether or not they joined the Catholic Church.

In the third place—and perhaps of greatest importance— whether a slave became a Protestant or a Catholic had a direct effect on the survival of his native music. For a West African in a Latin-Catholic colony soon discovered that a great many Catholic saints bore interesting resemblances to his own gods.[3] The church had pictures of the saints—inexpensive and plentiful chromolithographs—which suggested pointed parallels. St. Patrick, pictured driving the snakes out of Ireland, reminded the slave of his own Damballa, the snake god of the Dahomeans. So on St. Patrick's day, the slaves played the drum rhythms sacred to Damballa and worshipped both Damballa and St. Patrick at the same time and on the same improvised altar.

The ease with which West African and the Catholic religions fused—a process called syncretism by the anthropologists—as well as the extreme flexibility of the slave when it came to adopting new deities is strikingly illustrated in a photograph by Earl Leaf of a Haitian *vodun* altar. Among a variety of African charms and fetishes are several chromolithographs of Catholic saints and religious scenes, plus a forceful photograph of Admiral Ernest J. King of the United States Navy. Clad in a white uniform and staring resolutely forward, the admiral is obviously a powerful antidote to the forces of evil.

In the same manner and in a variety of ways, St. Anthony became associated with Legba, the Dahomean god of the crossroads, since both were imagined and pictured as tattered old men. John the Baptist, portrayed with a shepherd's crook, was

[3] See, for example, M. J. and F. S. Herskovits, *Trinidad Village* (New York: Alfred A. Knopf, 1947), pp. 327–31.

identified with Shango, the Yoruban god of thunder whose symbol is the ram. And St. Michael, pictured with a sword, called to mind Ogun, the Yoruban god of war. The identifications varied in different localities—in New Orleans, for example, Limba (Legba?) is still associated with St. Peter— but the over-all process was the same.

These parallels functioned as a kind of bridge to the New World over which West African music could be carried, modified, and preserved. And African rhythms survived more or less by accident. Here again, the Protestant religions of British colonies had no hierarchy of saints and, indeed, forbade any such pictures. The Baptist and Methodist denominations, which most actively proselytized for Negro members, strictly prohibited both dancing and drumming—the two outstanding characteristics of African religion—not so much as a safety precaution against revolts (the usual reason for prohibiting drumming in Catholic colonies) but as a matter of religious principle. So African music either disappeared or went underground.

Parenthetically, the West Africans had no inherent or 'instinctive' sense of rhythm which would have survived in any case. They came from a culture which happened to have fantastically complicated rhythms but only those rhythms survived which in one way or another were permitted to do so. A good part of the West African musical heritage, however, survived unconsciously—through attitudes, motions, habits, points of view, mannerisms, and gestures carried down from generation to generation without thought or plan.

A child might absorb some part of African rhythms, for example. In her *Slave Songs of the Georgia Sea Islands,* Lydia Parrish prints parallel photographs of three native women in West Africa pounding corn in a pestle and three American Negro Women in Georgia pounding rice. The sticks and the pestles are very similar but the important point is that both groups appear to be singing rhythmically as they pound. In the Georgia photograph, a little child is standing close by in rapt attention, absorbing the entire performance.

What light do these general patterns, formed in connection with the development of the slave trade and the changed New World environment, throw on the origins of jazz? We are still in the process of filling out the patterns which helped and hindered the survival of African music in the New World, but we can already pin down the dominant tribal style that existed in certain areas. Further, we know that these musical characteristics tended to survive in Latin-Catholic colonies and to disappear or go underground in British-Protestant colonies.

This is not to say that jazz evolved in Latin-Catholic surroundings because of the greater prevalence of African music, or even that going underground in British-Protestant surroundings contributed indirectly to the evolution of jazz—although, as we shall see, there may be some truth in both hypotheses. It is enough to observe that the elements of West African music which contributed to the blend that became jazz were certainly present and active in the New World. In the following pages we shall examine a variety of musical blendings in various parts of the New World in an effort to reconstruct the pattern that led to jazz.

The West Indies and the United States

Each island in the West Indies is a sort of musical test-tube in which West African and European musics have been mixed in more or less known quantities, thus furnishing possible clues as to what must have happened in the United States. No one island, of course, has exactly the same combination of ingredients, and the United States has a still different and perhaps more complicated mixture of its own. Although the results vary, the over-all pattern of blending is the same.

At one extreme is Dutch Guiana, located in the northern part of South America, where the Bush-Negroes live. It is jungle country and, from the first, many slaves escaped inland where they flourished. A wide sampling of the music of Dutch Guiana has been recorded by Herskovits and analyzed by Kolinski, who found : 'With the exception of a few songs, the music of the Bush-Negroes displays traits that are essentially African." In fact, since African music has been influenced by ours in recent times, Bush-Negro music, it has been suggested, is more African than African music today. Kolinski also discovered that the songs of the coastal Negroes, who lived in a predominantly European culture, were about 23 per cent African. Thus, in Dutch Guiana we find a pattern of survival ranging from a little less than one-quarter to almost total retention.

Haiti is a more complicated but more illuminating example. Haiti was supplied with slaves by French traders, among others, and the French planters preferred Dahomeans. Hence it is not surprising that although Courlander found traces of at least thirty-seven African tribes in Haiti, he found the dominant culture to be Dahomean.[2] Today Haiti is probably the most 'primitive' island this side of Africa. As Courlander says :[3]

> On the plantations and off, the Negroes never forgot the drum rhythms of their own countries, nor their ancestors and deities. They never forgot how to make fine drums. And whether the drum was of a Congo pattern, or Ibo, or Arada, all men listened to it, and danced in the light of the smoking oil lamps.

[1] See M. J. and F. S. Herskovits, *Suriname Folk-Lore* (New York: Columbia University Press, 1936), p. 517.

[2] Harold Courlander, *Haiti Singing* (Chapel Hill : The University of North Carolina Press, 1939), p. 4 *et passim*.

[3] *Ibid.* p. 5.

The Arada tribe is Dahomean and its members are practitioners of *vodun*. (For twelve years, from 1847 to 1859, *vodun* was virtually the official religion of Haiti.) At the same time, just about everyone in Haiti is a member of the Catholic Church. *Vodun* and Catholicism have merged, for the Haitian peasant gladly adopts the Catholic religion to reinforce his African beliefs.

On a field trip to Haiti in 1953, I witnessed a *vodun* ceremony presided over by a young *houngan,* or head priest, named Dr. Jean Dieudonné. He looked so much like the late saxophonist Charlie Parker that it made me uneasy. For three or more hours, the *hounsis,* or priests and priestesses, danced and sang a regular response to the *houngan's* cries, while the drum trio pounded away hypnotically. In a back room was an oven-like altar, containing a snake, sacred to Damballa, and on top of this altar was a second, smaller altar, containing a blond baby doll of the Coney Island variety and a statuette of the Madonna, twin symbols of Ezulie, goddess of fertility and chastity.

About eleven o'clock the lid blew off. Drinking from a paper-wrapped bottle, the *houngan* sprayed some liquid out of his mouth in a fine mist and the *hounsis,* touched by the spray, became seized with religious hysteria, or 'possessed' much like an epileptic fit. The rest of the group kept the 'possessed' ones from hurting themselves. I saw one young and stately priestess, who had earlier impressed me with the poise and dignity of her dancing, bumping across the dirt floor in time with the drums. The spirit of Damballa, the snake god, had entered her.

I shall never know how much of the performance was authentic. The drums, and the rhythms played upon them, were Dahomean. The whole ceremony was similar to, but decidedly more orderly than, some revival meetings—both white and Negro—that I have observed in the United States. This was probably because in Haiti they had a formal goal, namely possession, and it was reached in a highly ritualized fashion. I noticed that several *hounsis,* emerging from possession, simply sat down and fell into a peaceful sleep.

Secular African rhythms have survived in Haiti, too, in the *coumbite* (Dahomean : 'dokpwe'), or communal work-group. Their songs are similar to our own work songs. On the other hand, predominantly European mixtures, such as the *meringue* with its French folk melodies, also occur in Haiti. The Haitian *meringues* sometimes sound a little like our rag-time without the force and drive.

These parallels between Haitian and American music help to establish an over-all pattern. Both Haiti and New Orleans, for example, were Latin-colonial—French and Spanish—until the early 1800's. Africans from the same tribes arrived in both areas. In fact, many slaves came to New Orleans direct from Haiti during the revolution, brought there by fleeing French planters. The chief difference is that, from this time on, New Orleans but not Haiti felt the influence of British Protestant-ism, American variety, and sudden prosperity.

In 1885, a correspondent of the New York *World,* watching the dancing of the Negroes in New Orleans' Congo Square, asked a colored lady what the dance was. 'C'est le Congo,' she replied.[4] The Congo, as such, is no longer danced in New Orleans, but it is still danced in Haiti, along with the Bamboula, the Juba, the Calinda, and the Counjaille—dances that are mentioned frequently by early visitors to New Orleans. The Haitian versions, which have remained more or less untouched, are probably similar to the early New Orleans dances which have disappeared.

[4] As quoted in *Jazzmen,* edited by Ramsey and Smith (New York : Harcourt, Brace & Company, 1939), p. 8.

Another pattern for comparison occurs in Cuba.[5] The music varies from Yoruba rhythms to Spanish songs. This wide range reflects Cuba's historical background accurately. For many years a Spanish possession, into which Africans were smuggled as late as the 1880's, Cuba became a republic in 1902. Unlike Haiti, Cuba welcomed outside influences, in particular American capital, and has become prosperous more recently.

We are better acquainted with certain Cuban music because Cuba has its own Tin-Pan Alley, which in recent years has been closely linked with our own. The tango and its rhythms, which became the rage of New York City in 1914 over the protests of educators and clergymen, are a development of the Habanera (Havana). The word 'tango' is of African origin and the dance, according to Slonimsky, illustrates what the Africans in Cuba could do with an English country dance.

Of the native Cuban dances, the Habanera, Guajira, Punto, and Guaracha contain strong Spanish elements, while the Rhumba, Conga, Son Afro-Cubano, Mambo, and Cha-Cha are predominantly African. The chief difference, of course, is the rhythm. And even the amount of rhythm in any one dance can vary. The rhumba, which is by far the most popular outside of Cuba, is consistently diluted for Western ears and has become a fixture at fashionable American night clubs. Played by a real Afro-Cuban band, however, the true rhumba can develop into a rhythmic holocaust.

These dances and their rhythms show us only the surface of Cuban music. There is a lively religious group in Cuba known at Los Santos, or The Saints, which is quite similar to the folowing of Daddy Grace and Father Divine in the United States. The Saints, dressed in pure white, stage elaborate

[5] See F. Ortiz, *La Africania de la Musica Folklorica de Cuba* (Havana, 1950), *passim*.

religious rituals which culminate in possession, much like our own revival meetings. But the musical instruments for such occasions consist of Yoruban drums, shaped like hour glasses, and the drumming and singing are in the Yoruban style.

Another and more important brand of West African music is sung, danced, and played by secret societies, or *cabildos,* in Cuba.[6] The chief cults are the Arara from Dahomey (Haitian 'Arada,' the practitioners of *vodun*), the Kimbisa from the Congo, the Lucumi from the Slave Coast, and the Abakwa from the region of the Niger River. Each has its own type of West African instrument, rhythm, and dialect. The Abakwa, members of which are slightingly known as 'Nanigos,' is the most important and includes members of other cults and even a few whites.

These secret societies actually continue organizations that existed in Africa. They have been outlawed, whenever the political situation needed a scapegoat, but on the other hand they are also asked to furnish the rhythmic propulsion for the annual Mardi Gras. The Cuban dancer, drummer, and composer, Chano Pozo, was a member of the Abakwa and became the hit of Mardi Gras. Pozo had a direct impact on jazz when he joined the Dizzy Gillespie band in 1947.

In a search for Pozo's antecedents I was taken to the Cayo Hueso, or slum district, of Havana. I met his grandmother in a narrow, crowded alley where dozens of families live outdoors all year round. As the only white man and in the company of a brown-skinned guide, I met with silent hostility. My guide actually did not dare ask the pipe-smoking old lady if she were born in Africa. Later, I met Pozo's father, a shoeshine 'boy,' and learned that the son was two generations from Africa. Puzzled tears came to the father's eyes as he asked me why his

[6] See Harold Courlander, album notes, 'Cult Music of Cuba,' Folkways LP 410.

oldest and last surviving son had been murdered in Harlem. (I had heard only unprintable rumors.)

It was not difficult to find drummers in Cuba. In a bare tenement room I recorded the songs and rhythms of the various secret societies. The drummers knew most of them, but their favorites were Yoruban and derived from the Lucumi cult. The most impressive member was dedicated to Chango, the Yoruban thunder god, known as Shango in Trinidad. Another, in praise of 'Legua,' was similar to the rhythms of the Dahomean Legba, the guardian of the crossroads in Haiti.

What patterns occur in Cuba? Like Haiti, Cuba duplicates the Latin-Catholic background of New Orleans up to 1803. Unlike Haiti, Cuba has become relatively prosperous in recent years. Neither Haiti nor Cuba, however, felt the influence of British Protestantism until very recently. No jazz evolved in Cuba, and yet Cuban popular music and the dances associated with it have spread over the Western world. The mixture of Spanish and African music, in varying amounts, seems to be a highly palatable product.

Perhaps a more significant pattern for comparison occurs in Trinidad, for here we find the additional influence of British Protestantism.[7] Originally Spanish, Trinidad admitted Catholic colonists—mostly French—from 1783 to 1797, when it became a British colony and English planters moved in. Thus, the aristocracy of the island still consists of Spanish, French, and British families, in that order. In our time, laborers have been imported from the Orient—Chinese and East Indians—and with the discovery of oil, Trinidad has prospered.

The music of Trinidad runs the gamut from predominantly European to essentially West African. The Calypso, Trinidad's best-known creation, can be heard in the United States in a

[7] See M.J. and F.S. Herskovits, *Trinidad Village* (New York: Alfred A. Knopf, 1947), *passim*.

diluted version in such popular hits as 'Rum and Coca-Cola,' or in Trinidad in a more rhythmic version in a West African style. It is derived, in part, from the biting West African songs of ridicule and is still used as a political weapon when more direct means would bring reprisal. It also contains, according to some theorists, the melody and harmony of French folk songs, a dialect of several languages, and African rhythms. Its influence is now felt throughout the West Indies.

Like Haiti and Cuba, nevertheless, Trinidad has its African cult, or secret society, music. Much of this is Yoruban and dedicated to Shango, the god of thunder. The instruments have changed however, for when drums were banned, Trinidad Negroes adopted tambos—bamboo sticks tapped on the ground one at a time. When tambos were banned—with some reason, for they made formidable weapons—Trinidadians invented the steel band. The vogue of the steel band has invaded many other lands in the West Indies, and has even reached New York. (After hearing a steel band at the Jazz Roundtable at Music Inn, composer Henry Cowell scored part of a new symphony for steel drums.) Just one type of instrument is used : a drum made from the top of a huge oil barrel, heated and hammered until it responds with a variety of notes when struck in certain spots. Trinidad drummers march a hundred strong during a festival, playing the latest pop tune amidst a boiler factory of sound.

The special significance of Trinidad's background, however, lies in the rather early existence of Protestantism. When England took over in 1797, Catholicism and African fetish were already partly fused. The northern religion did not make much headway except with a small group of converts to the Baptist faith in Toco, a village in the northeastern part of the island. They are called Shouters with some accuracy, for they generated enough excitement and noise to be officially banned.

Unlike The Saints in Cuba, the Trinidad Shouters banned dancing and drumming, according to the Baptist rules. Hand-clapping and foot-stamping evolved to take the place of the drums, and the ceremonies became famous for their revivalist power and frenzy. Complaints poured in from a radius of several miles whenever the Shouters held a meeting. Here is a new pattern : Protestantism superimposed upon a mixture of African and Catholic rule, leading to revival music such as is found in the United States.

A recording of the Shouters, made by Herskovits, furnishes an amazing parallel. The tune is 'Jesus Lover of My Soul,' a standard hymn from the Moody and Sankey hymn-book. Beginning in a very stolid manner, the Shouters intone the tune 'as written.' Gradually, rhythms are introduced; one singer starts to imitate a drum, another begins to clap on the off-beat, a third introduces a falsetto cry. Soon the call-and-response pattern dominates the performance, which builds into a rhythmic jamboree of such intensity that it might well produce religious possession.[8]

The recording is a capsule demonstration of the Africaniza-tion of a British hymn. In the space of four minutes, the Euro-pean elements are transformed into African elements. Thus, when people of African descent perform European hymns, according to the prohibitions of Protestant religion, the music seems to bear a strong resemblance to one of the precursors of jazz in the United States—the shouting spiritual. Add Euro-pean instruments and you have something very near to early jazz.

Another pattern for comparison occurs in the Bahamas, which had little or no Latin-Catholic influence. The outstand-ing fact about the Bahamas is their poverty, relieved in recent

[8] This recording is in the archives of the Department of Anthropology at Northwestern University.

years by the tourist business. Their contact with the United States has been close for a century and a half. Bimini was a busy port during Prohibition and, in 1954, I found that the latest rhythm-and-blues hits from Harlem were played on juke boxes in the Negro section of Nassau. The keen admiration for the United States is symbolized by the fact that the so-called 'natives' prefer a Buick to a Rolls-Royce. Social distinctions are hard and fast, nevertheless, for the Bahamas are a typical British colony.

The music of the Bahamas is very similar to the music of the United States.[9] There are, however, subtle differences. The calypso influence is stronger but its current exponent, Blind Blake, acknowledges the early influence of Bessie Smith. Spirituals called 'ant'hems' are still sung in the old American style, as well as the latest gospel songs. Except for the addition of a formidable Salvation Army band accompaniment, the services of the Sanctified Church are similar to those held in the United States, where the denomination originated.

And yet drumming on native drums in the African manner still flourishes (Folkways LP 440), although all the jazz in the Bahamas came from the United States. Why? Perhaps because there was no Latin-Catholic background to assist in a blending. Perhaps because the United States emerged from colonial status at an early date. This meant social upheaval which broke down colonial attitudes, sharpened awareness of Negro-white relationships, and permitted the Negro to integrate himself more completely with the dominant culture. In the stable British colonial relationships of the Bahamas, unchanged because of one ruling class, poverty, and a lack of industrial development, class distinctions insulated Negro from white. African drumming may have survived simply by default, but

---

[9] See M. W. Stearns, album notes, 'Religious Songs and Drums of the Bahamas,' Folkways LP 440.

later, it became an asset to festivals and the tourist trade, and was encouraged.

Martinique, on the other hand, was colonized by the French in 1635 and has remained a French colony ever since. The music of the island, much like that of Haiti, runs the gamut from West African cult music to French folk songs. Unlike Haiti, Martinique remained a French colonial possession, and a musical blending resulted that is very close to New Orleans Creole music, even to the clarinet and trombone style and instrumentation. Music from the Select Tango dance-hall in Fort de France documents in the Bechet-like clarinet, the Ory-like trombone, and the raggy piano, playing waltzes, galops, and mazurkas with a kind of 'jazzy' rhythm (Dial LP 402). This Martinique music is slightly less martial, more complex rhythmically, and a little lighter than the Creole music of New Orleans, which is a demonstrable component of jazz.

What conclusions can we draw from the known patterns in Dutch Guiana, Haiti, Cuba, Trinidad, the Bahamas, and Martinique? West African religious music such as *vodun* survived best of all, because it was highly formalized and could mix with elements of Christianity, especially Catholicism. Where Protestanism existed, the blending took the direction of shouting revival music. Above all, a Latin-Catholic environment appears to have assisted the survival of African qualities.

In general, the cities and especially New Orleans (but cf. also Mobile and Charleston) seem to have evolved a blend of march music and satirical love song similar—even in instrumentation—to the Afro-French music of Martinique. On the other hand, the countryside, dominated by Protestant religions in the United States, seems to have evolved the style of the preacher and shouting congregation as in Toco, Trinidad. And then, of course, both traditions began to mix and blend in the southern United States in an endless variety of ways.

Living in New Orleans in 1880, Lafcadio Hearn wrote: 'the melancholy, quavering beauty and weirdness of the Negro chant are lightened by the French influence, or subdued and deepened by the Spanish.'[10] The contrasting music of Cuba and Martinique seems to bear out this insight—the former blending Spanish and the latter French music with West African. Again, prosperity certainly hastened the development and extended the influence of the merging wherever it occurred. Could it be that the Latin-Catholic background of New Orleans gave the West African musical heritage a head start in the blending of Europ an and African musics, which was later slowed down and t. d underground by the gradual advent of Protestantism afte. the Louisiana Purchase? Then, in turn, could this double process of speed-up and slow-down have forced a more radical integration, creating a new combination and a new music?

[10] H. E. Krehbiel, *Afro-American Folksongs* (New York: Schirmer, 1914), p. 134.

JOHN GREENWAY

The Migratory Workers*

But what is left of the IWW songbook after these defects are considered makes it the first great collection of labor songs ever assembled for utilitarian purposes—indeed, few collections since the publication of the first "little red songbook" equal it. In it first appeared the greatest American labor song, "Solidarity Forever," and such worthy songs of lesser stature as "The Workers' Funeral Hymn" and "The Red Flag." Historically, it is of first importance as a record of a conscious effort to carry economic and social discontent to the singing stage, which some writers believe is a necessary precedent to action. In the field of folksong scholarship, the IWW songbook is significant for its preservation of original compositions which potentially are folk material. Some observers might page through the Wobbly book and condemn the entire collection as either bombast or doggerel, neither of which can conceivably get into the stream of folklore, but such arbitrary judgments are always rash. The Wobblies' "Where the Fraser River Flows" has little to recommend it, for example. It is not the worst of the IWW parodies, certainly, but neither does it have any of those qualifications that seem to be prerequisites for admission to the highly selective folk tradition:

> Fellow workers pay attention to what I'm going to mention,
> For it is the clear contention of the workers of the world;
> That we should all be ready, true-hearted, brave and steady,
> To rally round the standard when the Red Flag is unfurled.

> REFRAIN : Where the Fraser river flows, each fellow worker knows,
> They have bullied and oppressed us, but still our Union grows.

* From *American Folk Songs of Protest* by John Greenway, copyright 1953 by the University of Pennsylvania Press.

And we're going to find a way, boys, for shorter
hours and better pay, boys,
And we're going to win the day, boys, where the
river Fraser flows.

But then Aunt Molly Jackson submits as her own composition
a song containing these stanzas :

Fellow workers, pay attention
To what I'm going to mention;
Now this is the intention
Of the workers of the world.

To march in under our union banner,
To sing and shout our slogan,
And build one powerful union
For the workers of the world.

We are going to find a way, boys,
To shorter hours and better pay, boys,
Yes, we are learning the way, boys,
As lots of bosses know.[1]

The bulk of the songs contained in the IWW songbook are
parodies of gospel hymns and sentimental songs which have
firmly established themselves in American esteem, such as "Just
Before the Battle, Mother," "Love Me and the World is
Mine," and "That Tumble Down Shack in Athlone." But no
recognized composition, whatever its original nature, was safe
from parody when the Wobbly song maker was hunting for a
tune to fit a set of lyrics. Thus, "Onward, Christian Soldiers"
becomes "Onward, One Big Union"; "Marching Through
Georgia" becomes "Paint 'er Red";[2] "Barcarolle" becomes

[1] The direction of borrowing in this transmission is clearly determined in other stanzas of Aunt Molly's song by her use of certain words,
not usually in her vocabulary, present in the Wobbly song.

[2] Attributed to Ralph Chaplin in the IWW songbooks, but Chaplin in
his autobiography, *Wobbly*, shifts the responsibility for this embarras-
sing composition to an obscure song writer. "Paint 'er Red" was one of the
Wobblies' great songs.

"Farewell Frank"; "The Toreador Song" becomes "We
Come"; and even "Lillibullero," the seventeenth-century
incendiary song that was said to have caused the loss of three
kingdoms, turn up as "Workers of the World."

From a literary aspect, the most consistently good songs
emanating from the Wobbly composers are the elegies written
for their fallen comrades. The pretentiousness which results in
bombast, the iconoclasm which results in compositions of
poor taste, and the hack work which results in doggerel are
rarely found in the elegies. The imminence of violent death
which hung over all the Wobblies when most of these songs
were written was brought close to them when they commem-
orated the victim of a lynching mob or vengeful justice, and
consequently purged their songs of insincerity and questionable
humor.

In spite of its defects, which are many, the many fine features of the "little red songbook" firmly establish it as a land-
mark in the history of singing labor.

Unquestionably the greatest song yet produced by American
labor is "Solidarity Forever," written to the tune of "John
Brown's Body" by Ralph Chaplin. Chaplin was one of the
leaders of the early Chicago faction of the IWW and right-
hand man to Big Bill Haywood, but soon after his release from
prison in 1923 he underwent that change of heart experienced
by so many youthful radicals. He has lived to hear "Solidarity
Forever" used against him.

SOLIDARITY FOREVER

When the union's inspiration through the workers' blood shall
    run,
There can be no power greater anywhere beneath the sun.
Yet what force on earth is weaker than the feeble strength
    of one?

But the union makes us strong.

Solidarity forever!
Solidarity forever!
Solidarity forever!
For the union makes us strong.

Is there aught we hold in common with the greedy parasite
Who would lash us into serfdom and would crush us with his
    might?
Is there anything left for us but to organize and fight?
For the union makes us strong.

It is we who plowed the prairies; built the cities where they trade;
Dug the mines and built the workshops; endless miles of railroad
    laid.
Now we stand, outcast and starving, 'mid the wonders we have
    made;
But the union makes us strong.

All the world that's owned by idle drones, is ours and ours alone.
We have laid the wide foundations; built it skyward stone by
    stone.
It is ours, not to slave in, but to master and to own,
While the union makes us strong.

They have taken untold millions that they never toiled to earn.
But without our brain and muscle not a single wheel can turn.
We can break their haughty power; gain our freedom while we
    learn
That the union makes us strong.

In our hands is placed a power greater than their hoarded gold;
Greater than the might of armies, magnified a thousand-fold.
We can bring to birth the new world from the ashes of the old,
For the union makes us strong.

Some of the turgid rhetoric of the latter stanzas of "Solidarity Forever" has been burned out in the alembic of folk

transmission. The pattern of the usual adaptation is a retention
of the first stanza and chorus, intact, and a complete discarding of the subsequent stanzas for improvised stanzas less pre-
tentious and more relevant to the situation at hand :

> The men all stick together and the boys are fighting fine;
> The women and the girls are all right on the picket line.
> No scabs, no threats can stop us as we all march out on time,
> For the union makes us strong.

From a strike at the Safeway Stores in West Oakland,
California, to force the management to hire Negro clerks,
comes this variant :

> Safeway thinks America is only for one race;
> To earn a living, white must be the color of your face.
> But we believe in democracy for everyone
> So we'll picket till our job is done.

Surprisingly enough, there were lady Wobs among the members of this toughest of all unions, and some of them, like Katie
Phar and Elizabeth Gurley Flynn, attained prominence in the
leadership. This song was composed in prison by Vera Moller,
another member of this Amazonian band.

WE MADE GOOD WOBS OUT THERE
(Tune : "Auld Lang Syne")

> Though we be shut out from the world
> Here worn and battle-scarred,
> Our names shall live where men walk free
> On many a small red card.
>
> So let us take fresh hope, my friend,
> We cannot feel despair.
> Whate'er may be our lot in here,
> We made good Wobs out there.

When we were out we did our bit
To hasten Freedom's dawn.
They can't take back the seeds we spread,
The truths we passed along.

'Tis joy to know we struck a blow
To break the master's sway
And those we lined up take the work
And carry on today.

Though we be shut out from the world,
And days are long and hard,
They can't erase the names we wrote
On many a small red card.

So let us take fresh hope, my friend,
Above our prison fare,
Whate'er may be our lot in here,
We made good Wobs out there.

"Dump the Bosses off Your Back" is a selection, taken at random, from the many gospel hymn parodies in the *Little Red Song Book*.

DUMP THE BOSSES OFF YOUR BACK

(Tune : "Take It to the Lord in Prayer")

Are you poor, forlorn, and hungry,
Are there lots of things you lack?
Is your life made up of misery?
Then dump the bosses off your back.

Are your clothes all patched and tattered,
Are you living in a shack?
Would you have your troubles scattered?
Then dump the bosses off your back.

Are you almost split asunder?
Loaded like a long-eared jack?
Boob—why don't you buck like thunder
And dump the bosses off your back?

All the agonies you suffer
You can end with one good whack.
Stiffen up, you orn'ry duffer,
And dump the bosses off your back.

One of the most successful organizing drives of the IWW was among the lumber and sawmill workers of the Northwest. After the AFL twice failed in attempting to establish a union, the Wobblies succeeded, but at the cost of the usual number of their shock troops. The most violent struggle took place at Everett, Washington, in the summer of 1916, after a long strike was about to collapse because of repeated beatings of strikers by police. August 19 saw the police begin an offensive designed to clear out the remaining pickets, but when the story of the beatings got abroad more Wobbly expendables moved into Everett. A strong force of police overwhelmed them also. Faithful to the principle of "one big union," the IWW gathered a force large enough to contend with the police, loaded two steamers full of men, and sailed from Seattle to Everett. But the police had been warned of the attempted invasion, and before the ships could dock they swept the decks with gunfire. Five Wobblies were killed and thirty-one were wounded, but they fought back, and when the battle ended, there were two dead and fourteen wounded among the deputies.

EVERETT, NOVEMBER FIFTH

". . . and then the fellow worker died, singing 'Hold the Fort' . . ."

Out of the dark they came; out of the night
Of poverty and injury and woe—

With flaming hope, their vision thrilled to light—
Song on their lips, and every heart aglow;

They came, that none should trample labor's right
To speak, and voice her centuries of pain.
Bare hands against the masters' armed might!
A dream to match the tolls of sordid gain!

REFRAIN : Song on his lips, he came;
Song on his lips, he went;
This be the token we bear of him—
Soldier of Discontent.

And then the decks went red; and the grey sea
Was written crimsonly with ebbing life.
The barricade spewed shots and mockery
And curses, and the drunken lust of strife.

Yet, the mad chorus from the devil's host,
Yea, all the tumult of that butcher throng,
Compound of bullets, booze, and coward boast,
Could not outshriek one dying worker's song!

At the height of the recent Flying Saucer furor, a letter to
the editor of a Philadelphia newspaper ventured the explanation, "They're pieplates—left over from the pie in the sky we
were promised years ago." Possibly many of the younger
generation missed the implication, but the older readers recalled Joe Hill's most famous song.

One evening late in 1910 Joe Hill walked into the Portland,
Oregon, IWW hall with a song he had written to the tune of
the popular Salvation Army gospel hymn, "In the Sweet Bye
and Bye." He gave it to the secretary of the local, George
Reese, who handed it to Mac McClintock, the local's "busker,"
or tramp entertainer. Mac sang it to the men idling in the hall,
and the tremendous applause that greeted its rendition convinced Reese that they had something. He and McClintock

revised the song, and printed it in their little song leaflet which two years later was adopted by the IWW as the official song-book of the union. Hill was invited to join the Wobblies, and so began his fabulous career.

THE PREACHER AND THE SLAVE

Long-haired preachers come out every night
Try to tell you what's wrong and what's right;
But when asked about something to eat,
They will answer with voices so sweet:

REFRAIN: You will eat, bye and bye
In that glorious land above the sky (way up high)
Work and pray, live on hay,
You'll get pie in the sky when you die (that's no lie).

And the starvation army they play,
And they sing and they clap and they pray,
Till they get all your coin on the drum,
Then they tell you when you're on the bum:

If you fight hard for children and wife—
Try to get something good in this life—
You're a sinner and bad man, they tell,
When you die you will sure go to hell.

Workingmen of all countries, unite,
Side by side for freedom we'll fight;
When the world and its wealth we have gained
To the grafters we'll sing this refrain:

You will eat, bye and bye,
When you've learned how to cook and to fry;
Chop some wood, 'twill do you good,
And you'll eat in the sweet bye and bye.

Among labor unions Hill's version of "Casey Jones" has become more popular than the original railroad ballad. It is one of the few songs that no labor song anthologist would dare leave out. According to popular history, it was composed for a Southern Pacific strike in 1910, but company records and newspapers show no evidence of a strike of the magnitude described in Hill's story of the song's composition having taken place in that year. Harry McClintock says it was written for the "Harriman strike of 1911."

CASEY JONES, THE UNION SCAB

The workers on the S.P. line to strike sent out a call;
But Casey Jones, the engineer, he wouldn't strike at all.
His boiler it was leaking, and its drivers on the bum,
And his engine and its bearings, they were all out of plumb.

REFRAIN : Casey Jones kept his junk pile running;
Casey Jones was working double time;
Casey Jones got a wooden medal
For being good and faithful on the S.P. line.

The workers said to Casey, "Won't you help us win this strike?"
But Casey said, "Let me alone, you'd better take a hike."
Then Casey's wheezy engine ran right off the worn-out track,
And Casey hit the river with an awful crack.

Casey Jones hit the river bottom;
Casey Jones broke his bloomin' spine;
Casey Jones was an Angelino
He took a trip to heaven on the S.P. line. . . .

The angels got together, and they said it wasn't fair,
For Casey Jones to go around a-scabbing everywhere.
The Angels' Union Number 23, they sure was there,
And they promptly fired Casey down the Golden Stair.

Casey Jones went to Hell a-flying.
"Casey Jones," the Devil said, "Oh fine!
Casey Jones, get busy shoveling sulphur—
That's what you get for scabbing on the S.P. line."

A version of Joe Hill's "Casey Jones," collected by Duncan Emrich among the western miners, records an exercise of one of the Wobblies' chief weapons, sabotage:

The workers got together, they said it wasn't fair
For Casey to go around in his cabin everywhere.
Someone put a bunch of railroad ties across the track,
And Casey hit the river with an awful crack.[3]

After hearing a similar stanza sung by a group of Wobblies in 1913, Harry F. Ward was impressed by the vociferous applause that greeted the lines telling of the workers' revenge. He continues,

Still another ballad tells gleefully how the cheated laborer buys a piece of gaspipe to lie in wait for the employment shark who has robbed him. This is partly the naïve revelation by simple folk of that terrible disregard for human life which is one of the outstanding facts of our industrial process. More than that, we have here the voice of men with whom life is rarely safe . . . men for whose lives society has scant respect may be expected to reciprocate the feeling and make it concrete. "We care no more for your food supply in time of strike than you cared for ours in ordinary times," was what the English strikers told remonstrant England after they had tied up transportation. These men whom the I.W.W. is organizing have less restraint.[4]

"Workers of the World, Awaken!" is probably Joe Hill's best serious song. It is one of the long tradition of compositions written in jail.

---

[3] "Songs of the Western Miners," *California Folklore Quarterly,* Vol. 1 (1942), p. 216.
[4] "Songs of Discontent," *Methodist Review,* September, 1913, p. 728.

WORKERS OF THE WORLD, AWAKEN!

Workers of the world, awaken!
Break your chains, demand your rights.
All the wealth you make is taken
By exploiting parasites.
Shall you kneel in deep submission
From your cradles to your graves?
Is the height of your ambition
To be good and willing slaves?

REFRAIN : Arise, ye prisoners of starvation!
Fight for your emancipation;
Arise, ye slaves of every nation
In one union grand.
Our little ones for bread are crying,
And millions are from hunger dying;
The end the means is justifying,
'Tis the final stand.

If the workers take a notion,
They can stop all speeding trains;
Every ship upon the ocean
They can tie with mighty chains;
Every wheel in the creation,
Every mine and every mill,
Fleets and armies of the nation
Will at their command stand still.

Join the union, fellow workers,
Men and women, side by side;
We will crush the greedy shirkers
Like a sweeping, surging tide.
For united we are standing,
But divided we will fall;
Let this be our understanding—
"All for one and one for all."

Workers of the world, awaken!
Rise in all your splendid might;
Take the wealth that you are making,

It belongs to you by right.
No one will for bread be crying,
We'll have freedom, love, and health
When the grand red flag is flying
In the Workers' Commonwealth.

Y. M. SOKOLOV

Folklore of the Peoples of the USSR*

It is difficult to survey the Russian folk creation of the Soviet era apart from the creation of all the fraternal peoples of the USSR.

Even in the past, both the recent and the remote past, Russian folklore absorbed into itself the artistic influences of the culture of neighboring and even of distant peoples of the West and East, and in its turn it enriched many other peoples by the wealth of its poetry. In the first part of this course we have had occasion to speak at some length concerning the researches of scholars on the question of the cultural intercourse of the West and the East, an intercourse in which the Russian people have played a very vital part. We recall, likewise, what has been said about the presence of a very great number of "migratory" motifs in the Russian *byliny,* religious verses, tales, and so forth. As we have seen, a great role was played in the poetic exchanges by the professional popular poets and artists of ancient Russia—the buffoons and the jesters.

Observations upon the history of folklore among the other (non-Russian) peoples of the USSR indicate that among them, also, oral poetry frequently broke down the artificial barriers which had been established among the various peoples by the efforts of the Church and the governmental authorities, and which stirred up chauvinism and sectional hostility. Popular poetry frequently took no account of the boundaries of states or of languages or of religions. An outstanding example is the activity of Sayat Nova, the famous *ashug* of the Transcaucasian region in the eighteenth century, who can justly be

* From *Russian Folklore* by Academician Y. M. Sokolov (Translated by Catherine Ruth Smith), copyright 1950 by The MacMillan Company.

claimed as their own national poet not only by the Armenians, but also by the Georgians and the Azerbaiijanians. He did his creative work in three languages, and contributed a great deal toward the poetic exchange among the three peoples who had often been enemies. Such is the activity of many of the *ashugi* of Daghestan with its many tribes; their songs quickly passed over from one language into another, as, for example, the songs of Suleyman Stalsky, even in the period before the revolution. Such is the activity of many of the *akyny* and *zhirshi* of Kazakhstan and Kirghizia, in particular the activity of Dzhambul Dzhabayev, whose songs have been spread abroad not only through the Kazakh villages, but also far beyond the boundaries of Kazakhstan.

But none the less, the development of the national poetry of each of the peoples of former tsarist Russia was accomplished, on the whole, in an isolated manner, without organic connection with the poetry of other lands. This is not what we see now, in our socialist land, where such a powerful impression has been made upon all of life and culture by the great friendship of the peoples, established by the genius of Lenin and Stalin.

The oral creative art of the peoples of the USSR is a striking manifestation of genuine internationalism, and at the same time of the national culture of each country.

The Soviet folklore of all the peoples of the Soviet Union is a most valuable historical document, an indication of the close union in which all the peoples of the socialist motherland live. Through a survey of the thematics of the oral poetry of the most diverse Soviet peoples, may be clearly seen the unity of moods and experiences, expressed in works of the greatest diversity of languages and form, yet permeated with common ideas and emotions.

The October Revolution awoke the creative powers of the

laboring masses among all the peoples of the Soviet Union. Even as early as 1918, Lenin wrote of the "splendid scope which the great revolution had given to popular creative art,"[1] and also wrote of the "independent, historical creation of the majority of the population, above all, of the majority of the laboring people."[2] These words of the great leader referred, above all, to the social life, to the political and economic structure, but, beyond a doubt, they can be extended also to all the aspects of Soviet culture, including folk art, and in particular popular oral poetry.

Concerning the creative flights of the laboring people as a result of the victories of the October Revolution, and with regard to the birth of new songs and the decisive changes in the character of the popular poetry, that folk poet of Kazakhstan, Dzhambul, wearer of the Order,* has beautifully said:

My joy came in the October Revolution,
The Moscow Decree brought me joy,
With a new song I came to the assembly,
And along with Dzhambul, Kazakhstan burst into song.
Since that time, like a youth, I am burning with happiness;
I am giving my best songs to my motherland.[3]

In the history of the world, it is not possible to point out another stupendous event which could be compared with the October Revolution, in the power of its influence on the creative art of the toiling masses of the people. In the history of the world, it is impossible to find any other event which, in such a short period of time, has brought about such profound changes in the existence of popular creation. The old narrow

[1] V. I. Lenin, *Collected Works*, XXII, p. 376.
[2] *Ibid.*, p. 440.
[3] Dzhambul, *Songs and Poems* (State Literary Press, 1938), p. 85.
* Order of Lenin, civil order of merit bestowed for exceptional public service. — Ed.

social and national barriers have been broken down. The working people have drawn their breath in freedom, filling their lungs with the fresh air of the vast and boundless spaces which have been opened up before the peoples of the USSR. With beautiful picturesqueness the Tadjik singer and workman Alimdzhanov has expressed these feelings:

> You have opened to us all the doors of the world,
> Great Lenin, the giant of the ages.[4]

During the twenty years of the socialist regime, there have been extremely powerful changes in the world view as expressed in the popular poetry.

The profound talents of the laboring people revealed themselves in all their brilliance at the time of the collapse of the old regime of oppression and violence, which had embittered the folk consciousness and the folk poetry in every way.

The masterly national-minority policy of Lenin and Stalin liberated the numerous peoples of tsarist Russia from a twofold oppression—that of the tsarist autocracy, and that of the power of the local national aristocracy and bourgeoisie. Now, summing up the total achievements of the Soviet regime, we may state that among all the peoples of the USSR there exists a new Soviet poetry, "national in form and Socialist in content" (J. V. Stalin). . . .

[4] *Creative Art of the Peoples of the USSR (Pravda*, 1937), p. 179.

EDWARD SAPIR

Language as a Historical Product: Drift*

Everyone knows that language is variable. Two individuals of the same generation and locality, speaking precisely the same dialect and moving in the same social circles, are never absolutely at one in their speech habits. A minute investigation of the speech of each individual would reveal countless differences of detail—in choice of words, in sentence structure, in the relative frequency with which particular forms or combinations of words are used, in the pronunciation of particular vowels and consonants and of combinations of vowels and consonants, in all those features, such as speed, stress, and tone, that give life to spoken language. In a sense they speak slightly divergent dialects of the same language rather than identically the same language.

There is an important difference, however, between individual and dialect variations. If we take two closely related dialects, say English as spoken by the "middle classes" of London and English as spoken by the average New Yorker, we observe that, however much the individual speakers in each city differ from each other, the body of Londoners forms a compact, relatively unified group in contrast to the body of New Yorkers. The individual variations are swamped in or absorbed by certain major agreements—say of pronunciation and vocabulary—which stand out very strongly when the language of the group as a whole is contrasted with that of the other group. This means that there is something like an ideal linguistic entity dominating the speech habits of the members of each group, that the sense of almost unlimited

* From *Language,* by Edward Sapir, copyright 1921 by Harcourt, Brace and Company, Inc., copyright 1949 by Jean Sapir. Reprinted as a Harvest Book, Harcourt, Brace and Company, Inc.

freedom which each individual feels in the use of his language is held in leash by a tacitly directing norm. One individual plays on the norm in a way peculiar to himself, the next individual is nearer the dead average in that particular respect in which the first speaker most characteristically departs from it but in turn diverges from the average in a way peculiar to himself, and so on. What keeps the individual's variations from rising to dialectic importance is not merely the fact that they are in any event of small moment—there are well-marked dialectic variations that are of no greater magnitude than individual variations within a dialect—it is chiefly that they are silently "corrected" or canceled by the consensus of usage. If all the speakers of a given dialect were arranged in order in accordance with the degree of their conformity to average usage, there is little doubt that they would constitute a very finely intergrading series clustered about a well-defined center or norm. The differences between any two neighboring speakers of the series[1] would be negligible for any but the most microscopic linguistic research. The differences between the outermost members of the series are sure to be considerable, in all likelihood considerable enough to measure up to a true dialectic variation. What prevents us from saying that these untypical individuals speak distinct dialects is that their peculiarities, as a unified whole, are not referable to another norm than the norm of their own series.

If the speech of any member of the series could actually be made to fit into another dialect series,[2] we should have no true barriers between dialects (and languages) at all. We should merely have a continuous series of individual variations extending over the whole range of a historically unified linguistic area, and the cutting up of this large area (in some cases embracing parts of several continents) into distinct dialects and languages would be an essentially arbitrary proceeding with

no warrant save that of practical convenience. But such a conception of the nature of dialectic variation does not correspond
to the facts as we know them. Isolated individuals may be
found who speak a compromise between two dialects of a
language, and if their number and importance increases that
may even end by creating a new dialectic norm of their own,
a dialect in which the extreme peculiarities of the parent dialects are ironed out. In course of time the compromise dialect
may absorb the parents, though more frequently these will
tend to linger indefinitely as marginal forms of the enlarged
dialect area. But such phenomena—and they are common
enough in the history of language—are evidently quite secondary. They are closely linked with such social developments as
the rise of nationality, the formation of literatures that aim to
have more than a local appeal, the movement of rural populations into the cities, and all those other tendencies that break
up the intense localism that unsophisticated man has always
found natural.

The explanation of primary dialectic differences is still to
seek. It is evidently not enough to say that if a dialect or
language is spoken in two distinct localities or by two distinct
social strata it naturally takes on distinctive forms, which in
time come to be divergent enough to deserve the name of
dialects. This is certainly true as far as it goes. Dialects do
belong, in the first instance, to very definitely circumscribed
social groups, homogeneous enough to secure the common
feeling and purpose needed to create a norm. But the embar-
rassing question immediately arises: If all the individual
variations within a dialect are being constantly leveled out to
the dialectic norm, if there is no appreciable tendency for the
individual's peculiarities to initiate a dialectic schism, why
should we have dialectic variations at all? Ought not the
norm, wherever and whenever threatened, automatically to

reassert itself? Ought not the individual variations of each locality, even in the absence of intercourse between them, to cancel out to the same accepted speech average?

If individual variations "on a flat" were the only kind of variability in language, I believe we should be at a loss to explain why and how dialects arise, why it is that a linguistic prototype gradually breaks up into a number of mutually unintelligible languages. But language is not merely something that is spread out in space, as it were—a series of reflections in individual minds of one and the same timeless picture. Language moves down time in a current of its own making. It has a drift. If there were no breaking up of a language into dialects, if each language continued as a firm, self-contained unity, it would still be constantly moving away from any assignable norm, developing new features unceasingly and gradually transforming itself into a language so different from its starting point as to be in effect a new language. Now dialects arise not because of the mere fact of individual variation but because two or more groups of individuals have become sufficiently disconnected to drift apart, or independently, instead of together. So long as they keep strictly together, no amount of individual variation would lead to the formation of dialects. In practice, of course, no language can be spread over a vast territory or even over a considerable area without showing dialectic variations, for it is impossible to keep a large population from segregating itself into local groups, the language of each of which tends to drift independently. Under cultural conditions such as apparently prevail to-day, conditions that fight localism at every turn, the tendency to dialectic cleavage is being constantly counteracted and in part "corrected" by the uniformizing factors already referred to. Yet even in so young a country as America the dialectic differences are not inconsiderable.

Under primitive conditions the political groups are small, the tendency to localism exceedingly strong. It is natural, therefore, that the languages of primitive folk or of non-urban populations in general are differentiated into a great number of dialects. There are parts of the globe where almost every village has its own dialect. The life of the geographically limited community is narrow and intense; its speech is correspondingly peculiar to itself. It is exceedingly doubtful if a language will ever be spoken over a wide area without multiplying itself dialectically. No sooner are the old dialects ironed out by compromises or ousted by the spread and influence of the one dialect which is culturally predominant when a new crop of dialects arises to undo the leveling work of the past. This is precisely what happened in Greece, for instance. In classical antiquity there were spoken a large number of local dialects, several of which are represented in the literature. As the cultural supremacy of Athens grew, its dialect, the Attic, spread at the expense of the rest, until, in the so-called Hellenistic period following the Macedonian conquest, the Attic dialect, in the vulgarized form known as the "Koine," became the standard speech of all Greece. But this linguistic uniformity[3] did not long continue. During the two millennia that separate the Greek of to-day from its classical prototype the Koine gradually split up into a number of dialects. Now Greece is as richly diversified in speech as in the time of Homer, though the present local dialects, aside from those of Attica itself, are not the lineal descendants of the old dialects of pre-Alexandrian days.[4] The experience of Greece is not exceptional. Old dialects are being continually wiped out only to make room for new ones. Languages can change at so many points of phonetics, morphology, and vocabulary that it is not surprising that once the linguistic community is broken it should slip off in different directions. It would be too much to expect a locally diversified language to develop along strictly parallel lines. If once the speech of a locality has begun to drift on its own account, it is practically certain to move further and further away from its linguistic fellows. Failing the retarding effect of dialectic inter-influences, which I have already touched upon, a group of dialects is bound to diverge on the whole, each from all the others.

In course of time each dialect itself splits up into subdialects, which gradually take on the dignity of dialects proper while the primary dialects develop into mutually unintelligible languages. And so the budding process continues, until the divergences become so great that none but a linguistic student, armed with his documentary evidence and with his comparative or reconstructive method, would infer that the languages in question were genealogically related, represented independent lines of development, in other words, from a remote and common starting point. Yet it is as certain as any historical fact can be that languages so little resembling each other as Modern Irish, English, Italian, Greek, Russian, Armenian, Persian, and Bengali are but end-points in the present of drifts that converge to a meeting-point in the dim past. There is naturally no reason to believe that this earliest "Indo-European" (or "Aryan") prototype which we can in part reconstruct, in part but dimly guess at, is itself other than a single "dialect" of a group that has either become largely extinct or is now further represented by languages too divergent for us, with our limited means, to recognize as clear kin.[5]

All languages that are known to be genetically related, i.e., to be divergent forms of a single prototype, may be considered as constituting a "linguistic stock." There is nothing final about a linguistic stock. When we set it up, we merely say, in effect, that thus far we can go and no farther. At any point in the progress of our researches an unexpected ray of light may reveal the "stock" as but a "dialect" of a larger group. The terms dialect, language, branch, stock—it goes without saying —are purely relative terms. They are convertible as our perspective widens or contracts.[6] It would be vain to speculate as to whether or not we shall ever be able to make larger historical syntheses than were at one time deemed feasible, just as students of culture have been able to show historical connections between culture areas or institutions that were at one time believed to be totally isolated from each other. The human world is contracting not only prospectively but to the backward-probing eye of culture-history. Nevertheless we are as yet far from able to reduce the riot of spoken languages to a small number of "stocks." We must still operate with a quite considerable number of these stocks. Some of them, like Indo-European or Indo-Chinese, are spoken over tremendous reaches; others, like Basque,[7] have a curiously restricted range and are in all likelihood but dwindling remnants of groups that were at one time more widely distributed. As for the single or multiple origin of speech, it is likely enough that language as a human institution (or, if one prefers, as a human "faculty") developed but once in the history of the race, that all the complex history of language is a unique cultural event. Such a theory constructed "on general principles" is of no real interest, however, to linguistic science. What lies beyond the demonstrable must be left to the philosopher or the romancer.

Notes

1. In so far as they do not fall out of the normal speech group by reason of a marked speech defect or because they are isolated foreigners that have acquired the language late in life.

2. Observe that we are speaking of an individual's speech as a whole. It is not a question of isolating some particular peculiarity of pronunciation or usage and noting its resemblance to or identity with a feature in another dialect.

3. It is doubtful if we have the right to speak of linguistic uniformity even during the predominance of the Koine. It is hardly conceivable that when the various groups of non-Attic Greeks took on the Koine they did not at once tinge it with dialectic peculiarities induced by their previous speech habits.

4. The Zaconic dialect of Lacedaemon is the sole exception. It is not derived from the Koine, but stems directly from the Doric dialect of Sparta.

5. Though indications are not lacking of what these remoter kin of the Indo-European languages may be. This is disputed ground, however, and hardly fit subject for a purely general study of speech.

6. "Dialect" in contrast to an accepted literary norm is a use of the term that we are not considering.

7. Spoken in France and Spain in the region of the Pyrenees.

PAUL RADIN

The Systematization of Ideas*

From speculative discussion for its own sake we shall now turn to the more usual subjects of philosophical interest, the systematization of the various ideas concerning the origin of the world, and the nature of things. Some of the concepts underlying these attempts at systematization have already been discussed before, others such as those embodied in the creation myths of various tribes we must postpone to the chapter on monotheism. In this chapter we will limit ourselves exclusively to the definite philosophical implications found in certain cosmological myths and related material, and still further circumscribe our inquiry by discussing only Polynesian data. I do not feel that any objection can legitimately be advanced against thus limiting ourselves to a very restricted ethnological province, for in a tentative work like the present, our object must be to demonstrate the existence, among people customarily regarded as primitive, of certain intellectual tendencies and accomplishments. The question of their universality, while important, can for the time being be relegated to the background.

The Polynesians have long been known for their unusually elaborate cosmological chants. In these chants, many of them possessing a beauty of thought and expression that can be still felt in the translation, a complete cosmogony is outlined containing not only an account of the origin of the world and the earth but what is to all appearances a fairly definite theory of the origin of consciousness. I say this advisedly for I can find no other interpretation for the first five lines of the following Maori chant. The story of creation is divided into four

* From *Primitive Man as Philosopher* by Paul Radin, copyright 1957 by Dover Publications, Inc.

large periods, each one showing within itself a secondary and progressive evolution. The first period, which as I said contains a theory of the development of consciousness, is as follows :

> From the conception the increase,
> From the increase the swelling,
> From the swelling the thought,
> From the thought the remembrance,
> From the remembrance, the desire.[1]

It is only after the development of physical and psychical differentiation and of personal consciousness—so we must interpret these lines—that an external world can be apprehended. This is the first period. It is with this external world, or better with what is outside the perceiving self, that the second period is concerned. One is naturally inquisitive about the transition between the two periods and here our unknown Maori philosopher is both stimulating and suggestive. He does not apparently regard the external world as having been created from, or as responding to, what he has predicated as the last stage of the first period, namely, desire; but he assumes that the second period was created by the *word*. Is it too far-fetched to see herein an attempt to obviate the necessity of ascribing the existence of the external world to thought or will, by the predication of a mediating principle, the *word;* that is, by what represents the first articulate and external expression of thought, remembrance, and desire? I do not think so. To people more qualified than myself, however, do I leave the task of interpreting the following lines, which give the account of the second cosmic period. The problem of the origin of matter is here most skillfully dodged—or shall I say delayed— in the most approved manner of the early evolutionists :

[1] Richard Taylor, *Te Ika A Maui.*

> The word became fruitful;
> It dwelt with the feeble glimmering;
> It brought forth night;
> The great night, the long night,
> The lowest night, the loftiest night,
> The thick night to be felt,
> The night to be touched, the night unseen.
> The night following on,
> The night ending in death.[2]

Here we have evolutionism *in excelsis*. The absolute consistency and inevitableness of this thinking—call it intuitive or definitely rational as you wish—is simply appalling. From desire came the word. But this first phase of articulateness creates nothing. It merely *dwells* with the feeble glimmering. Is this feeble glimmering to be construed as the dawn between non-consciousness and consciousness? Our Maori philosopher leaves this unresolved. Then follows the description of the absoluteness of night perfect in its kind; the night that can be touched but is yet unseen, the lowest yet the highest, the night that follows on, but ends in death. Yet this night has one distinctive quality which philosophically is fundamental—it can be apprehended, and thus becomes quite different from that night which the Maori describe as existing when, unborn, they dwelt within the womb of their mother, the earth.

The third period represents the genealogical history of matter. It is strictly parallel to the account given in the first period of the origin of consciousness.

> From the nothing the begetting,
> From the nothing the increase,
> From the nothing the abundance,
> The power of increasing, the living breath;
> It dwelt with the empty space,
> It produced the atmosphere which is above us.

[2] *Journal of the Polynesian Society*, XVI, p. 113.

As compared with the first period there is a flaw in the evolutionary account. Nothing leads to begetting, increase, abundance and the power of increasing, the living breath. Apparently our ancient philosophic friend, after having delayed the vexatious problem of how something could have arisen out of nothing, throws all logic and caution to the winds and hurdles over the question. Let us not throw stones; he has some illustrious successors.

The fourth period is philosophically not so interesting. Light is about to appear and with it our problems become dissipated.

> The atmosphere which floats above the earth,
> The great firmament above us, the spread-out space
>   dwelt with the early dawn,
> Then the moon sprang forth;
> The atmosphere above dwelt with the glowing sky.
> Forthwith was produced the sun;
> They were thrown up above as the chief eyes of heaven;
> Then the heavens became light,
> The early dawn, the early day.
> The midday. The blaze of day from the sky.

Where such remarkable chants are developed one naturally expects that the philosophy in one version may be better or worse than in another. I wish to quote one such version which logically is better, although the Maori philosopher simplified his problem and instead of positing the question of mind and matter, frankly assumed both from the very beginning. He still further simplified the problem of the origin of the mind by assuming a divine mind, the deity Io. Although everything superficially comes into existence as the *fiat* of Io, this version contains in reality a profounder understanding of development than did our first:

> Io dwelt within the breathing-space of immensity.
> The universe was in darkness, with water everywhere.

There was no glimmer of dawn, no clearness, no light.
And he began by saying these words,
That he might cease remaining inactive.
"Darkness, become a light-possessing darkness."
(He) then repeated these selfsame words in this manner,
That he might cease remaining inactive.
"Light, become a darkness-possessing light."
And again an intense darkness supervened.
Then a third time he spake saying :
"Let there be darkness above,
Let there be one darkness below (alternate),
Let there be darkness unto Tupua,
Let there be darkness unto Tawhito,
A dominion of light,
A bright light."
And now a great light prevailed.
(Io) then looked to the waters which compassed him
    about and spoke a fourth time saying,
"Ye waters of Tai-kama, be ye separate,
Heaven be formed." Then the sky became suspended.
"Bring forth, thou Tupua-hono-nuku."
And at once the moving earth lay stretched abroad.[3]

Even at the risk of wearying the reader I cannot refrain
from giving one more chant, a Tahitian creation hymn, in its
entirety. Much of its content is contained in the two chants already quoted but this third chant has some new features, new
subleties, and bears the impress of a different type of tempera-
ment and personality :

He abides—Taaroa by name—
In the immensity of space.
There was no earth, there was no heaven,
There was no sea, there was no mankind;
Taaroa calls on high;
He changed himself fully.
Taaroa is the root;

[3] *Journal of the Polynesian Society,* XVI, p. 113.

Turn and look this way.
On Tara-rua's distant peak now
Shines the light of coming day—
The dawn of eating-man and feats of war.[6]

All the speculations so far quoted have been couched in fairly abstract terms. But there was another kind of cosmological speculation not uncommon among the Polynesians where the ideas were drawn primarily from the domain of plant life. Thus among the Maori we have the following periods:

1. *Te Pu* (origin, source, root, base, foundation).
2. *Te More* (tap-root; figuratively, cause).
3. *Te Weu* (rootlet, fibers).
4. *Te Aka* (long, thin roots; stem of climbing plant).
5. *Te Rea* (growth).
6. *Te Wao-nui* (primeval forest).
Here the plant analogies stop and we find
7. *Te Kune* (pregnancy, conception, form acquired).
8. *Te Whe* (sound, as of creaking of tree branches).
9. *Te Kore* (non-existence).
10. *Te Po* (night).

From night then came the Sky-father and the Earth-mother; from them, in turn, the god Tane and from him finally man.[7]

We have in our discussion of the Polynesian material so far been carried only to the period of the creation of the sky and the earth. Naturally speculation did not stop there. The same feeling for an evolutionary systematization which we saw evinced for the development of the cosmos is shown for the period subsequent to the appearance of the sky and earth and for the origin of man himself. The order of creation among the Maori ran as follows:

1. The waters of ocean that are in the world, these were all

[7] *Journal of the Polynesian Society,* III, p. 158.

created by the waters; and then grew out of them the land, the earth, which on maturity was taken to wife by the Sky-father.

2. Next were created the trees of all kinds, to clothe the skin of the earth which had heretofore been naked.

3. Next were created the minor vegetation growing each after its own kind.

4. Next were created the reptiles and insects of every kind

5. Next were created the animals, dogs of every species.

6. Next were created the birds of different kinds to dwell on the plains and in the woods of the earth and on lady-ocean also.

7. Next were created the moon, the sun, and all the stars. When this had been accomplished, the "world of light" became permanent.

8. Next and finally were created the first woman and her daughter, from whom sprang mankind.[8]

The Maori informant added the following characteristic note: "Each one of these, from the very first down to the creation of man, mentioned each in his own period, growing up in its own time, increasing in its own period, living in its own period, endowed after its own manner and time. Each had its own time of conception or sprouting. We now understand that this was the nature of all things, that each thing has its female counterpart through which it conceives."

From the origin of man the Maori developed a type of speculation whose counterpart I have yet to find. Now as a rule, in creation myths, the creation of man is comparatively simple. He is generally created directly by the deity either out of nothing, out of a portion of the deity, or out of the cosmic material that already exists. Here nothing of the kind occurs. From the very beginning it is assumed that man can arise only in the proper biological manner, from a female. The problem

[8] S. Percy Smith, "The Lore of the Whare-Wananga," *Memoirs of the Polynesian Society,* III, pp. 135–137.

that then confronts the gods is to discover the appropriate female. This is not so easy to determine, because the Maori gods were sharp logicians in whom Anatole France would have taken keen delight. They argued that their own kind must be excluded, for from gods only gods can be born. They soon realized that the type of female required would have to be created *de novo* and they proceeded to create her, after having first agreed that the mammalian method of reproduction was to be followed, that of reptiles and birds having been examined and found wanting. The myth follows :

Then Tane and his elder brother asked one another, "By what means shall we raise up descendants to ourselves in the world of light?" Their elder brother said, "Let us seek a female that may take on our likeness and raise up off-spring for us in the world of light." Some suggested they should fetch some of the female Apas (divine messengers) of the twelve heavens. But the older brother replied, "If we fetch our females from there, then all our descendants will be gods like ourselves. Rather let us take of the earth, that it may be said they are the descendants of the earth." Hereupon it was agreed to search for such a female.

The family of gods now dispersed by two and two to search for the female. Every place was sought out but not one single thing was found suitable to take on the functions of a female similar to the female Apas of the conjoint heavens. All assembled again—none had found anything.

It was then decided by the gods to ascertain or no whether the female was to be found in any of the living beings that had been appointed to dwell in the world (i.e., the animals, insects, etc.). For all females of living things conceive. An examination of the offspring was made. Some were found partly appropriate, some not. The reptiles have their particular issue in the form of eggs; they were not found suitable on examination and so were discarded. It was considered better that something which produced after its own kind or bodily shape should be adopted—and hence offspring by eggs was assigned to birds. It was now obvious that the kind of female required from which the *iho-tangata* (the form or likeness and attributes of man) could be born, was not to be found.

So the gods all assembled again to declare their various ideas. And then spoke Ro-iho, Ro-ake, and Hae-puru to Tane. "O Tane, what is it ye are seeking?" Tane replied, "We are searching the way to the female." The three then said, "Try the earth at Kura-waka and commence your operations there for in that place is the female in a state of virginity and potentiality; she is sacred for she contains the likeness of man."

The gods then went off to seek the earth at Kura-waka. Here they formed a body in the likeness of a woman and completed the arrangements of the head, the arms, the bust, the legs, the back, and the front; and then the bones. Here ended the work of the elder brethren. Then followed the arrangements of the flesh, the muscles, the blood, and the fat. On the completion of these parts the breath of life was assigned to Tane to place in the nostrils, the mouth, and the ears. That was done. Then for the first time the breath of man came forth— the eyelids opened, the pupils saw, and the hot breath of the mouth burst forth, the nose sneezed. After this the body was taken to the altar at Muritakina where all the proceedings were voided (i.e., where all evil influence of earthly origin was removed and the first woman became a fitting recipient of the germ of life).

The parts were at first all made separately in different places but afterwards gathered and joined together and on completion, it was said to be a human body. It was Io and one of his messengers who implanted the thoughts and the living spirit.[9]

[9] *Ibid.*, pp.138–141.

LAWRENCE ELLIOT

The Remarkable Eskimo Artists of Baffin Island*

Thirteen hundred miles due north of Ottawa, beyond the farthest reaches of Hudson Bay, a scattering of tiny buildings clings to a high rise of rock. This is the settlement of Cape Dorset, on Baffin Island—a Canadian government outpost, trading center for perhaps 350 semi-nomadic Eskimos, and surely the most astonishing art colony in the world.

The artists can neither read nor write; yet here, where the arctic winds shriek and winter cold can kill in seconds, they have developed a hauntingly original folk art. Their pictures, sketched by the flickering light of a seal-oil lamp, have made the incredible leap from the bleak and lonely barrens to marbled galleries and salons on three continents. Their names —Tudlik, Niviaksiak, Kenojuak—are acclaimed in the rarefied realm of international art.

The Eskimo prints from Cape Dorset, first shown in 1959, excited the critics and captivated thousands. Museums rushed to buy examples for their collections, vied for the defaced stone blocks and sealskin stencils on which they were made. Prints meant to sell for $15 to $95 were soon being traded for as much as $1000.

The Eskimos were puzzled by all the excitement. They do not think of themselves as artists. They are hunters, as their fathers were, and the place of a *tituktowak* (print) in the Eskimo scheme of things is best indicated by the literal meaning of the word : small-marks-you-make-with-your-hand. Making a picture is something to while away the long hours when gales howl and even the mightiest hunters dare not leave camp. But when the winds are still again, a man must strike out across the tundra in search of walrus, seal, whale, bear.

* Reprinted from *The Reader's Digest,* September, 1962. Copyright 1962 by The Reader's Digest Association, Inc.

For this is the land of the quick and the dead. The grim struggle to survive is all-important. The frozen ground yields nothing to appease a man's hunger, or clothe his body, or shelter his family. And yet the land is endlessly fascinating to the Eskimos. "The *kaluna* (white man) sees only the harshness and feels only the cold," says Tùdlik. "But this is our home, and we can see its beauty."

They see, too, the essential mystery of life. Searching back into their dreams and fears and perplexities, they experience feelings not easy to talk about. So a hunter returns empty-handed—and draws a mischievous Talluliyak, the sea goddess who perversely lured the seals away from his harpoon. Another ponders the brilliant northern lights— and makes a picture of the gods playing catch in that other world, creating ghostly flashes as they throw seal skulls across the night sky.

Some of the pictures are direct, urgent. "To hunt the great bear," Niviaksiak once said, "you must *feel* like a bear." And his art shows the mammoth white beast poised for fight, or hunching low on an ice floe—stark portrayal of the quarry at bay.

Cape Dorset is one of the oldest settlements in North America. For 3,000 years Eskimos have camped by its steep shore and fished its winding fjords. And for almost that long they have been revealing themselves in an art whose primitive purity has been undiluted by outside influence. With no tools but crude knives, they carved on odd bits of driftwood, antlers, ivory from a walrus tusk, the soft arctic soapstone exposed by an ebb tide—anything that came to hand. They had an almost eerie power of observation, the hunter's total familiarity with his world. They knew the lost look of an injured seal, and they wrested it from the lifeless stone. They knew the exuberance of the fisherman returning home with a full string, and they shaped it from a piece of ivory.

To this inscrutable land 14 years ago came a young Canadian artist, James Houston, for a season of painting the austerely beautiful arctic landscapes. The magic and mystery of the north took hold of him. He stayed two years—and when he finally did return south, it was only to wangle an assignment as an officer for the Department of Northern Affairs and to marry his Canadian fiancée. Then he returned with her to Cape Dorset.

Ellie Houston found three frame buildings and some tents housing a Hudson's Bay Co. store, a nurse, a teacher and ten Eskimo families. Some 300 other Eskimos, in three- and four-family groups, ranged across the 18,000-square-mile Foxe Peninsula, and once a year came to the village to trade white-fox skins for cartridges, fish nets and cloth.

Ellie loved the life almost from the beginning. She taught the women to bake bread, and Jim found time to paint glittering icebergs and the long scarlet sunrise.

The Eskimos had never known anyone like this soft-spoken, picture-making *kaluna*. Saumik, they called him—the left-handed one. They were soon visiting the Houston's hut, grinning as Jim and Ellie stumbled over an Eskimo word but secretly gratified at the couple's persistent efforts to learn.

One evening Kananginak, a distinguished hunter, brought a gift for Saumik—a small soapstone carving of a seal. Houston needed only one look to recognize its worth. "It was magnificent" he says.

In halting Eskimo, Jim Houston asked if Kananginak could carve another seal. The hunter was puzzled. He had already made a seal. Why would he want to make another? A walrus, then? Ah, that was a challenge. Kananginak had never made a walrus. He went off to find some stone.

When the Eskimos learned that the carvings pleased Houston, they brought him more. Convinced that the outside world would respond to these unique expressions of a unique people, Houston prepared to take some south. First, though, he presented the villagers with a fine rifle. "It is for the carvings," he said. They stared at him, awestruck.

In Montreal and Toronto and Ottawa, wherever Houston showed the carvings, the reaction was: "Where can I buy one?" Encouraged by the Department of Northern Affairs, Houston made a marketing arrangement with the Canadian Handicrafts Guild, then returned north to convince unbelieving natives across the eastern arctic that there were people who would pay money for their soapstone figures. For the first time the Eskimos of Canada had a source of income independent of the trapline.

One afternoon in 1957, Oshaweetuk, the carver, fingered a package of Jim Houston's cigarettes. "It must be tiresome for someone to paint this same picture on every package," he said. Trying to explain the process of printing, Houston took down one of Oshaweetuk's own delicately incised walrus tusks and lightly spread it with ink. Then he put a piece of paper over it and pressed gently until the picture on the tusk was faithfully transferred.

Oshaweetuk was entranced. "We could do that!" he cried —and instantly it occurred to Houston that the people of Cape Dorset could, indeed, be taught to adapt their artistry from stone to paper. Houston obtained leave from the Department and, drawing on his savings, flew to Japan. There, for four months, he studied with 72-year-old Unichi Hiratsuka, acknowledged master in a land where the printing craft had reached its peak. When he came back to Cape Dorset, an artistic revolution was in the making.

One decision was automatic: the basic art must remain the Eskimos' own, and the materials would be those they had always used. Hewn with a hand-ax, a block of stone was filed smooth and polished, and on this surface the artist cut in low relief forms and figures to be colored and gently rubbed off onto tissue-thin paper. All that winter the little heated *senlavik* (craft center) hummed with activity. Men and women brought their sketches, watched the newly taught print-makers re-create their art on paper.

The first small collection was exhibited at the Shakespeare Festival in Stratford, Ontario. A few months later, when 1500 prints went on sale in Montreal, 600 were bought the first day, including copies for the Tate Gallery in London, the Museum of Fine Arts in Montreal and the Museum of Modern Art in New York. Within weeks, dealers across Canada and the United States were clamoring for more.

But there would be no more until the following year's collection was ready. For, with Jim Houston's help, the people of Cape Dorset had formed a cooperative and made some important decisions. To avoid sacrificing the artists' ever-fresh individuality, only a limited number of designs, chosen and priced by an independent committee, would be printed. Of the 54 copies made before the stone was broken, 50 were to be sold and four kept as a permanent record in Ottawa and Cape Dorset. Each artist and print-maker would be paid for his work. The balance of the income (there was $20,000 that first year) was to be plowed back into the co-op.

The 1960 print collection earned more than $60,000 and the 4150 prints sold in 1960—the work of some 25 artists—brought over $80,000. Last Spring, the co-op decided to finance and build its own store, then hired a *kaluna* to operate it—the first time in Canadian history that the traditional roles of Eskimo and white man had been reversed.

Though each family now has warm clothing and every hunter his own rifle, nothing is essentially different. The people must still move across the frozen tundra in search of the seal and the great bear, and their lives remain beset by the same hardship with which their ancestors lived and died. This, the old ones will tell you, is the way it must be.

But even the stern stoicism of the Eskimos was shaken by the death of Niviaksiak, perhaps the greatest of the Eskimo artists. His life and strange passing have become an arctic legend.

Often Niviaksiak would seclude himself on a small island to ponder the mysteries of life. Two years ago he grew obsessed with the great white bear. He knew it to be an inscrutable creature, its passions as deep and mysterious as man's own. For months he neither carved nor drew anything but the bear. Some say he probed too deeply, that there are things better left unknown.

Then on a still, cold morning in winter Niviaksiak led a hunting party to a camp 40 miles north of Cape Dorset where, one afternoon, they returned to find their canoe smashed. Niviaksiak and a companion followed fresh polar-bear tracks until suddenly, they stood face to face with the great white creature. Niviaksiak threw his rifle to his shoulder, but he never fired. Instead, he cried out, "Ah, it is dark! I am falling." He dropped to the snow, and his companion fled.

Next day the hunters returned. Niviaksiak's body was untouched. The bear tracks ended abruptly, on precisely the spot where beast and hunter had faced each other for the last time.

The *kaluna* would search for medical clues to the mystery, but the Eskimos know that Niviaksiak had, indeed, come too close to the great bear's secrets with his art and his pondering. He had been struck down by the spirits, and their earthly instrument had then vanished into thin air.

Bibliography

The literature of folklore has become so specialized and so voluminous that even if consideration were restricted to English-language publications or North American materials any gesture toward full representation would be either incomplete or too voluminous for inclusion here. The editors have chosen, then, to remind readers that both the *Journal of American Folklore* and *Southern Folklore Quarterly* publish annual bibliographies. Also, the American Folklore Society began quarterly publication of *Folklore Abstracts* in 1963. Thus current or recent folklore bibliography is relatively easy of access.

For general orientation to the field and for excellent bibliographies related to various folklore genres, the following titles should prove useful to the beginning student.

Botkin, Benjamin A., *A Treasury of American Folklore*. New York : Crown Publishers, Inc., 1944.

Brewster, Paul G., *American Non-Singing Children's Games*. Norman, Oklahoma : University of Oklahoma Press, 1953.

Clarke, Kenneth and Mary, *Introducing Folklore*. New York : Holt, Rinehart and Winston, Inc., 1963.

Coffin, Tristram P., *The British Traditional Ballad in North America*. Philadelphia : The American Folklore Society, Bibliographical and Special Series, No. 2, 1951.

Dorson, Richard, *American Folklore*. Chicago : University of Chicago Press, 1959.

Haywood, Charles, *A Bibliography of North American Folklore and Folksong,* rev. ed. New York : Dover Publications, 1961.

Lawless, Ray M., *Folksingers and Folksongs: A Handbook of Biography, Bibliography, and Discography.* New York : Duell, Sloan & Pearce-Meredith Press, 1960.

Opie, Peter and Iona, *The Lore and Language of Schoolchildren.* Oxford : The Clarendon Press, 1960.

Taylor, Archer, *English Riddles from Oral Tradition.* Berkeley : University of California Press, 1951.

———, *The Proverb.* Cambridge : Harvard University Press, 1931.

Thompson, Stith, *The Folktale.* New York : Holt, Rinehart and Winston, Inc., 1946.

Wilgus, D. K., *Anglo-American Folksong Scholarship since 1898.* New Brunswick, N.J. : Rutgers University Press, 1959.

White, Newman Ivey, and Paul F. Baum, general eds., *The Frank C. Brown Collection of North Carolina Folklore,* 7 vols. Durham, N.C. : Duke University Press, 1952-1964.

Index